THOMAS AQUINAS

BIBLICAL
THEOLOGIAN

THOMAS AQUINAS

BIBLICAL THEOLOGIAN

EDITED BY ROGER NUTT &
MICHAEL DAUPHINAIS

EMMAUS
ACADEMIC

www.emmausacademic.com
Steubenville, Ohio

EMMAUS
A C A D E M I C

Steubenville, Ohio
www.emmausacademic.com
A Division of The St. Paul Center for Biblical Theology
Editor-in-Chief: Scott Hahn
1468 Parkview Circle
Steubenville, Ohio 43952

Library of Congress Cataloging-in-Publication Data
Names: Aquinas the Biblical Theologian (Conference) (2019 : Ave Maria
  University), author. | Nutt, Roger W., editor. | Dauphinais, Michael,
  1973- editor.
Title: Thomas Aquinas, biblical theologian / edited by Michael Dauphinais
  and Roger Nutt.
Description: Steubenville : Emmaus Academic, [2020] | Includes
  bibliographical references. | Summary: "In the past 800 years, it's
  possible that no other theologian has shaped the Church's understanding
  of God, man, and herself more than St. Thomas Aquinas. Many people are
  familiar with his most famous work, the Summa Theologiae, but fewer know
  of his important role as a biblical theologian. Aquinas' primary work
  was biblical theology. His biblical commentaries are invaluable in the
  ongoing work of Scripture study. This book contains essays delivered at
  a three-day conference to explore some of Aquinas' most important
  contributions to the field"-- Provided by publisher.
Identifiers: LCCN 2020021676 (print) | LCCN 2020021677 (ebook) | ISBN
  9781645850373 (hardcover) | ISBN 9781645850380 (paperback) | ISBN
  9781645850397 (ebook)
Subjects: LCSH: Bible--Theology--Congresses. | Thomas, Aquinas, Saint,
  1225?-1274--Congresses.
Classification: LCC BS543 .A65 2019 (print) | LCC BS543 (ebook) | DDC
  230/.2092--dc23
LC record available at https://lccn.loc.gov/2020021676
LC ebook record available at https://lccn.loc.gov/2020021677

Cover design and layout by Emily Demary

Cover image: *Saint Thomas Aquinas* (1511) by Fra Bartolomeo

TABLE OF CONTENTS

DOGMATIC AND MORAL CONSIDERATIONS

FOREWORD

The essays in this volume were originally delivered as papers at a conference on "Aquinas the Biblical Theologian," hosted by Ave Maria University (February 7–9, 2019) and sponsored by the Aquinas Center (Ave Maria, Florida) and the St. Paul Center for Biblical Theology (Steubenville, Ohio). Nearly two hundred scholars attended, and seventy presented papers in the course of a busy weekend. Both the quantity and the quality of the work exceeded the organizers' high expectations.

On the first full day of the conference, at the start of his plenary address, John Boyle noted that a generation ago such a conference could not have happened. When he began studying Aquinas and Scripture some forty years before, barely a handful of scholars shared his interest. What a difference one generation has made.

Conference co-host Matthew Levering deserves some of the credit for that remarkable growth. He has been widely recognized for awakening the interest of younger scholars. He observes: "The recent recovery of Aquinas's biblical commentaries has made Aquinas's use of Scripture something of a hot topic."[1]

Even with this newfound appreciation, Aquinas is viewed—in most of academia—as a medieval systematic theologian. There is good reason for this. His unique comprehension of the speculative elements that contribute to the coherent unity and constructive science of theology remains unmatched.

Yet, it is unlikely that Aquinas would be happy in this narrow niche. His days at the University of Paris were spent almost entirely in the classroom as a Master of the Sacred Page, devoted to exegesis of Scripture. These lectures were transformed into his many volumes of biblical commentary. This, and not philosophy, was his domain.

---

[1] Matthew Levering, *Paul in the Summa Theologiae* (Washington, DC: The Catholic University of America Press, 2014), xi.

Thomas, in fact, never taught a class on Aristotle.

John Boyle notes: "Indeed, Thomas may well have thought his Scripture commentaries to be his most important works. If we distinguish so sharply systematic from biblical theology, Thomas would not."[2]

Beyond the commentaries, the centrality of Scripture for Aquinas is evident in the two Summas, which contain around twenty-five thousand explicit biblical citations. Thomas considered the Summas to be compilations of the truths that were diffuse and sometimes obscure in Scripture. As Jean-Pierre Torrell observes: "Sacred Scripture intimately penetrates Thomas's work."[3]

In his classic study *Toward Understanding St. Thomas*, Marie-Dominique Chenu proposed, around the middle of the last century, that Aquinas's *Summa Theologiae* should be read and understood in terms of "biblical theology." This is not simply on account of its thousands of explicit biblical quotations but because it is based on "the theologically primary function of Scripture as source and framework of theology," the fruit of his thoughtful theological exegesis.[4]

What Chenu proposed should have seemed obvious. It was not, however, and it had not been since Thomas's own lifetime. For many reasons, the value of his work for philosophy and systematic theology increased in the centuries following his death. But the world seemed to forget that he was, in his own day, considered primarily a teacher of Scripture. Because the Bible was revealed by the God who created the world, Thomas considered it to be the most reliable guide to the world and life in it. One of his earliest biographers, the Dominican Bernard Gui wrote (during Thomas's canonization process): "His knowledge was like an overflowing river of scriptural doctrine, sprung from the fount of Wisdom on high and then branching out through all the variety of his writings."[5]

---

[2] John F. Boyle, "St. Thomas Aquinas and Sacred Scripture," *Pro Ecclesia* IV.1 (1995): 92–93.

[3] Jean-Pierre Torrell, *Aquinas's Summa: Background, Structure, and Reception* (Washington, DC: The Catholic University of America Press, 2005), 72.

[4] Wilhelmus G.B.M. Valkenberg, *Words of the Living God: Place and Function of Holy Scripture in the Theology of St. Thomas Aquinas* (Leuven: Peeters, 2000), 189; citing M.-D. Chenu, *Toward Understanding St. Thomas* (Chicago, Regnery, 1964), 253–60.

[5] Kenelm Foster, O.P., *The Life of St. Thomas Aquinas: Biographical Documents* (Baltimore: Helicon, 1959), 51.

In the late twentieth century, the academy began to recover this memory of Thomas. Certain fashions in scholarship made the recovery inevitable, among them a fascination with patristic exegesis, but also the emergence of a new school of canonical exegesis. In the postmodern academy, anything was possible. Even Thomas could once again find his place.

Since then, Emmaus Academic Press has established a reputation for producing scholarly books of classic pedigree and lasting value. One of its ongoing projects (carried on in collaboration with the Aquinas Institute) is The Aquinas Project, which involves the translation and publication of St. Thomas's *Opera Omnia*—including all of his biblical commentaries. Some of these volumes will appear in English for the first time when they appear in Emmaus Road's catalogue.

This present collection can rest easy on the same shelves as those venerable volumes. Its contributors have made it worthy.

What is most edifying to me, however, is not the curiosity or skill of the scholars involved in these great works. It is rather the thirst for truth and holiness that I detect when I read these papers and when I encounter their authors. This volume, then, celebrates a new springtime of unexpected growth in a long-neglected—yet extremely important—area of biblical and theological inquiry as well as Thomistic Studies. This is a great contribution. It promises a future of delightful scholarship still to come.

SCOTT W. HAHN
Franciscan University of Steubenville

THE PLACE OF CHRIST AND THE BIBLICAL NARRATIVE IN AQUINAS'S THEOLOGY OF REVELATION*

MICHAEL DAUPHINAIS
Ave Maria University

For Aquinas, Jesus Christ and the biblical narrative may be described as revelation. This view is not shared by all. For instance, the illustrious Thomist Fr. Leo Elders offers the following analysis of Aquinas and revelation:

> St. Thomas holds that revelation is primarily something taking place in the human intellect and not a visible historical event or an ontological structure such as the person of Jesus Christ. According to St. Thomas it consists formally in the illumination of the mind by God [*Summa theologiae* II-II, q. 176, a. 2; *Summa contra gentiles* III, ch. 154]. The events as such, recorded in the Bible, and in particular in the gospels, are not yet revelation in the strict sense of the term: the insight into their significance, given by God to the apostles and the evangelists, constitutes revelation.[1]

Elders contrasts his emphasis on revelation as intellectual illumina-

---

* Leo J. Elders, S.V.D., "Aquinas on Holy Scripture as the Medium of Divine Revelation," in *La doctrine de la revelation divine de saint Thomas d'Aquin*, ed. Leo J. Elders, Studi Tomistici 37 (Vatican: Libreria Editrice Vaticana, 1990), 132–52, at 132.

tion to the contemporary emphasis on revelation as historical events.[1] Elders affirms *Dei Verbum* in its teaching that "Christ the Lord [is the one] in whom the full revelation of the supreme God is brought to completion,"[2] but cautions that such language must be interpreted broadly and may not serve as precise theological language. Although I agree with Elders's proper concern to safeguard the understanding of revelation in its cognitive dimension as imparting the truth about God and his saving plan, I will suggest that Elders fails to appreciate how Aquinas understands revelation in and through the biblical narrative and Christ.

Gustave Martelet, S.J., who took a less traditional approach to theology than Fr. Elders, nonetheless similarly alleges that Aquinas fails to appreciate Christ as revelation. He offers the following criticism of the role of Christ and revelation in Aquinas:

> Considered from the perspective of its theological structure in the order of teaching (*ordo doctrinae*), the *Tertia Pars* is therefore a Soteriology of the sinner, but not a Christology of the revealer. . . . Has one said everything about Christ that one must say when one presents Christ as the Savior? Should the overarching plan of the teaching of this holy science remain in such darkness about the sovereign identity of Christ as the revealer?[3]

---

[1] Elders describes the contemporary view as seeing historical events as the means by which "God reveals himself, Jesus himself being the supreme revelation" ("Aquinas on Holy Scripture," 134).

[2] Second Vatican Council, Dogmatic Constitution on Divine Revelation *Dei Verbum* (November 18, 1965), §7.

[3] Gustave Martelet, S.J., "Theologie und Heilsökonomie in der Christologie der 'Tertia Pars,'" in *Gott in Welt: Festgabe für Karl Rahner* (Freiburg im Breisgau: Bassel, 1964), 3:3–42, at 3:42: "Zweifellos offenbart uns der Christus der Tertia etwas Wesentliches über die Trinität, nämlich daß die ganze Trinität uns erlöst. Die Tertia, unter dem Blickpunkt des ihren theologischen Aufbau bestimmenden „ordo doctrinae" betrachtet, ist also eine Soteriologie des Sünders, nicht aber eine Christologie des Offenbarers. Und um alles mit einem Worte zu sagen: das Problem des Aufbaus der Summa erscheint uns am Ende dieser Studie als ein Problem der trinitarischen Christologie. Hat man von Christus alles gesagt, was man sagen muß, wenn man ihn als den Heilbringer darstellt? Soll der Gesamtplan der heiligen Wissenschaft didaktisch die souveräne Identität Christi mit dem Offenbarer in solcher Dunkelheit lassen?" (translation mine). This criticism was taken up in several later treatments of Aquinas. For example, Yves Congar, O.P., writes: "It must be acknowledged that St. Thomas has neglected this first

I agree with Martelet that a proper Christology ought to attend to both his salvific and revelatory roles. I disagree, however, with his allegation that Aquinas leaves theology in the dark about Christ as the revelation of God.

The present essay argues that Aquinas has a thoroughly biblical and Christological theology of revelation. Christ communicates to his followers and to the Church the saving truth about God and his plan for the salvation of the human race. Furthermore, the Bible itself is both witness to and part of Christ's saving and revealing action. The full phenomenon of revelation as saving truth includes its communication and its reception. Revelation's intellectual reception takes place within the providential story of salvation as it reaches its definitive fulfillment in the mission of the Son of God. Seen in this light, Aquinas's theology is properly biblical, historical, intellectual, Christological, and Trinitarian. This essay presents four interrelated aspects of how we might receive properly Aquinas's presentation of divine revelation: first, Aquinas's treatment of prophecy as the mode of revelation; second, Aquinas's treatment of *sacra doctrina* and revelation; third, Aquinas's presentation of Christ as teacher of rev-

---

aspect [how we also know the intimate mystery of God through Jesus Christ], at least in the *Summa*: there he does not show Christ as the revealer of God, a theme nevertheless biblical and traditional" ("Le Moment 'Economique' et le Moment 'Ontologique' dans la sacra doctrina," in *Mélanges offerts a M.-D. Chenu Maitre en Théologie*, Bibliothèque Thomiste 37 [Paris: Vrin, 1967]: 135–87, at 185n170). Congar's remark here is a criticism of E. Mersch, "Le Christ mystique, centre de la théologie comme science," *Nouvelle revue théologique* 61 (1934): 449–75, and "L'object de la théologie et le 'Christus totus'" *Recherches de science religieuse* 26 (1936): 129–57; these two are reprinted synthetically in *La theologie du Corps mystique* (Paris: Desclée de Brouwer, 1944), 1:56–115. In support, Congar cites Martelet, "Theologie und Heilsökonomie," 3:28–42. Catherine LaCugna writes: "By the time Thomas does come to *oikonomia* proper, it is 'the economy of the saved, of those who belong to Christ, and not the economy of the revelation of the Trinity in Christ'" (*God For Us: The Trinity and Christian Life* [San Francisco: Harper Collins, 1991], 149 [citing Martelet, "Theologie und Heilsökonomie," 3:41]). Anne Hunt writes: "The Trinity, although known only through revelation, is elaborated by Aquinas in refined metaphysical terms in *Prima Pars* of the *Summa Theologiae* while the death and resurrection of Jesus Christ are treated in *Tertia Pars* under the rubric of the return of the rational creature to God (*motus rationalis creaturae in Deum*). Clearly Aquinas's emphasis is on the redemptive effect rather than the revelatory aspect of Jesus' death and resurrection" (*The Trinity and the Paschal Mystery: A Development in Recent Catholic Theology* [Collegeville, MN: Liturgical Press, 1997], 5).

elation; and fourth, Aquinas's consideration of the human nature of Christ as the instrument of revelation. All of these together will substantiate the claim that Christ's salvific mission is present throughout Aquinas's doctrine of revelation.

Revelation and Prophecy

Aquinas indisputably links revelation with prophecy and vice versa. Prophecy thus signifies primarily the divine illumination of the mind of the recipient of such revelation. Does this mean that revelation should be restricted properly to interior intellectual illumination, thus eschewing the accompanying historical events? I will argue that this restriction is based upon a misunderstanding and risks a caricature of Aquinas's theology of revelation as being ahistorical and divorced from the drama of salvation history. Instead, Aquinas's view of revelation includes both the communication and the reception of the biblical narrative as truth. Revelation may be exclusively illumination for *angels*, who are immaterial and live and have their being in aeviternity and to whom God reveals himself by implanting species in their minds, but for *human beings*, who are material, who move in time and so realize themselves in history, it is not so.[4]

Let us consider a central aspect of Aquinas's treatment of prophetic revelation. Aquinas writes, "the gift of prophecy consists in the mind itself being illumined [*in ipsa illuminatione mentis*] so as to know an intelligible truth [*ad cognoscendum intelligibilem veritatem*]."[5] Aquinas then continues to describe the nature of these intelligible truths: "Prophetic revelation [*prophetica revelatio*] extends

---

[4] *In* II *sent.*, d. 9, q. 1, a. 3: "Our hierarchy is distinguished from the angelic in that ours is perfected by the divine light veiled through sensible similitudes, whether in the sacraments or in the metaphors of the Scriptures; but the angelic is perfected by a simple, absolute light [nostra hierarchia distinguitur ab angelica in hoc quod nostra perficitur divino lumine velato per similitudines sensibiles tam in sacramentis quam in metaphoris Scripturarum; sed angelica perficitur lumine simplici et absolute]." Unless otherwise stated, all translations of the works of Aquinas are my own.

[5] *Summa theologiae [ST]* II-II, q. 176, a. 2. Translations of the *Summa theologiae* are from the translation by the Fathers of the English Dominican Province (New York: Benziger Brothers, 1920–1925), with minor modifications.

not only to future events relating to man, but also to divine realities [*ad res divinas*]." Prophetic revelation thus serves as a means by which God instructs human beings about his plans for our salvation and about himself.[6]

Aquinas employs the adapted Aristotelian language of "intellectual lights" to describe parallel levels of insight into the realities presented to the mind typically through the senses. He will speak of the natural light of the intellect, the light of grace, the light of prophecy, and even up to the light of glory by which the blessed behold God. As such, the light of prophecy functions in a manner parallel to yet distinct from that of the natural light of the intellect. The natural light of the intellect is that by which "the intellect knows chiefly the first principles of all things known naturally"; such natural light illumines the intellect as its "abiding and complete form."[7] This natural light is seen in the questions of children—"What is it?" and "Why?"—questions through which children seek to understand the meaning of the world around them.

In contrast to the natural light of our intellect, the light of prophecy allows the intellect to receive "the principle of things pertaining to supernatural knowledge," which Aquinas describes simply

---

[6] These divine realities include both "those which are to be believed by all and are matters of 'faith,' and . . . yet higher mysteries, which concern the perfect and belong to 'wisdom'" (*ST* II-II, q. 171, prol.).

[7] *ST* II-II, q. 171, a. 2. Aquinas elsewhere draws a similar parallel between the light of natural reason and the light of grace in human knowledge of God: "The knowledge which we have by natural reason contains two things: images derived from the sensible objects; and the natural intelligible light [*lumen naturale intelligibile*], enabling us to abstract from them intelligible conceptions. Now in both of these, human knowledge is assisted by the revelation of grace. For the intellect's natural light is strengthened by the infusion of gratuitous light; and sometimes also the images in the human imagination are divinely formed, so as to express divine things better than those do which we receive from sensible objects, as appears in prophetic visions; while sometimes sensible things, or even voices, are divinely formed to express some divine meaning; as in the Baptism, the Holy Ghost was seen in the shape of a dove, and the voice of the Father was heard, 'This is My beloved Son' (Matt. 3:17)" (*ST* I, q. 12, a. 13, corp.). Aquinas continues: "From the images either received from sense in the natural order, or divinely formed in the imagination, we have so much the more excellent intellectual knowledge, the stronger the intelligible light is in man; and thus through the revelation given by the images a fuller knowledge is received by the infusion of the divine light" (*ST* I, q. 12, a. 13, ad 2).

MICHAEL DAUPHINAIS

as "God himself."[8] The light of prophecy is a transitory insight into divine realities, since the proper vision of God's essence is complete only in heaven.[9] Were the light of prophecy to abide in the human intellect, then the intellect would have to have God himself as the principle of its knowledge, proper only to the light of glory. That light is that by which God sees himself perfectly and by which the blessed in heaven behold God according to the perfection of their created modes of being.[10] Although it is not the light of glory, the light of prophecy is a participation in the light of glory.

Prophecy is an imperfect form of divine revelation adapted to the present state of the human race. Aquinas describes prophecy as "something imperfect in the genus of Divine revelation."[11] Aquinas presents this conclusion by referring to 1 Corinthians 13:8—"Prophecies shall be made void" and "we prophesy in part"—then citing 13:10—"When that which is perfect is come, that which is partial shall be done away"—to show that revelation will be perfected in heaven. Participating in the perfect mode of divine revelation by which the blessed see God (*comprehensors*), prophetic revelation guides us in the present life as wayfarers (*viatores*) journeying through history

---

[8] *ST* II-II, q. 171, a. 2.

[9] This is also why Aquinas distinguishes grace as a habitual form from prophecy as a temporary form: "Every gift of grace raises man to something above human nature, and this may happen in two ways. First, as to the substance of the act—for instance, the working of miracles, and the knowledge of the uncertain and hidden things of Divine wisdom—and for such acts man is not granted a habitual gift of grace. Secondly, a thing is above human nature as to the mode but not the substance of the act—for instance to love God and to know Him in the mirror of His creatures—and for this a habitual gift of grace is bestowed" (*ST* II-II, q. 171, a. 2, ad 3).

[10] See *ST* I, q. 12. This is also why Aquinas will call *sacra doctrina* a participation in the knowledge of God and the blessed (see *ST* I, q. 1).

[11] *ST* II-II, q. 171, a. 4, ad 2. Aquinas continues the theme of graced participation in the heavenly perfection when he treats the gift of understanding (*intellectus*) and the sixth beatitude—"Blessed are the pure of heart for they shall see God"—which accompany the virtue of faith: "The sight of God is twofold. One is perfect, whereby God's Essence is seen: the other is imperfect, whereby, though we see not what God is, yet we see what He is not; and whereby, the more perfectly do we know God in this life, the more we understand that He surpasses all that the mind comprehends. Each of these visions of God belongs to the gift of understanding; the first, to the gift of understanding in its state of perfection, as possessed in heaven; the second, to the gift of understanding in its state of inchoation, as possessed by wayfarers" (*ST* II-II, q. 8, a. 7).

6

to its culmination.[12] As such, prophetic revelation occurs within the contingent necessity of the created order.

The participatory nature of prophetic revelation necessitates a dimension within the created, historical order. Aquinas describes the light of prophecy as a divine light: "Prophetic knowledge comes through the Divine light [*per lumen divinum*], whereby it is possible to know all things both Divine and human, both spiritual and corporeal; and consequently the prophetic revelation extends to them all."[13] This divine light unifies all prophetic revelations. Aquinas describes this unity as follows: "The formal element in prophetic knowledge is the Divine light, which being one, gives unity of species to prophecy, although the things prophetically manifested by the Divine light are diverse."[14] All prophetic revelation thus is unified by the divine

---

[12] Revelation here parallels the passage from the present state of the new law to the state of heaven. Aquinas writes: "As Dionysius says (*Eccl. Hier.* v), there is a threefold state of mankind; the first was under the old law; the second is that of the new law; the third will take place not in this life, but in heaven. But as the first state is figurative and imperfect in comparison with the state of the Gospel; so is the present state figurative and imperfect in comparison with the heavenly state, with the advent of which the present state will be done away as expressed in that very passage (1 Cor. 13:12): 'We see now through a glass in a dark manner; but then face to face'" (*ST* I-II, q. 106, a. 4, ad 1). Reginald Garrigou-Lagrange argues that *sacra doctrina* persists in a perfected state when the theologian comes to the beatific vision, as the imperfect finds perfection: "The theologian who is still a wayfarer, believes the principles transmitted by God revealing and proposed by the Church; and thus his theology is truly a subordinated science, but as yet imperfect. But when this theologian afterward attains to the beatific vision or comes into possession of it, then he not only believes but sees the principles transmitted to him by God through the beatific vision, or in the Word, and he still can, outside the Word, make use of his discursive theology, which then is truly not only a subordinated science, but a perfect one. Thus with the attainment of the beatific vision faith is made void, but not theology. St. Thomas's conclusion concerns sacred theology as it is in itself, and this can be in the theologian either as wayfarer, or as one of the blessed or possessors of God" (*The One God: a Commentary on the First Part of St. Thomas' Theological Summa*, trans. Dom Bede Rose [St. Louis, MO: B. Herder, 1943], 45).

[13] *ST* II-II, q. 171, a. 3.

[14] *ST* II-II, q. 171, a. 3, ad 3. "Now the principle of those things that are prophetically manifested by the Divine light is the first truth, which the prophets do not see in itself. Wherefore there is no need for their knowing all possible matters of prophecy; but each one knows some of them according to the special revelation of this or that matter" (*ST* II-II, q. 171, a. 4). Thomas also writes: "Prophecy denotes Divine knowledge as existing afar off. Wherefore it is said of the prophets

light, namely, God's own knowledge of himself shared with others. Such knowledge unifies revelation as a unified set of truths and also unifies revelation across all space and time, and thus in the historical unfolding of creation. Recalling Aquinas's careful exposition of the reality of God as the source of all created being, we can see that the divine light extends to all created realities, both those of the natural and those of the supernatural orders.[15] The truths that prophetic revelation communicates necessarily have a unity in God's truth and also a unity in God's providential ordering of history.[16] Prophecy thus has a historical dimension.

Not only does prophecy possess a historical dimension for Aquinas; prophecy unveils the providential ordering of history. Although Aquinas treats prophecy toward the end of the *secunda secundae* of the *Summa theologiae* [*ST*], prophetic revelation takes place within the history of the covenants and the laws, which Aquinas treats at length in the *prima secundae*.[17] Prophecy includes not only the Old

---

(Heb. 11:13) that 'they were beholding . . . afar off.' . . . The prophetic vision is not the vision of the very essence of God, and . . . the prophets do not see in the Divine essence Itself the things they do see, but . . . they see them in certain images, according as they are enlightened by the Divine light" (*ST* II-II, q. 173, a. 1). By consequence, although the divine essence is one, the divine perfections, for example, are not synonymous (see *ST* I, q. 13).

15 As Josef Pieper helpfully shows in his essay "On the 'Negative' Element in the Philosophy of St. Thomas Aquinas" (trans. Fred Weick, *CrossCurrents* 4, no. 1 [1953]: 46–56), Aquinas consistently treats truth within the relation between creator and creation. The human mind is measured by the reality of natural creation and in turn measures the reality of the artifacts it makes, and so the divine intellect measures the truth of all created realities. Things are truth insofar as they conform to God's knowledge of himself. Recall that God's knowledge of created realities is not something other than his knowledge of himself. God's knowledge of things measures them and brings them into being by a conjoined act of his will. Aquinas describes God's knowledge of all created realities as "a knowledge of approbation" or "a knowledge of approval" (*ST* I, q. 14, a. 8).

16 Jean-Pierre Torrell, O.P., examines the larger question of whether Aquinas has a sufficiently historical approach to theology. Referring to the work of Ghislain Lafont, he writes, "the author powerfully and pertinently underscores the extent to which Thomas consciously forced himself to respect the order of biblical revelation [l'auteur souligne avec force et pertinence à quel point Thomas s'est efforcé consciemment de respecter l'ordre de la Révélation biblique]" (Torrell, "Saint Thomas et l'histoire: État de la Question et Pistes de Recherches," *Revue thomiste* 105 [2005]: 355–409).

17 For example, see *Super Gal* 4, lec. 2, on Gal 4:4—"But, when the fullness of the time was come, God sent his Son, made of a woman, made under the law"—where

Testament future-oriented prophecy of how God will act in Jesus Christ but also the New Testament witness to how God has in fact acted in Jesus Christ.

Aquinas makes his presumption evident in an almost off-hand-ed remark about Jesus teaching his apostles.[18] In describing the role of prophecy in forming judgments about the truth, he writes: "The intellectual light is divinely imprinted on the human mind [lumen autem intelligibile quandoque quidem imprimitur menti humanae divinitus] sometimes for the purpose of judging of things seen by others, as in the case of Joseph [interpreting dreams in Egypt] . . . and of the apostles whose understanding our Lord opened 'that they might understand the scriptures' (Luke 24:45)."[19] In this latter ex-ample, Aquinas refers to the climactic scene of the disciples on the way to Emmaus, who encounter the risen Jesus. Luke there describes Jesus as explaining the meaning of the (now) Old Testament scrip-tures: "And beginning with Moses and all the prophets, he interpret-ed to them in all the scriptures the things concerning himself" (Luke 24:27). Aquinas presents the apostles being taught by the risen Jesus as a paradigmatic case of prophecy.

Let us consider what is happening when the risen Jesus teaches the apostles. The apostles receive the light of prophecy by which they have insight into divine realities and into how God has fulfilled his promises to Israel in the death and resurrection of Jesus. This pro-phetic insight, moreover, occurs through two modes: first, through the human words of Jesus explaining to them the meaning of the Scripture, and second, by the divine power of Jesus opening their minds to receive a truth rooted in God's revelation.

Aquinas describes the internal and external character of reve-

---

Aquinas comments: "Two reasons are given why that time was pre-ordained for the coming of Christ. One is taken from His greatness: for since He that was to come was great, it was fitting that men be made ready for His coming by many indications and many preparations. 'God, who, at sundry times and in divers manners, spoke in times past to the fathers by the prophets, last of all in these days hath spoken to us by his Son' (Heb 1: 1). The other is taken from the role of the one coming: for since a physician was to come, it was fitting that before his coming, men should be keenly aware of their infirmity, both as to their lack of knowledge during the Law of nature and as to their lack of virtue during the written Law. Therefore it was fitting that both, namely, the Law of nature and the written Law [legem naturae et legem Scripturae], precede the coming of Christ."
[18] See Pieper, "'Negative' Element."
[19] ST II-II, q. 173, a. 2.

9

lation when he comments on Jesus's words "No one can come to me unless the Father, who has sent me, draws him" (John 6:44): "External revelation has the power to attract us along with an interior impulse that incites and moves us to believe. And so the Father draws many to the Son by the impulse of a divine action, moving a person's heart from within to believe: 'it is God who is working in us, both to will and to accomplish' (Phil 2:13)."[20] Revelation includes the interior divine illumination as well as the external historical revelation given in Christ's fulfillment of the biblical narrative and its ongoing reception in the Church.

This is not the only time that Aquinas links prophecy to teaching. Aquinas presents prophetic revelation as a divinely elevated form of teaching. He argues that prophecy includes both "the judgment which depends on the inflow of intellectual light" and "the acceptance or representation of things, which is effected by means of certain species": "Human teaching may be likened to prophetic revelation in the second of these respects, but not in the first. For a man represents certain things to his disciple by signs of speech, but he cannot enlighten him inwardly as God does. But it is the first of these two that holds the chief place in prophecy, since judgment is the complement of knowledge."[21] Again, we see that prophetic revelation includes both interior illumination and external speech.

When Aquinas comments on the story of Jesus and the Samaritan woman at the well, he describes Christ as both a prophet and, yet, more than a prophet, since he himself enlightens the prophets.[22] Unlike other prophets, he does not see certain divine and human realities through a transitory prophetic light; instead, Christ sees them in their fullness, and thus teaches them to others as the incarnate

---

[20] *Super Ioan* 6, lec. 5 (Marietti no. 935).
[21] *ST* II-II, q. 173, a. 2. This passage is cited by Andrew Wood, "Thomas Aquinas and Joseph Ratzinger's Theology of Divine Revelation: A Comparative Study" (PhD diss., Australian Catholic University, 2018), 96.
[22] See *Super Ioan* 4, lec. 2 (Marietti no. 596): "And so she says, Sir, I see that you are a prophet. As if to say: You show that you are a prophet by revealing hidden things to me. It is clear from this, as Augustine says, that her husband was beginning to return to her. But he did not return completely because she regarded Christ as a prophet: for although he was a prophet—'A prophet is not without honor except in his own country' (Matt 13:57)—he was more than a prophet, because he produces prophets: 'Wisdom produces friends of God and prophets' (Wis 7:27)."

Word.[23] In his *De veritate*, Aquinas affirms two acts belonging to prophecy: "One is principal, namely sight, and the other is secondary, namely, announcing."[24] The prophet receives in order to teach. Thus, Christ is the perfect prophet, the perfect teacher, who sees God with the fullness of vision and then announces that vision to everyone beginning with his disciples.[25]

Christ is not only the revealer as subject; he is also the object of revelation as saving truth. This is evident when Aquinas comments on Jesus's words to the Samaritan woman: "You have had five husbands, and the man you have now is not your husband." Unfolding the spiritual meaning of the passage, Aquinas says that she sees Christ only through her five senses, without full intellectual sight. Jesus's intention was to bring her to a "spiritual understanding so that she might believe there was something divine about Christ":

> We should rather say, you have had five husbands, i.e., the five senses, which you have used up to this time; but the man you have now, i.e., an erring reason [*rationem errantem*], with which you still understand spiritual things in a sensual way [*qua spiritualiter dicta adhuc carnaliter intelligis*], is not your husband, but an adulterer who is corrupting you. Call your husband, i.e., your intellect, so that you may really understand me [*idest intellectum, ut intelligas me*].

Christ, the incarnate Word, forms the object of her proper vision; Christ alone can be seen through the receptive understanding proper to the intellect. Moreover, Christ alone is the proper object of the intellect: Christ is the one for which the intellect was made in this created order. Aquinas states the necessity of coming to know Christ in his

---

[23] *Super Ioan* 4, lec. 2 (Marietti no. 594).

[24] *De veritate* q. 12, aa. 9 and 13, cited by Wood when he observes that the act of prophecy for Aquinas includes both the prophetic vision and its announcement by the prophet ("Thomas Aquinas and Joseph Ratzinger's Theology of Divine Revelation," 90).

[25] Dominic Legge, O.P., writes: "Christ as man is truly a prophet who reveals to men the mysteries of God, and whose prophetic knowledge comes to him as a gracious gift from the Holy Spirit. Yet Christ is greater than every other prophet; possessing the fullness of the Holy Spirit, Christ's prophetic knowledge surpasses that of all others" (*The Trinitarian Christology of Thomas Aquinas* [New York: Oxford University Press, 2017], 184).

Commentary on Colossians: "Is our intellect filled by knowing Christ? I say that it is because in him 'are hid all the treasures of wisdom and knowledge.'"[26] The divine light illumines the intellect of the believer to see Christ, to know Christ, as he is in his human and divine reality.[27]

Revelation and the Communication of *Sacra Doctrina*

This section considers *sacra doctrina* and its communication primarily through the lens of revelation.[28] *Revelatio* appears twenty-seven

---

[26] *Super Col* 2, lec. 1 (Marietti no. 81), commenting on Col 2:3: "[Christ Jesus] in whom are hid all the treasures of wisdom and knowledge."

[27] In his *De veritate*, Aquinas distinguishes two ways in which people beheld Christ: with corporeal vision and with intellectual vision. He does so in reference to John the Baptist's singular recognition of Jesus of Nazareth: "That John pointed out Christ physically does not belong to prophetic sight in the way we are now speaking about the comparison of prophecy. Rather, it belongs to the declaration of prophecy. Also, that he saw Christ bodily did not give his prophecy a more perfect nature, but was a concession greater than prophecy given him by God. Hence, Luke (10:24) says: 'Many prophets and kings have desired to see the things that you see' [quod hoc quod Ioannes Christum digito demonstravit non pertinet ad visionem propheticam, prout nunc de prophetiae comparatione loquimur, sed magis ad denuntiationem. Hoc etiam quod Christum corporaliter vidit, non ei dedit prophetiam perfectioris rationis, sed fuit quoddam munus divinitus concessum amplius quam prophetia; unde dicitur Luc. X, 24: multi reges et prophetae voluerunt videre quae videtis, et cetera]" (*De veritate*, q. 12, a. 12, ad 3). It should be admitted that Aquinas at least once speaks of the superiority of supernatural intellectual vision alone: "Thus, it is clear that the pure sight of understanding, which has judgment alone without supernatural reception, is inferior to that which has judgment and the reception of imagination. But the sight of understanding which has judgment and supernatural reception is more noble than that which has judgment and the reception of imagination. In this respect we must concede that prophecy which contains the sight of understanding alone is more worthy than that which has sight of imagination joined to it" (*De veritate*, q. 12, a. 12). It appears to me that this is meant in reference to the prophets of the Old Testament as they sought for Christ: their vision of Christ could not yet be the unique combination of internal and external vision made possible in the Incarnation. Such might be said for Christ himself as the perfection of prophecy in which the beatific light of glory overflowed into the light of prophecy (and into the perfection of infused and acquired knowledge). This will be treated in a later section.

[28] *Sacra doctrina* will usually be left untranslated. Perhaps the best English translation available is "holy teaching" as used by Victor White, O.P., *Holy Teaching:*

times, noun and verbal forms combined, in the first question of *ST*
I. The entire discussion of *sacra doctrina* and the manner in which it
is both a *scientia* (a scientific body of knowledge) and a *sapientia* (a
wisdom) presuppose the phenomenon of divine revelation.[29] By ex-
amining the role of revelation in the context of *sacra doctrina*, we will
see how Aquinas presents revelation in its biblical and Christological
dimensions.

Revelation's decisive role strikes the reader in the very first article
of *ST* I, q. 1. Aquinas asks whether a *doctrina* beyond the philosophical sciences is necessary. Aquinas argues that there needs to be a *doctrina* "according to divine revelation [*secundum revelationem divinam*]
in order to bring about human salvation."[30] In the second article of
this first question, Aquinas presents *sacra doctrina* as a subalternate
scientia, a *scientia* that borrows its principles from a higher *scientia*.
Here he again employs the idea of revelation: "*Sacra doctrina* is a *scientia* because it proceeds from principles established by the light of a
higher *scientia*, namely, the *scientia* of God and the blessed. Hence,
just as the musician accepts on authority the principles taught him
by the mathematician, so *sacra doctrina* accepts principles revealed to
it by God [*doctrina sacra credit principia revelata sibi a Deo*]."[31] *Sacra
doctrina* is a receptive *scientia* that borrows from the light of glory by

---

The Idea of Theology according to St. Thomas Aquinas (London: Blackfriars, 1958),
8. The translation "sacred doctrine" risks misunderstanding, since the word
"doctrine" has a passive meaning referring to what is taught. The word "teaching" more properly also includes the activity of handing it on. Developing this
foundational insight, Francis Martin helpfully observes Aquinas's multi-layered
presentation of *sacra doctrina*: "In Aquinas's mind, there is something called *sacra
doctrina* that is necessary for salvation. . . . As commentators rightly maintain,
[in *ST*, I, q. 1] he is consistent throughout in his use of the term. Consistency,
however, is not the same as univocity, and thus van Ackeren, who holds that
the term refers uniformly to the act of teaching, and O'Brien, who sees it as a
counterpoint to the body of philosophic disciplines taught at Paris, have, in my
opinion, restricted the term unduly and not respected the suppleness of Aquinas's
account. In brief, the term *sacra doctrina* applies to several diverse realities under
the aspect of what they have in common, namely the action of 'causing someone
to know' the truth(s) they need in order to attain the goal God has set for human
existence" (*Sacred Scripture: The Disclosure of the Word* [Naples, FL: Sapientia,
2005], 2–3).

[29] I leave the word *scientia* untranslated, since the Aristotelian notion of an intellectual *scientia* is distinct from modern understandings of empirical science.

[30] *ST* I, q. 1, a. 1.

[31] *ST* I, q. 1, a. 2.

which the blessed are united to God and God knows himself. Aquinas argues in the third article that *sacra doctrina* is one *scientia*, again by showing the role of revelation: "Sacred Scripture considers things precisely under the formality of being divinely revealable [*divinitus revelabilia*], since whatever has been divinely revealed [*divinitus revelata*] shares in [*communicant*] the one precise formality of the object [*in una ratione formali obiecti*] of this science."[32] *Sacra doctrina*—and its written expression in *sacra Scriptura*—are united as being divinely revealable.

Aquinas defends the nobility of *sacra doctrina* by arguing that it "does not accept its principles from other sciences, but immediately from God through revelation."[33] All of *sacra doctrina* thus comes about by divine revelation, as the principles are given by God himself. This immediacy of *sacra doctrina* presupposes the unique role of the incarnate Word in its communication. When he discusses the virtue of faith, Aquinas draws a parallel between the revelation of *sacra doctrina* and the Incarnation when he says that the Incarnation is likewise necessary for human salvation: "The mystery of Christ's Incarnation and passion is the way by which men obtain beatitude."[34] In the context of his *Commentary on John*, Aquinas makes explicit that *sacra doctrina* rests on the revelation of Jesus Christ. Aquinas offers an interpretation of John 1:1—"In the beginning was the Word"—in light of Origen's emphasis on "the beginning" (*archē* in Greek; *principia* in Latin) as the principle of all things. Aquinas then argues that whatever has a principle or beginning also has an order:

> Order is found in learning; and this in two ways: as to nature [*secundum naturam*] and as to ourselves [*quoad nos*], and in both cases we can speak of a beginning [*archē; principia*]. . . . As to nature, in Christian doctrine [*disciplina Christiana*] the beginning and principle of our wisdom is Christ, inasmuch as he is the wisdom and Word of God, i.e., in his divinity. But as

---

[32] *ST* I, q. 1, a. 3: "Quia igitur sacra Scriptura considerat aliqua secundum quod sunt divinitus revelata, secundum quod dictum est, omnia quaecumque sunt divinitus revelabilia, communicant in una ratione formali obiecti huius scientiae. Et ideo comprehenduntur sub sacra doctrina sicut sub scientia una." Aquinas here uses the phrases *sacra doctrina* and *sacra Scriptura* interchangeably.
[33] *ST* I, q. 1, a. 5, ad 2: "Non enim accipit sua principia ab aliis scientiis, sed immediate a Deo per revelationem."
[34] *ST* II-II, q. 2, a. 7.

to ourselves, the beginning is Christ himself inasmuch as 'the Word has become flesh' (John 1:14), i.e., by his Incarnation. [35]

Thus, in and of itself, *sacra doctrina* is simply the Word, God's eternally perfect understanding of himself. For us, in this created, historical order, the principle of *sacra doctrina* is the Word incarnate. Recall that, for Aquinas, a *scientia* is virtually contained in its principles. [36] Thus, we may conclude that it is true to affirm that *sacra doctrina* is virtually contained in the Word incarnate. In commenting on Colossians, Aquinas succinctly summarizes the centrality of Jesus Christ: "the mystery of God the Father, which mystery is Christ [*mysterii Dei Patris, quod est Christus*]." [37] Christ is—and reveals—the mystery of God.

We observe the same pivotal role of revelation in the first question when Aquinas considers *sacra doctrina* as a wisdom. [38] Both philosophical and theological wisdoms consider God as the highest principle of being. Philosophical wisdom considers God as knowable through the perfections and principles in creatures; theological wisdom, however, treats God as "he is known himself to himself alone [*sibi soli de seipso*]." [39] God is the first cause, pure act, sheer to-be-ness

---

[35] *Super Ioan* 1, lec. 1 (Mareitti no. 34). In his *In I an. post.* lec. 1, Aquinas relates *doctrina* and *disciplina*, teaching and learning: "For the names *doctrina* and *disciplina* pertain to the learning process, doctrine being the action exerted by the one who makes us know, and discipline the reception of knowledge from another [Nomen autem doctrinae et disciplinae ad cognitionis acquisitionem pertinet. Nam doctrina est actio eius, qui aliquid cognoscere facit; disciplina autem est receptio cognitionis ab alio]."

[36] *ST* I, q. 1, a. 7: "The object of the principles and of the whole science must be the same, since the whole science is contained virtually in its principles [idem autem est subiectum principiorum et totius scientiae, cum tota scientia virtute contineatur in principiis]."

[37] *Super Col* 2, lec. 1 (Marietti no. 80), on Col 2:2: "That their hearts may be consoled, being instructed in charity and unto all riches of fullness of understanding, unto the knowledge of the mystery of God the Father and of Christ Jesus."

[38] See Mark F. Johnson, "God's Knowledge in Our Frail Mind: The Thomistic Model of Theology," *Angelicum* 76, no. 1 (1999): 25–45. Johnson argues that Aquinas broadly classifies *sacra doctrina* as *scientia* (*ST* I, q. 1, a. 2) and more specifically classifies theology as wisdom (a. 6). In both instances, *sacra doctrina* moves from God to human beings.

[39] *ST* I, q. 1, a. 6. In his *Commentary on Colossians*, Aquinas writes that "some people do not have the Word, and so they do not have *sapientia*" (*Super Col* 3, lec. 3 [Marietti no. 166]).

knowing himself to be.[40] Aquinas then continues to say that theological wisdom is God's eternal act of knowing himself "communicated/shared with others by means of revelation [*et aliis per revelationem communicatum*]."[41] *Sacra doctrina* is this divine self-communication given to and received by the rational creature in this providential order.[42] Combined with the insight of the preceding paragraph, we may affirm that Aquinas presents *sacra doctrina* as the divine self-communication in the Word incarnate.

In his *De veritate*, Aquinas devotes question 12 to prophecy and there connects prophecy to the same theme of divine self-communication to others.[43] In fact, the communication of God via prophecy is so fitting to God and to human nature that Aquinas asks whether prophecy is natural for us. He then draws the distinction that, although this is natural, but not necessary, for God, it is not natural to man: "To communicate His goodness is natural for God in the sense that it is in harmony with His nature and not in the sense that He communicates it because of some necessity of His nature. For such communication is made by the divine will in keeping with the order of wisdom which distributes His goods to all in an orderly way."[44] Thus prophetic revelation is the gratuitous and wise act by which God communicates his goodness to rational creatures by elevating their natural powers to receive a graced mode of understanding and so enter into a communion with God.

Aquinas reiterates this foundational divine self-communication when he introduces his consideration of the Incarnation at the beginning of *ST* III. There he explicates the suitability of the Word becoming flesh by drawing upon the theme from Pseudo-Dionysius that goodness seeks to communicate itself to others; in Latin, he writes "se aliis communicet," the same expression he used in treating

---

[40] Aquinas considers God's knowledge of himself to be the same as his *esse* and his *essentia* (*ST* I, q. 14).

[41] *ST* I, q. 1, a. 6.

[42] Reinhard Hütter writes, "*sacra doctrina* is first and foremost the *act* of faith adhering to the First Truth in the concrete instance of its self-communication as apostolically mediated and interpreted by the *doctrina Ecclesiae*" ("Transubstantiation Revisited: *Sacra Doctrina*, Dogma, and Metaphysics," in *Ressourcement Thomism: Sacred Doctrine, the Sacraments, and the Moral Life*, ed. Reinhard Hütter and Matthew Levering [Washington, DC: Catholic University of America Press, 2010], 21–79, at 33).

[43] *De veritate*, q. 12, a. 3.

[44] *De veritate*, q. 12, a. 3, ad 17.

sacra doctrina as wisdom, "et aliis per revelationem communicatum." Aquinas then argues that the highest goodness ought to communicate itself to creatures in the highest manner ("summo modo se creaturae communicet"). Aquinas draws the conclusion with a quote from Augustine's *De Trinitate* to show that God has in fact done so: "[God joined] created nature to Himself [so] that one Person is made up of these three—the Word, a soul, and flesh."[45] The Incarnation is the highest manner of God's communication of himself to creatures—first and foremost in the created human nature assumed by the Word. The communication to creatures of God's perfect knowing of himself through revelation thus comes from the communication of God's perfection to creatures in the Incarnation.

Thus, the thesis of the present exposition is that it is erroneous to present Aquinas's theology of revelation as exclusively an interior illumination of the human mind to come to know supernatural realities. Aquinas sees the interior illumination as conjoined to events of history, the drama of the covenants, spoken words, and visible signs. He summarizes Christ in his assumed human nature (*secundum quod homo*), or according to the flesh, as our way of coming to God (*tendendi in Deum*).[46] And so, when Aquinas treats the way of truth, he does not address some exclusively interior illumination. Instead, as he writes in the prologue to *ST* III, our Savior "showed us in himself the way of truth [*viam veritatis nobis in seipso demonstravit*]."[47]

---

45 *ST* III, q. 1, a. 1. It is interesting to note many similar themes in Aquinas's treatment of the Incarnation and Augustine's in *De Trinitate* 13. The immediate context of this quote from *De Trinitate* 13.22 is that the Incarnation ("One person now out of three elements, God, soul and flesh") provides hope for humanity's participation in the divine life, "seeing that human nature could so be joined to God."

46 *ST* I, q. 2, prol.

47 *ST* III, prol.: "Forasmuch as our Savior the Lord Jesus Christ, in order to 'save His people from their sins' (Matt. 1:21), as the angel announced, showed unto us in His own Person the way of truth, whereby we may attain to the bliss of eternal life by rising again, it is necessary, in order to complete the work of theology, that after considering the last end of human life, and the virtues and vices, there should follow the consideration of the Savior of all, and of the benefits bestowed by Him on the human race" (cited by René Latourelle in *Theology of Revelation*, as cited by Wood, "Thomas Aquinas and Joseph Ratzinger's Theology of Divine Revelation," 71).

Revelation and Christ the Teacher

In explanation of the statement with which this essay began—that Aquinas does not properly understand revelation to concern historical events—Fr. Elders writes as follows: "According to St. Thomas revelation is a communication of knowledge and so he writes that it is given *'per modum cuiusdam doctrinae* (under the form of teaching).'"[48] The truth of this affirmation, however, does not exclude the historical and external components associated with teaching. For Aquinas, *doctrina* is not merely what is taught, but includes the activity of the teacher.[49] In his *Commentary on the Posterior analytics*, Aquinas juxtaposes the simultaneous realities of teaching and learning: "For the words *doctrina* and *disciplina* pertain to the learning process, *doctrina* being the action of one who makes something known, and *disciplina* the reception of knowledge from another."[50] We may draw from this simultaneous presence of teaching and learning one further implication: there can be neither teaching nor learning without a teacher and a student. We ought then to expect to find a *sacer doctor* of this *sacra doctrina*; a holy teacher of this holy teaching.[51] Thus, it comes

---

[48] Elders, "Aquinas on Holy Scripture," 134, citing *ST* II-II, q. 171, a. 6.

[49] See White, *Holy Teaching*, 8, where he draws upon Aquinas's commentary on the *Posterior analytics*, in which Aquinas describes *doctrina* as "the activity of one who makes something known" (8n1).

[50] *In I an. post.*, lec. 1: "Nomen autem doctrinae et disciplinae ad cognitionis acquisitionem pertinet. Nam doctrina est actio eius, qui aliquid cognoscere facit; disciplina autem est receptio cognitionis ab alio." This is the fuller quotation referenced by White, *Holy Teaching*, 8n1.

[51] Avery Dulles, S.J., presents the following insightful, but undeveloped, relation between Christ's teaching and divine revelation: "In his Christology (*Summa theologiae* III, qq. 1–59), St. Thomas has much to say about the revelatory function of the incarnate Word. Although he looks upon Christ's revelatory work primarily as 'teaching,' he considers this teaching office concretely, as fulfilled not simply in his verbal discourse, but in his whole visible presence and activity, including the example of his life, his passion, and his resurrection. Thus Thomas does not look upon revelation in merely propositional terms, as some have insinuated" (*Revelation Theology: A History* [New York: Herder and Herder, 1961], 43). Dulles's comments help to circumvent any misunderstandings concerning Christ as teacher. Christ exercises his revelatory function through the totality of his teaching not only through his words and doctrines, his parables, and epigrams, but also through his life, passion, and resurrection. The teaching of Christ includes the totality of his being as the eternal Word of the Father who has assumed a human nature.

as no surprise to discover that Aquinas indeed speaks of Christ as the "first and chief teacher [*primus et principalis doctor*] of spiritual *doctrina* and faith."[52]

What does it mean to call Christ the first and principle teacher of *sacra doctrina*?[53] First, it is helpful to observe Aquinas's attention to Christ's relationship to God's covenant with Israel. Christ does not come out of nowhere, but comes as one who has been prepared for by the prophets and the Old Law. The Old Law and the New Law are two parts of the divine law by which God heals and elevates human beings to their supernatural end of union with him.[54] Aquinas relates the two laws to each other as imperfect to perfect, as the immature to the mature, as the prefiguration to the fulfillment. He cites Augustine's *Against the Manicheans*, to affirm "little difference [*brevis differentia*] between the law and the Gospel, fear and love," playing on the similarity of sound between the Latin words *timor et amor*.[55] Aquinas presents the New Law of Christ as the fulfillment of the biblical narrative. In his *Commentary on John*, Aquinas makes this explicit: "Christ's actions [*facta Christi*] are midway between the events [*facta*] of the Old Testament and of the New Testament. . . . Christ's actions are the rule and exemplar of the things that are done in the New Testament, and they were prefigured by the fathers of the Old Testament."[56] Christ himself offers in all that he does the definitive meaning of both the Old and New Laws. The Incarnation thus does not serve as merely a datum of revelation, but as the historical disclosure of saving truth.

We need to interpret thoughtfully Aquinas's presentation of the relation of the Old and New Laws as one of the imperfect and the perfect. First, recall that the imperfect and the perfect belong to the

---

[52] *ST* III, q. 7, a. 7: "Now Christ is the first and chief teacher of spiritual doctrine and faith, according to Heb. 2:3,4: 'Which having begun to be declared by the Lord was confirmed unto us by them that heard Him, God also bearing them witness by signs and wonders.' Hence it is clear that all the gratuitous graces were most excellently in Christ, as in the first and chief teacher of the faith [*in primo et principali doctore fidei*]." Note that all of q. 7 treats of Christ's grace as an individual man, "de gratia eius secundum quod est singularis homo" (*ST* III, q. 7, prol.).

[53] See also the focused treatment of Christ the teacher found in Paweł Klimczak, O.P., *Christus Magister: Le Christ Maître dans les commentaries évangéliques de saint Thomas d'Aquin* (Fribourg, CH: Academic Press, 2013).

[54] *ST* II, q. 91, a. 5.

[55] *ST* II, q. 91, a. 5.

[56] *Super Ioan* 12, lec. 3 (Marietti no. 1626).

same species: so the immature grows into the mature, the boy into the man. With this characterization, Aquinas rejects any Marcionite view that would reject the Old Testament or fundamentally oppose the New to the Old. The Old Law comes to completion in the New Law since the Old Law was intrinsically ordered to the rejection of idols, to the right worship of God, and to its fulfillment in Christ.[57]

Second, it is helpful to note how Aquinas uses the language of perfection in general. Aquinas quotes Aristotle to affirm that "a thing is perfect when it is able to produce its like [*potest alterum tale facere quale ipsum est*]."[58] A tree thus reaches perfection when it is able to spread its seed. The human being reaches maturity when it can reproduce its life in its physical, intellectual, moral, and spiritual dimensions. So, to describe the New Law as perfect in relation to the Old Law means that the New Law can reproduce its like.

The perfect law has the perfect teacher. As the incarnate God, Christ can reproduce himself, his life, and his operation in the lives of those who follow him through the conjoined invisible missions of the Son and the Holy Spirit. Aquinas says that "it was fitting that the perfect law of the New Testament should be given by the incarnate God immediately."[59] Aquinas echoes the teaching of perfection in the Incarnation in his *Commentary on Hebrews*: "Although God speaks in both the New and the Old Testaments, He speaks more perfectly in the New, because in the Old he speaks in the minds of men, but in the New through the Son's Incarnation."[60] This quote, perhaps more than any other, supports the thesis of this essay that Aquinas considers Christ properly as revelation. Prophetic revelation in the Old Testament was necessarily in the minds of the prophets, since Christ had not yet become incarnate; but in the New Testa-

---

[57] Aquinas lists three distinct reasons (*rationes*) for the sacrifices of the Old Law: "God wished these sacrifices to be offered to Him, in order to prevent idolatry; in order to signify the right ordering of man's mind to God; and in order to represent the mystery of the Redemption of man by Christ" (*ST* I-II, q. 102, a. 3, ad 1).

[58] *De potentia*, q. 2, a. 1. The *sed contra* continues: "Now God the Father is perfect. Therefore he can produce his like, and beget a Son." The body of the article continues this theme: "I answer that it is in the nature of every act to communicate itself as far as possible. . . . Now the Divine nature is supreme and most pure act: wherefore it communicates itself as far as possible."

[59] *ST* I-II, q. 98, a. 3.

[60] *Super Heb* 1, lec. 1 (Marietti no. 15); see Wood, "Thomas Aquinas and Joseph Ratzinger's Theology of Divine Revelation," 98.

ment, revelation is no longer thus conceived. The divine law reaches its perfection in Jesus Christ as the perfect teacher.

The perfect teacher gives the perfect law in both internal and external dimensions. Aquinas describes the New Law as principally the grace itself of the Holy Spirit given to those who believe in Christ.[61] Aquinas also teaches that the New Law is an external, written law. These secondary elements instruct the faithful in how to receive and to use that grace. Such instruction comes "both by word and [by] writing, both as to what they should believe and as to what they should do."[62] Aquinas thus describes the *ratio* of the writings of the New Law insofar as they dispose us to the grace of the Holy Spirit and direct us to live in accord with such grace. The New Testament instructs the faithful to believe properly about Christ's divinity and humanity, moves their affections to turn from the world and to God, and exhorts them to the practice of virtue.[63]

So, if "the perfect law of the New Testament should be given by the incarnate God immediately," we now see that Christ gives the New Law in a twofold manner: first, he gives the grace of the Holy Spirit to the faithful; and second, he instructs the faithful with respect to their intellects, affections, and actions through the writings of the New Testament. Both aspects of the New Law, however, are unintelligible apart from their being "given by the incarnate God immediately." Recall here the earlier observation that Aquinas defends the nobility of *sacra doctrina* by arguing that it "does not accept its principles from other sciences, but immediately from God through revelation."[64] Moreover, we saw that, in his *Commentary on Hebrews*, Aquinas offered the formulation that "God speaks more perfectly through his Son's Incarnation." I want to suggest, therefore, that the New Law needs to be seen in a threefold manner, rather than a twofold one consisting merely in the internal grace of the Holy Spirit and the external writings of the New Testament. The third component of the New Law is its reality in its ongoing promulgation by Christ incarnate (*secundum quod homo*).

Let us now consider Aquinas's explicit treatment of the teaching

---

[61] *ST* I-II, q. 106, a. 1. As such, the New Law is the conjoined missions of the Son and the Holy Spirit (*ST* I, q. 43, a. 5, ad 2; a. 6).

[62] *ST* I-II, q. 106, a. 1.

[63] *ST* I-II, q. 106, a. 1, ad 1.

[64] *ST* I, q. 1, a. 5, ad 2: "Non enim accipit sua principia ab aliis scientiis, sed immediate a Deo per revelationem."

of Christ or the *doctrina Christi*. Aquinas addresses the teaching of Christ in a slightly quirky question about why Christ did not write a book or, perhaps more accurately, why Christ did not write the New Testament himself.[65] Aquinas here unveils three key insights into the teaching of Christ: first, his unparalleled dignity as a teacher (*doctor*); second, the excellence of his teaching (*doctrina*); and third, the way in which his teaching (*doctrina*) reaches others through his disciples. In these instances, we will see the centrality of the biblical and historical character of divine revelation.

For the first reason that Christ did not write down his own teachings, Aquinas turns to the excellence of Christ the teacher. He says that "Christ, as the most excellent of teachers [*doctor*], should employ the manner of teaching [*doctrina*] whereby His teaching [*doctrina*] is imprinted on the hearts of His hearers; wherefore it is written (Matt. 7:29) that 'He was teaching them as one having power.'"[66] Aquinas notes that the purpose of writing is nothing other than to share one's teaching. Christ thus accomplishes that purpose of writing by imprinting his *doctrina* directly on the hearts of his hearers. As shown earlier, the incarnate Word is the teacher of the New Law.[67] Consider how Aquinas describes a law as a dictate of reason. As such, a law is one intellectual agent speaking to another intellectual agent. As the communication of the New Law, revelation is God's speaking to his intelligent creatures. When Aquinas treats of teaching in his *De veritate*, he states: "Teaching [*doctrina*] implies the perfect activity of knowledge in the teacher or master [*in docente vel magistro*]."[68] In the case of *sacra doctrina*, its teacher has the perfect realization of knowledge. So, yes, revelation includes an interior illumination of

---

[65] See J. Mark Armitage, "Why Didn't Jesus Write a Book? Aquinas on the Teaching of Christ," *New Blackfriars* 89 (2008): 337–53.

[66] *ST* III, q. 42, a. 4.

[67] Aquinas explicitly identifies the *doctrina Christi* with the New Law of the Spirit: "Since the old Law was given under the form of sensible signs, therefore also was it fittingly written with sensible signs. But Christ's doctrine [*doctrina Christi*], which is 'the law of the spirit of life' (Rom. 8:2), had to be 'written not with ink, but with the Spirit of the living God; not in tables of stone, but in the fleshly tables of the heart,' as the Apostle says (2 Cor. 3:3)" (*ST* III, q. 42, a. 4, ad 2).

[68] *De veritate*, q.11, a.2. He continues here: "Hence, the teacher or master must have the knowledge which he causes in another explicitly and perfectly, as it is to be received in the one who is learning through instruction [*per doctrinam*]." See also ad 3: "God knows explicitly everything which man is taught by him. Hence, the character of teacher can suitably be applied to God."

the mind, but it also includes a teacher who makes possible that interior illumination. Aquinas writes in his *Commentary on John*, "Christ is the most excellent and sublime magister, and therefore his students are the most privileged students."[69] The ultimate external reality and speaker is Jesus Christ in his visible deeds and audible words—for both those who heard the God-man directly and those who come to know his teaching through the deeds and words of his disciples making known Jesus Christ.[70]

The greatest teacher must have the greatest *doctrina*. Aquinas secondly argues that the *doctrina Christi* was so excellent that it could not be written down. Here he pulls in the beautiful verse from John 21:25: "There are also many other things which Jesus did: which, if they were written every one, the world itself, I think, would not be able to contain the books that should be written." Aquinas interprets this in light of Augustine's comment that "we are not to believe that in respect of [physical] space the world could not contain them, . . . but that by the capacity of the readers they could not be comprehended." Aquinas then distinguishes between the understanding of a teaching and its written expression. He writes that, "if Christ had committed His doctrine to writing, men would have had no loftier thought of His *doctrina* than that which appears on the surface of the writing [nihil altius de eius doctrina homines existimarent quam quod Scriptura contineret]."[71] As was the case with the interior and exterior dimensions of the New Law, Aquinas presents the *doctrina Christi* as primarily Christ teaching himself in the hearts of his hearers and secondarily teaching in the actual written passages of the New Testament. Just as the teacher is of unparalleled dignity, so the *doctrina* is of unparalleled excellence. Aquinas summarizes the

---

[69] *Super Ioan* 8, lec. 1, as cited in Thomas O'Meara, O.P., *Thomas Aquinas Theologian* (Notre Dame, IN: University of Notre Dame Press, 1997), 135.

[70] The emphasis on the role of the Word incarnate as teacher by no means excludes the accompanying role of the Holy Spirit in divine teaching. Aquinas makes explicit the role of the Holy Spirit in *Super Ioan* 14, lec. 6 (Marietti no. 1958): "Even the Son himself speaking through the instrument of his humanity would be of no avail, unless he works interiorly through the Holy Spirit"; and "The Son, as the Word, gives us his teaching, but the Holy Spirit makes us capable of receiving that teaching" (as cited by Legge, *Trinitarian Christology of Thomas Aquinas*, 224–25).

[71] *ST* III, q. 42, a. 4. The word *existimarent* also appears in Luke 19:11 "Hæc illis audientibus adjiciens, dixit parabolam, eo quod esset prope Jerusalem: et quia existimarent quod confestim regnum Dei manifestaretur."

divine power of the *doctrina Christi*: "The teaching of Christ has the power both to illumine and to give life, because his words are spirit and life."[72] Christ is both the *doctor* and the *doctrina*, the teacher and the teaching. To put it differently, Christ teaches himself.[73]

The greatest teacher teaches by teaching through others. We learn more about revelation by considering the role of Christ's disciples in the order of his teaching, the third reason offered by Aquinas for Christ not writing down his own teaching. Aquinas says Christ taught in an orderly manner (*ordine*): "[Christ] Himself teaching His disciples immediately, and they subsequently teaching others, by preaching and writing: whereas if He Himself had written, His *doctrina* would have reached all immediately."[74] Christ's disciples participate in the communication of the *doctrina Christi* or the divine revelation.

In his *Commentary on John*, Aquinas describes God as sharing his "dignity of causality" by means of the testimony of the prophets and apostles: "Even though God could have illumined all men by himself and led them to a knowledge of himself, yet to preserve due order [*debitus ordo*] in things and to ennoble certain men, he willed that divine knowledge reach men through certain other men. 'You are my witnesses,' says the Lord (Isa 43:10)."[75] Revelation in Christ is communicated to others through the prophets' unveiling of the future and the apostles' unveiling of the past. In his *Commentary on Hebrews*, Aquinas writes: "The Old Testament was handed down to the patriarchs looking on from afar and seeing God from a distance; the New has been handed down to us, namely, to the apostles, who have seen him in his very person: 'That which we have heard, which we have seen with our eyes, and our hands have handled the Word of life, we declare unto you' (1 John. 1:1)."[76] The apostles handed on

---

[72] *Super Ioan* 8, lec. 1 (Marietti no. 1118).

[73] See also *De veritate*, q. 11, a. 3, ad 8: "A certain progression in faith appears in the disciples of Christ, so that at first they respected him as a wise man and a teacher, and later listened to him as God teaching them. Hence, a gloss a little further on says: 'Since Nathanael knew that Christ, though absent, saw what he had done in another place, which is a sign of the Godhead, he acknowledged that Christ was not only a teacher, but also the Son of God.'"

[74] *ST* III, q. 42, a. 4.

[75] *Super Ioan* 1, lec. 4 (Marietti no. 119).

[76] *Super Heb* 1, lec. 1 (Marietti no. 15). He continues here: "Hence, it is clear that that speaking was a promise: 'To Abraham were the promises made' (Gal. 3:16); but the New was a manifestation: 'Grace and truth came by Jesus Christ' (John

what they received from Christ.[77] In other words, the apostles become teachers through whom Christ teaches.

The apostles share in Christ's teaching by witnessing to Christ's deeds and words. Aquinas appeals to Augustine's formulation of the *totus Christus* to affirm one way in which Christ may be said to have written down his teaching: "Christ is the head of all His disciples who are members of His body. Consequently, when they put into writing what He showed forth and said to them, by no means must we say that He wrote nothing. . . . For at His command they, being His hands, as it were, wrote whatever He wished us to read concerning His deeds and words."[78] Aquinas here articulates that the human authors of the New Testament primarily wrote down "Christ's deeds and words" for us based upon their own witness of "what he showed forth and said to them." In commenting upon the last verse of John, Aquinas speaks of the vocation of the disciples to make known Christ their divine teacher. "For to write about each and every word and deed of Christ is to reveal the power of every word and deed. Now the words and deeds of Christ are also those of God."[79] Therefore, revelation as handed on by the Church retells Christ's deeds and words according to their prophetic meaning, namely, God's activity of revealing himself to the human race in the person of Jesus Christ. For Aquinas, Christ's deeds and words are indeed revelatory.

The apostles and scriptural authors share in the revelatory action of Jesus Christ. When Aquinas comments on faith, he affirms that

---

1:17). Also, in the Old he spoke in the prophets; in the New in his Son, who is the Lord of the prophets: 'The only begotten, who is in the bosom of the Father, he has declared him' (John 1:18)."

[77] For instance, Thomas the Apostle did not come to believe in the resurrection until he saw the risen Christ and listened to his words and actions. Aquinas comments on this episode: "Thomas 'saw one thing, and believed another' [St. Gregory: *Hom. xxvi in Evang.*]: he saw the man, and believing Him to be God, he made profession of his faith, saying: 'My Lord and my God'" (*ST* II-II, q. 1, a. 4, ad 1). The human authors of Scripture, moreover, play a necessary role in the communication of the saving *doctrina*. Aquinas says that divine revelation proceeds to us through certain human beings. Thus *sacra doctrina* includes individual facts, in addition to universal principles, in part "to establish the authority of those men through whom the divine revelation . . . has come down to us" (*ST* I, q. 1, a. 2, ad 2).

[78] *ST* III, q. 42, a. 4, ad 1.

[79] *Super Ioan* 21, lec. 6 (Marietti no. 2660): "Scribere enim per singula, signa et dicta Iesu Christi, est dictorum singulorum et factorum enucleare virtutem. Verba autem et facta Christi sunt etiam Dei."

"the truth of faith is sufficiently explicit in the teaching of Christ and of the apostles [*doctrina Christi et apostolorum*]."[80] Aquinas here identifies the teaching of Christ and the teaching of the apostles with each other. This identity allows Aquinas to say that "Holy Scripture contains the substance of divine revelation which is its source."[81] For Aquinas, divine revelation is God's pedagogy for the human race through the Incarnation and Pentecost as continued in Scripture and the Church.[82]

The present analysis of Christ the teacher returns to the earlier theme of prophetic revelation as rooted in the historical deeds and words of Jesus Christ and its proper reception by his disciples. When Aquinas comments on Christ's sitting down to teach in John, he explains that "sitting down" here refers to the divine condescension of the Incarnation as an act of revelatory teaching. Aquinas explains the reason for the Incarnation, "so that his *doctrina* might be more easily understood": "Because it was through the human nature that our Lord assumed that he became visible, and we began to be instructed in the divine matters more easily."[83] The Word made flesh

---

[80] *ST* II-II, q. 1, a. 10, ad 1. The full response here defends the ongoing role of the Church: "The truth of faith is sufficiently explicit in the teaching of Christ and the apostles. But since, according to 2 Pet. 3:16, some men are so evil-minded as to pervert the apostolic teaching and other doctrines and Scriptures to their own destruction, it was necessary as time went on to express the faith more explicitly against the errors which arose."

[81] *ST* I, q. 1, a. 2, ad 2. The fuller quote is "in order to establish the authority of those men through whom the divine revelation, on which this sacred Scripture or doctrine is based, has come down to us [tum etiam ad declarandum auctoritatem virorum per quos ad nos revelatio divina processit, super quam fundatur sacra Scriptura seu doctrina]" (cited by Elders, "Aquinas on Holy Scripture," 137). See also *ST* III, q. 42, a. 4: "Scripta ordinatur ad impressionem doctrinae in cordibus auditorium sicut ad finem." See Pim Walkenberg, "Scripture," in *The Cambridge Companion to the Summa Theologiae*, ed. Philip McCosker and Denys Turner (New York: Cambridge University Press, 2016), 48–61.

[82] Aquinas presents prophetic revelation as a *doctrina* passing from the divine teacher to the human learner: "Prophecy is a type of knowledge impressed on the prophet's intellect from a divine revelation; this happens after the manner of education [*per modum cuiusdam doctrinae*]. Now the truth of knowledge is the same in both the student and the teacher [*in discipulo et in docente*] since the student's knowledge is a likeness of the teacher's knowledge, just as in natural matters the form of what is generated is a certain likeness of the form of the generator" (*ST* II-II, q. 171, a. 6; cited and trans. by Fr. Matthew Lamb in his introduction to his translation of Aquinas's *Commentary on Ephesians*).

[83] *Super Ioan* 8, lec. 1 (Marietti no. 1122).

instructs the human race in divine realities. This is the heart of revelation for Aquinas.

REVELATION AND THE HUMAN NATURE OF THE INCARNATE WORD

Aquinas employs the theme of teaching throughout his treatment of the reception of divine revelation in faith. He writes of the virtue of faith as follows: "In order that a man arrive at the perfect vision of heavenly happiness, he must first of all believe God, as a disciple believes the master who is teaching him."[84] Just as the New Law is given immediately by the incarnate Son, so also God reveals himself immediately in the human nature of Jesus Christ. Such revelation much be received in faith; trust in God is paramount. Aquinas argues that trust gives us sufficient inducement to believe. He describes the believer as being "moved by the authority of divine teaching [*divinae doctrinae*] confirmed by miracles, and, what is more, by the inward instinct of God's invitation [*interiori instinctu Dei invitantis*]."[85] Then Aquinas shows the fruit of this assent: "Hence the believer does not believe lightly [*non leviter credit*]." The firmness of the assent stems from faith's grounding in divine revelation: "The faith of which we are speaking, does not assent to anything, except because it is revealed by God."[86] The firmness is an internal disposition rooted as well in the external order. The believer trusts in the miracles of Christ, the resurrection, the saving history of Israel, and the prophecies of Christ and their fulfillment. As the fruit of trust and charity, faith is the movement of the intellect to attain to the divine truth. Aquinas describes this assent as a kind of vision, "The light of faith [*lumen fidei*] makes us see what we believe."[87] In faith, we come to know divine realities. How does this knowledge come about?

As we have already seen, the incarnate Word plays a necessary role in the communication of divine revelation. Here we want to ex-

---

[84] *ST* II-II, q. 2, a. 3.

[85] *ST* II-II, q. 2, a. 9, ad 3. This article shows that the act of faith remains meritorious, since the believer has sufficient motive for believing (*ad credendum*) God speaking, but not for knowing (*ad scientiam*) without trust in God.

[86] *ST* II-II, q. 1, a. 1.

[87] *ST* II-II, q. 1, a. 4, ad 3.

amine how Aquinas treats the human nature of Christ as a con-joined—not separate—instrument of that revelation.[88] It is helpful to remember that Aquinas describes revelation in its perfected state as that by which the blessed see God in heaven; revelation in its imperfect state, within history, participates in that reality in a manner parallel to that in which *sacra doctrina* participates in the *scientia* of God and the blessed. Due to this participatory scheme, the faithful believe what the incarnate Word sees. Aquinas describes this instrumental relationship in faith as follows: "Faith is a kind of knowledge, inasmuch as the intellect is determined by faith to some knowable object. But this determination to one object does not proceed from the vision of the believer [*non procedit ex visione credentis*], but from the vision of Him who is believed [*a visione eius cui creditur*]."[89] The vision of him who is believed applies to the eternal Word in his assumed human nature.

What is the vision of him who is believed? What does Christ see? Drawing upon the reality of the assumption of a full human nature by the second person of the Trinity, Aquinas juxtaposes the knowledge appropriate to the human nature with that appropriate to the divine. The two knowledges are instrumentally ordered: the light of uncreated knowledge illuminates the light of created knowledge in Jesus Christ. The greater light gives light; the lesser light receives light. So the "light of knowledge is not dimmed, but rather is heightened in the soul of Christ by the light of the Divine knowledge, which is 'the true light which enlightens every man that comes into this

---

[88] *Summa contra gentiles* [*SCG*] IV, ch. 41, nos. 11–12: "The human nature of Christ, then, is compared to God as a proper and conjoined instrument is compared, as the hand is compared to the soul. . . . Therefore, nothing prevents our putting the union of the human nature to the Word in this way: that the human nature be, so to speak, an instrument of the Word—not a separated, but a conjoined, instrument; and the human nature, nonetheless, does not belong to the nature of the Word, and the Word is not its form; nevertheless the human nature belongs to his person."

[89] *ST* I, q. 12, a. 13, ad 3. He continues here: "Thus as far as faith falls short of vision, it falls short of the knowledge which belongs to science, for science determines the intellect to one object by the vision and understanding of first principles." Thus the intellect is not sufficient unto itself for the *scientia* of *sacra doctrina*, but requires the movement of the will in charity. For instance: "The intellect of the believer is determined to one object, not by the reason, but by the will, wherefore assent is taken here for an act of the intellect as determined to one object by the will" (*ST* II-II, q. 2., a. 1, ad 3).

world,' as is written [in] Jn 1:9."[90] When Aquinas asks whether Christ possessed the vision that belongs to the blessed, he again makes reference to the interplay of intellectual lights: "The soul of Christ, which is a part of human nature, through a light participated from the Divine Nature, is perfected with the beatific knowledge [*lumen participatum a natura divina perfecta est ad scientiam beatam*] whereby it sees God in essence."[91] When Aquinas affirms that Christ's human nature possessed infused knowledge as well, he states: "By this [infused] knowledge Christ knew all things made known to man by Divine revelation, whether they belong to the gift of wisdom or the gift of prophecy, or any other gift of the Holy Spirit."[92] Even though this may sound strange at first, Aquinas teaches that Christ's human nature receives the fullness of revelation.

When Aquinas considers whether Christ has acquired knowledge, he answers *yes*, but in the mode of discovery rather than trusting in the teachings of others.[93] He emphasizes Christ's unique role as the teacher of saving *doctrina*: "It was more fitting for Christ to possess a knowledge acquired by discovery than by being taught, especially since He was given to be the Teacher of all [*praesertim cum ipse daretur a Deo omnibus in doctorem*], according to Joel 2:23: 'Be joyful in the Lord your God, because He hath given you a Teacher

---

[90] *ST* III, q. 9, a. 1, ad 2.

[91] *ST* III, q. 9, a. 2, ad 1. The distinction, however, remains between the creator and creature, between the uncreated light and the created light: "Therefore, although the knowledge of the soul of Christ which He has in the Word is equal to the knowledge of vision as regards the number of things known, nevertheless the knowledge of God infinitely exceeds the knowledge of the soul of Christ in clearness of cognition, since the uncreated light [*lumen increatum*] of the Divine intellect infinitely exceeds any created light [*lumen creatum*] received by the soul of Christ; although, absolutely speaking, the Divine knowledge exceeds the knowledge of the soul of Christ, not only as regards the mode of knowing, but also as regards the number of things known, as was stated above" (*ST* III, q. 10, a. 2, ad 3).

[92] *ST* III, q. 11, a. 1, cited by Legge, *Trinitarian Christology of Thomas Aquinas*, 183. Legge shows how the perfection of Christ's human knowledge includes the invisible mission of the Holy Spirit (172–86).

[93] Aquinas makes the same distinction in *De veritate*, q. 11, a. 1: "There are two ways of acquiring knowledge. In one way, natural reason by itself reaches knowledge of unknown things, and this way is called discovery [*invention*]; in the other way, when someone else aids the learner's natural reason, and this is called learning by instruction [*disciplina*]."

of justice.'"[94] Christ serves as the teacher of all because his human nature is fully illuminated by divine light of knowledge.

Aquinas repeatedly emphasizes the uniqueness of the role of the human nature assumed by the eternal Word. In virtue of the hypostatic union, the soul of Christ receives the divine light "more perfectly than the rest of creatures [and] sees the First Truth itself, which is the Essence of God; hence it is written (John 1:14): 'And we saw His glory, the glory as it were of the Only-begotten of the Father,' 'full' not only of 'grace' but also of 'truth.'"[95] All of the blessed receive a "participation of the light that comes to them from the source of the Word of God." In *ST* I, Aquinas describes this divine light as the light of glory, a created participation in God's own vision of himself through himself.[96] Here he describes the light of glory as the light of the soul of Christ as both perfect and perfecting.[97]

When Aquinas treats the light of glory by which the blessed behold God's essence, he cites Psalm 36:10—"In thy light, we shall see light." In his commentary on this psalm, Aquinas considers "in thy light" according to four lights that come from God in degrees, all stemming from the inner-Trinitarian light: first, the natural light of the intellect; second, the light of grace; third, the light of glory; and fourth, the light of light, the Son proceeding from the Father.[98]

---

[94] *ST* III, q. 9, a. 4, ad 1.

[95] *ST* III, q. 10, a. 4. Aquinas continues here to emphasize the priority of the divine illumination of Christ's human soul: "And in this way the soul of Christ, which is filled with a more abundant light [*quae abundantiori impletur lumine*], knows the Divine Essence more perfectly than do the other blessed, although all see the Divine Essence in itself."

[96] *ST* I, q. 12, a. 2; a. 5.

[97] Aquinas employs the perfection and perfecting argument to support his determination that Christ enjoyed the beatific vision: "Now men are brought to this end of beatitude by the humanity of Christ, according to Heb. 2:10: 'For it became Him, for Whom are all things, and by Whom are all things, Who had brought many children unto glory, to perfect the author of their salvation by His passion.' And hence it was necessary that the beatific knowledge, which consists in the vision of God, should belong to Christ pre-eminently, since the cause ought always to be more efficacious than the effect" (*ST* III, q. 9, a. 2). Christ does not merely have the light of grace or the light of prophecy; instead, Christ's human nature possesses the light of glory. Nonetheless, he has all three insofar as the light of prophecy is a participation in the light of glory. It belongs to the perfection of Christ's human nature and its role as the instrument of the perfection of the human race that Christ possess the light of glory and the light of prophecy.

[98] *Super Psalmos* 35 (dhspriory.org/thomas/PsalmsAquinas/ThoPs35H36.htm).

Then, Aquinas considers "we shall see light" and identifies this visible light as "created truth, that is Christ, with respect to his human nature."[99] Christ's human nature perfects human nature in two ways: first, in its own vision of the Father, and second, in making that vision visible to the rest of human beings.

Christ thus perfects revelation in both receiving and communicating his vision of God. Aquinas emphasizes the role of the human nature of Christ in accomplishing our healing: "The humanity of Christ had the power of influencing [human beings] because it was united to the Word of God."[100] Aquinas further develops this theme of Christ as the light of vision in his *Commentary on Colossians*:

> Let us suppose that a person has a candle that is covered; he would not look then for another light, but wait for the light he has to become uncovered. And in the same way we do not have to look for wisdom anywhere but in Christ: "for I decided to know nothing among you except Jesus Christ and him crucified" (1 Cor 2:2). . . . In other words, if I had a book in which all knowledge was contained, I would seek to know only that book; similarly, it is not necessary for us to seek any further than Christ.[101]

Aquinas reiterates a similar theme in his discussion of wisdom at the beginning of the *Summa contra gentiles*. There he says that the Incarnation was ordered to communicate the truth: "And for this reason divine wisdom, clothed in flesh, declares that he came into the world to make known the truth, saying, 'For this I was born, and for this I have come into the world, to bear witness to the truth' (John 18:37)."[102] As the incarnate Word, Christ shares his wisdom, his *doctrina*, his truth with the human race for the sake of our salvation and final union with the triune God.

---

[99] *Super Psalmos* 35. Aquinas also says that "we shall see light" may be interpreted also to mean the light by which we see: "uncreated truth, by which we recognize and come to know other true things."

[100] *ST* III, q. 8, a. 2.

[101] *Super Col* 2, lec. 1 (Marietti no. 82), commenting on Col 2:3: "[Christ Jesus] in whom are hid all the treasures of wisdom and knowledge."

[102] *SCG* I, ch. 1, no. 2.

CONCLUSION

This essay proceeded in four parts. First, we showed how Aquinas understands prophetic revelation as the interior illumination of the understanding combined with external prophetic realities, including par excellence Jesus Christ. Second, we looked at how Aquinas understands *sacra doctrina* as God's sharing his own understanding of himself with human creatures through Jesus Christ. Third, we learned that Aquinas presents Christ as the teacher of divine revelation. Fourth, we saw that Aquinas holds that the human nature of Christ acts as the instrumental cause of the communication of divine revelation and as the perfection of its reception.[103]

The appearance in history of the incarnate Word forms the centerpiece of divine revelation for Aquinas. Christ teaches in a divine and human manner, in which the divine Son teaches through his human nature as a fully human instrument. Aquinas describes the rationale for the Incarnation: "He wished to draw near to us by taking flesh, [and so] He drew us to know Him more deeply [*magis nos ad se cognoscendum attraxit*]."[104] As the Incarnate divine teacher, he allows the faithful to know God in a graced and eventually glorified manner. In his *Commentary on John*, Aquinas explains God's wisdom in so drawing us to himself: "The manner in which we are drawn

---

[103] See Michael Sherwin, O.P., "Christ the Teacher in St. Thomas's *Commentary on the Gospel of John*," in *Reading John with St. Thomas Aquinas: Theological Exegesis and Speculative Theology*, ed. Michael Dauphinais and Matthew Levering (Washington, DC: Catholic University of America Press, 2005), 173–93.

[104] *ST* III, q. 1, a. 1, ad 3. Note also the quotation of Dionysius in which Aquinas considers an objection from Dionysius's *Mystical Theology* that says the more we are united to God in this life, "we are united to him as an entirely unknown [*omnino ignoto*]." In his response, Aquinas changes the *omnino* to a *quasi* and affirms that we are united to God "as to one seeming unknown" (*quasi ignoto*). Aquinas's response then affirms that "we know him more fully [*tamen plenius ipsum cognoscimus*]" (*ST* I, q. 12, a. 13, ad 1). He continues: "According as many and more excellent [*plures et excellentiores*] of His effects are demonstrated to us, and according as we attribute to Him some things known by divine revelation, to which natural reason cannot reach, as, for instance, that God is Three and One." Aquinas here gives the example of the baptism of Jesus at which the dove was visible and the Father's voice was heard. Thus, revelation comes in outward and inward dimensions. For a thorough treatment of how Aquinas receives and interprets Dionysius, see Bernard Blankenhorn, O.P., *The Mystery of Union with God: Dionysian Mysticism in Albert the Great and Thomas Aquinas* (Washington, DC: Catholic University of America Press, 2015), 317–440.

is appropriate [*congruus*], for God draws us by revealing and teaching."[105] Christ is not only savior; he is also is teacher and revealer.[106]

Contrary to the earlier interpretations of Elders and Martelet and those who have followed their interpretations, this paper has demonstrated that Aquinas does not separate Christ from revelation. Instead, for Aquinas, revelation is properly the fulfillment of the providential order of the biblical narrative in Jesus Christ. As developed in his *Summa theologiae* and in his biblical commentaries, Aquinas's theology of revelation shows that God reveals himself to us in the Incarnation, and so allows us to participate in God's own beatifying knowledge of himself.[107]

---

[105] *Super Ioan* 6, lec. 5 (Marietti no. 942).

[106] Legge develops the theme of the Word incarnate in both a revelatory and salvific role by focusing on the missions of the divine Persons—and their relation to the eternal processions—as foundational for Aquinas's Christology: "The Word's incarnation is thus the heart of the entire *dispensatio*, because it is through him, and through his manifestation of the Father, that we are brought back to the Father, 'the ultimate person to whom we return.' The Word incarnate is, indissociably, the agent of revelation and salvation" (*Trinitarian Christology of Thomas Aquinas*, 82, citing *In* I *sent.*, d. 15, q. 4, a. 1).

[107] The present essay develops a line of argumentation about Christ as revelation in Aquinas similar to that found in M. J. Le Guillou, O.P., *Christ and Church: A Theology of the Mystery*, trans. Charles Schaldenbrand (New York: Desclee, 1966) [originally *Le Christ et l'Eglise—Théologie du Mystère* (1963)]. Guillou summarizes his argument thus: "The theology of the *Tertia Pars* is truly the contemplation of the divine Wisdom incarnate, who has become for us the Word revealing God and His glory, and, at the same time, the saving Word. Christ is thus truly the *Mystery*: He is the plentitude of the divine Word which has been spoken to us, and He is, at the same time, considered in His humanity conjoined to the Word, the free and loving response which man offers to God in grace" (266). Likewise: "The Thomistic wisdom has frequently been reproached (even by its admirers) for its lack of an historical sense, and for its failure to do justice to the irreversible character of historical becoming. Nevertheless, this objection seems without justification when it is applied to the heart of St. Thomas's reflection, for in spite of certain insufficiencies which we will consider shortly, he was undoubtedly the first, and perhaps the only theologian, to have carried out a plan of such immense dimensions: it was his goal to establish the epistemological status of a theology capable of satisfying the need for the intelligible consistency of the faith, while at the same time preserving intact the full value of the economy of salvation. The Thomistic synthesis represents a unique moment in the history of reflection upon the data of revelation, and its excellence in this respect has remained unequaled even to the present day. As the *Sacra Doctrina* in the sense defined in the preceding chapters, it is a *theology* in the strongest sense of the term, since it seeks to contemplate all things in this light of wisdom in which God sees Himself and

Christ as revelation grounds the Christian life. Aquinas exhorts the faithful to stay close to Jesus Christ, "the way, the truth, and the life":

> If then, you ask which way to go, take Christ, for he is the way: "this is the way, walk in it" (Isa 30:21). . . .

> If you ask where to go, cling to Christ, for he is the truth which we desire to reach: "my mouth will utter truth" (Prov 8:7).

> If you ask where to remain, remain in Christ because he is the life: "he who finds me finds life and will have salvation from the Lord" (Prov 8:35).[108]

---

all things in Himself, *on the basis of the self-revelation which he has granted us in His Son, through Scripture and the tradition of the Church*. As the expression of the sapiential richness of the Word of God revealing the meaning of His action in history, *it is the theology of the Mystery of Christ*" (326).

[108] *Super Ioan* 14, lec. 2 (Marietti no. 1870).

Unless You Believe, You Will Not Understand: Biblical Faith according to Thomas Aquinas and Benedict XVI

Matthew J. Ramage
Ave Maria University

Introduction: We Are All Thomas Now

We find ourselves today inhabiting an age described by Charles Taylor as "secular." Indeed, ours is a very secular society in the sense that discourse about God and expression of our Christian faith in the public square are often characterized as an affront to other people's freedom, a danger that must be tightly curtailed in the name of tolerance. However, this is not the use of the word "secular" that I have in mind here in beginning this essay. In Taylor's parlance, "secularity" does not refer to a society being composed largely of nonreligious people but to it being one in which the path of faith is seen to be just one lifestyle option among others and no more obviously true than its alternatives. As James Smith puts it in his helpful book distilling Taylor's much longer work *A Secular Age*: "Faith is fraught; confession is haunted by an inescapable sense of its contestability. We don't believe instead of doubting; we believe while doubting. We're all Thomas now."[1]

---

[1]   James Smith, *How (Not) to Be Secular: Reading Charles Taylor* (Grand Rapids, MI:

One of the most oft-recurring questions in the lives of adult Christians of our age concerns the relationship between faith and doubt that Smith has pithily identified above. Believers often tend to think that their faith is supposed to be absolutely certain. However, the reality of belief experienced in the actual lives of the faithful today often appears to exist more along the lines described by Taylor and Smith than as described by Thomas Aquinas, for whom the presence of doubt is incompatible with faith. Accordingly, what I wish to do in the following pages is to show that the Catholic Church, especially as enshrined in the biblically infused thought of Thomas Aquinas, has something profound to say to those of us today who find ourselves caught in the situation described above. As a way of working toward this end, I will spend the first half of the essay teasing out what precisely it is that Aquinas thinks about the nature of faith and what biblical texts he uses to ground his approach, addressing the questions of what is meant by faith, what power of the soul faith resides in, and how much certitude faith enjoys, and finally the issue of the believer's need to affirm the entire faith.

After surveying Aquinas's biblical account of faith, I will turn in the final portion of this paper to Joseph Ratzinger / Benedict XVI to compare and contrast his approach with that of the Angelic Doctor, highlighting along the way the various biblical texts that inspire the emeritus Pontiff's theology of faith. These include some of the same ones that Aquinas reflects on in this regard, especially Isaiah 7:9, which lies behind the title of the present essay. As I will attempt to show, Ratzinger's account of the faith—inspired more directly by Pseudo-Dionysius and Bonaventure than by Thomas— envisions faith more as an existential virtue, rather than an intellectual one. In the end, however, my contention will be that it is important that we benefit from both *ressourcement* of the ancient and engagement with the modern—from the approaches of both Aquinas and Ratzinger—when it comes to articulating the nature of biblical faith. I thus hope to showcase the deep harmony that exists between Aquinas and Ratzinger in their biblically grounded contemplation of the virtue of faith.

Eerdmans, 2014), 21.

AQUINAS'S BIBLICAL ACCOUNT OF FAITH

What Is the Virtue of Faith?

The Angelic Doctor discusses the definition of faith (*fides*) in three key places: *De veritate*, the *secunda secundae pars* of the *Summa theologiae* [*ST*], and his commentary on Hebrews, all of which base their response on the definition of faith in Hebrews 11:1 ("Est autem fides sperandarum substantia rerum, argumentum non apparentium"). In *De veritate*, this definition is described as "very complete" yet "not in the sense as given according to the required form of a definition, but because in it there is sufficient mention of everything which is necessary for a definition of faith."[2] In *ST* II-II, likewise, Aquinas says that "this definition overlooks none of the points in reference to which faith can be defined, albeit the words themselves are not arranged in the form of a definition."[3] And in his commentary devoted specifically to Hebrews, Aquinas describes this definition of faith as "complete but obscure."[4]

A question arises in this definition from Hebrews 11:1: If faith is prior to hope, as we know from 1 Corinthians 13, then why does Hebrews 11 define it in terms of hope (*sperandarum substantia rerum*)? Thomas's answer is that, yes, of course, in the order of knowing, the intellect (which concerns faith) is prior to the will (which concerns hope), but when it comes to the order of movement within the act of faith, the will is prior. Accordingly, Aquinas finds the definition of faith in Hebrew 11 to be fitting, for a proper definition of faith has to include the order of the act of faith to its object, eternal happiness.[5]

And what of calling faith a "substance" (*substantia*)? For Aquinas this is simple: "We are wont to call by the name of substance, the first beginning of a thing, especially when the whole subsequent

---

2   *De veritate*, q. 14, a. 2, trans. James McGlynn (Chicago: Henry Regnery, 1953). All quotations of *De veritate* will come from this edition.

3   *Summa theologiae* [*ST*] II-II, q. 4, a. 1, trans. Fathers of the English Dominican Province (Westminster, MD: Christian Classics, 1981). All quotations of *ST* in translation will be from this translation.

4   *Super Heb* 11, lec. 1 (Marietti no. 252), in *Commentary on the Letter of St. Paul to the Hebrews*, trans. Fabian R. Larcher (Lander, WY: Aquinas Institute for the Study of Sacred Doctrine, 2012); paragraph numbers in citations of Thomas's Scripture commentaries will be the Marietti numbers.

5   *Super Heb* 11, lec. 1 (nos. 553–54).

thing is virtually contained in the first beginning."[6] In this way, we can say that the first self-evident principles are the substance of science, as the whole science is contained in them virtually. Thus, faith is rightly said to be the "substance of things to be hoped for," for the first beginning of things to be hoped for—eternal life—is already about in a virtual or inchoative manner by the assent of faith.

Two other words from Hebrews 11:1 briefly require our attention. By the words "of those things that appear not" (*non apparentium*), faith is distinguished from science and understanding (*a scientia et intellectu*), for these modalities of knowledge concern things which do indeed appear to us in the sense that our intellect is able to attain vision of them without the additional assistance of the will that faith requires. Meanwhile, the presence of the word "evidence" (*argumentum*), translated "conviction" by the RSV, distinguishes faith from both opinion and doubt, something I will be commenting on in more detail in another section below. Finally, describing faith as evidence also distinguishes it from all habits that are not cognitive, which leads us to our next topic.[7]

In What Power of the Soul Does Faith Reside?

Aquinas's understanding of faith operates on Augustine's definition of belief (*credere*) as "thinking with assent," or in Aquinas's words, "an act of the intellect narrowed to one thing by the command of the will."[8] Since this act of belief is called assent, says Aquinas, it must be about a proposition, in which truth or falsity is found.[9] Countering the objection that this act of assent would seem to lie more in the will than in the intellect, in question 2 of *ST* II-II, the Angelic

---

[6] *ST* II-II, q. 4, a. 1. For a discussion of how the entire substance—all articles—of the Christian creed are virtually contained in the affirmation of the two truths of God's existence and providence, see Matthew Ramage, *Dark Passages of the Bible* (Washington, DC: Catholic University of America Press, 2013), 93–108.

[7] *De veritate*, q. 14, a. 2.

[8] *Super Heb* 11, lec. 1 (no. 553); Augustine, *On the Predestination of the Saints* 1.5, trans. Peter Holmes and Robert Ernest Wallis, rev. Benjamin B. Warfield, NFPF1, vol. 5.

[9] *De veritate*, q. 14, a. 12: "Thus, when we say: 'I believe in the resurrection,' we must do this with reference to some time in which the resurrection occurred historically." Accordingly, for Aquinas the sense of "I believe in the resurrection" is "I believe that the resurrection is, was, or will be."

Doctor parses Augustine in this way: belief indeed is an act of the intellect, yet it is one in which the intellect is determined to its object by the will.[10] In *De veritate*, meanwhile, we find this exposition of what it means for the act of the intellect to be determined by the will: some things that are not enough to move the intellect are enough to move the will; as a result, in the act of belief, the intellect's proper action is caused not by itself but by the will.

Because of this determination, Aquinas says that the intellect of the believer is "held captive" by the will insofar as, "in place of its own proper determinations, those of something else are imposed on it."[11] Thomas grounds this dynamic in 2 Corinthians 10:5: "We destroy arguments and every proud obstacle to the knowledge of God, and take every thought captive to obey Christ."[12] Although I doubt that Paul had the relationship of intellect and will in mind when penning this verse, Aquinas's use of the text strikes me as brilliant—and deeply Pauline. As Paul has it in his other letter to the Corinthians, the word of the Cross is folly in the eyes of those who are wise in the ways of this world, but in truth, the foolishness of God is wiser than men (see 1 Cor 1:17–25).

We may add a Pascalian note here and say that faith appears as foolishness to the intellect untutored by grace because the heart has its reasons of which reason knows nothing—in other words, because the will's adherence to the good moves the intellect in a way that it would not be able to if left to its own power. And, of course, there is also the causality of grace that moves the whole act, as we read in Aquinas's classic definition of belief in *ST* II-II, q. 2, a.9: "Believing is an act of the intellect assenting to the divine truth at the command of the will moved by the grace of God."[13]

In *ST* II-II, q. 4, a. 2, and *De veritate*, q. 14, a. 2, Aquinas considers objections to his view of faith as a cognitive act, objections claiming Augustine's authority in support of the view that faith resides in the affective part (*in parte affectiva*) rather than the cognitive part (*in parte cognoscitiva*) of the soul—in other words, that it resides

---

[10] *ST* II-II q. 2, a. 1: "Assent is taken here for an act of the intellect as determined to one object by the will."
[11] *De veritate*, q. 14, a. 1.
[12] Unless otherwise indicated, translations in the biblical text that follows will be taken from the RSV.
[13] See also *Catechism of the Catholic Church*, §155.

in the will (*in voluntate*).[14] In the *sed contra* of the *ST* II-II article, we find Thomas citing 1 Corinthians 13:12: "For now we see in a mirror dimly, but then face to face." Since vision is in the intellect, Aquinas reasons, faith too must be. Belief is immediately an act of the intellect, because the object of the act is the true, which pertains properly to the intellect.[15] In the reply to objection 1, Thomas then spells out directly what he thinks Augustine means and how his objector has it wrong: "Augustine takes faith for the act of faith, which is described as *depending on* the believer's will, in so far as his intellect assents to matters of faith at the command of the will."[16] Aquinas might be putting words into Augustine's mouth, but I think it is a theologically accurate articulation of the relationship between the intellect and will in the act of faith.

In objection 3 of the *ST* passage, meanwhile, Aquinas wishes to address the related contention that: "Faith is not in the speculative intellect, since this is not concerned with things to be sought or avoided. . . . Likewise, neither is it in the practical intellect, the object of which is some true, contingent thing, that can be made or done." The objector references Galatians 5:6 to drive home his point: "Faith work[s] through love."[17] In his reply, Thomas contends that faith's residence in the speculative intellect is evidenced by its object, the First Truth, which is the end of all our desires and actions. He then parses Galatians 5:6 in this manner: faith works through love just as the speculative intellect becomes practical by extension.[18] Clearly, faith must be distinct from charity if it is said to work through it.

In the next article of *ST* II-II, q. 4, Thomas takes up the question of whether charity is faith's form. The objector sees a problem in this, given that faith is in the intellect but charity resides in the will. In reply, he says that this would be a good objection if we were speaking of intrinsic form, but when we call charity the form of the virtues, we are not talking about the intrinsic form of natural things.

---

[14] *ST* II-II, q. 4, a. 2, obj 1; Augustine, *On the Predestination of the Saints* 1.10: "The passage, 'For who makes you to differ? And what have you that you received not?' [1 Cor 4:7] refers to that very faith which is in the will of man." In the Latin text of *De veritate*, this citation is attributed to a letter of Augustine to Consentius, but I have been unable to track down what precise line he intends to reference.

[15] *ST* II-II, q. 4, a. 2.

[16] *ST* II-II, q. 4, a. 2, ad 1 (emphasis added).

[17] *ST* II-II, q. 4, a. 2, obj. 3.

[18] *ST* II-II, q. 4, a. 2, ad 3.

Rather, voluntary acts like faith take their species from their end, the will's object. Charity is the form of the voluntary act of faith, then, in the sense that it *quickens* the act of faith.[19]

In *De veritate*, q. 14, a. 2, we find further arguments to aid our endeavor of answering the question of whether faith resides in the intellect or in the will. There are various opinions regarding this question, Thomas says. Some, for example, have said that faith is in both the affective and cognitive powers ("in utraque vi, scilicet affectiva et cognitiva"). Aquinas rejects this possibility, reasoning that an act cannot be in two powers equally. Acknowledging this, some—like the objector in the *ST* passage—then say that faith is principally in the affective power. But neither does this ring true to Thomas, who now invokes Augustine's authority to remind us that belief implies some thought (belief is thinking with assent), which of course belongs to the cognitive power of man.[20]

Although faith resides in the speculative intellect, Aquinas does say that it is nevertheless the remote occasion (*remota occasio*) of doing something, occasioning the doing through the mediation of charity (*mediante caritate*). Accordingly, faith is not in the speculative intellect absolutely, but only insofar as it is subject to the will ("non est in intellectu speculativo absolute, sed secundum quod subditur imperio voluntatis").[21] In other words, although that which comes from the will can be said to be accidental to the intellect, it is nevertheless essential to faith ("quamvis illud quod est ex parte voluntatis possit dici accidentale intellectui, est tamen fidei essentiale"). In a helpful analogy, Thomas reminds us that something similar occurs in the case of temperance, for which the element of reason is essential, even though it is accidental to the concupiscible appetite considered alone.[22] Nevertheless, if the intellect is to follow the command of the will promptly, it needs its own perfective habit, and this we call faith.

Thomas addresses the Augustinian objection directly in his answer to the difficulty in objection 3, arguing that, when Augustine says that faith lies in the will, he is "talking about the act of faith, which, indeed, is said to be in the will not as in a subject, but as in

---

[19] *ST* II-II, q. 4, a. 3.
[20] *De veritate*, q. 14, a. 4.
[21] *De veritate*, q. 14, aa. 4–5.
[22] *De veritate*, q. 14, a. 3, ad 10.

a cause, in so far as it is commanded by the will."[23] Again, I am not
sure whether Augustine himself had consciously thought this out as
clearly as Aquinas makes it seem, but it is nevertheless consistent
with the above contention that faith must be distinct from charity if
it is said to work by means of it.

On the subject of how Aquinas construes the relationship of the
intellect and will in faith, one last note from his extensive commentary on Galatians 5:6 merits our attention:

> *For in Christ Jesus*, i.e., in those who live in the faith of
> Christ, *neither circumcision nor uncircumcision avails anything*,
> i.e., they make no difference; but faith, not unformed, but
> the kind that *works by charity*: *Faith without works is dead* (Jas
> 2:26). For faith is a knowledge of the Word of God—*That
> Christ may dwell by faith in your hearts* (Eph 3:17)—which
> Word is not perfectly possessed or perfectly known unless
> the love which it hopes for is possessed.[24]

I find this text to be incredibly interesting. Once again, faith is clearly
understood here to be an intellectual virtue. However, in this passage,
Thomas accentuates the reality that faith's knowledge is not perfectly
possessed unless it is accompanied by love. This is going to connect
closely with the thought of Benedict XVI, according to whom love
itself is a source of knowledge. While they understand the virtue of
faith in different ways, the two theologians share the deep conviction
that head knowledge itself is insufficient—not just for salvation, but
for the possession of the intellectual virtue of faith itself.

The Certitude of Faith

Aquinas holds that faith is the most certain of all knowledge in this
life, yet he is also keenly aware of the objection many of us still harbor
seven centuries later: if faith is eminently certain, then why is it so
easy to doubt? The Angelic Doctor answers in this profound passage:

[23] *De veritate*, q. 14, a. 4, ad 3.

[24] *Super Gal* 5, lec. 2 (no. 286), in *Commentary on the Letter of St. Paul to the Galatians and Ephesians*, trans. F. R. Larcher (Lander, WY: Aquinas Institute for the
Study of Sacred Doctrine, 2012).

It may well happen that what is in itself the more certain may seem to us the less certain on account of the weakness of our intelligence, "which is dazzled by the clearest objects of nature; as the owl is dazzled by the light of the sun." Hence the fact that some happen to doubt about articles of faith is not due to the uncertain nature of the truths, but to the weakness of human intelligence; yet the slenderest knowledge that may be obtained of the highest things is more desirable than the most certain knowledge obtained of lesser things.[25]

This in brief is how Aquinas accounts for the reality that the light of faith, though in itself the brightest of all lights available to us here below, appears "dark" in the eyes of so many. While sin surely plays a part in our inability to grasp divine truth, for Aquinas, the very nature of our created intellect is inadequate to the task of piercing the depths of supernatural truth in this life. Thus, not everyone who struggles with faith does so because they are living a life of habitual grave sin. In point of fact, the history of Catholic spirituality teaches us that many of the greatest saints—Mother Teresa, Thérèse of Lisieux, and Faustina, to name just a few—struggled with spiritual darkness, not despite their holiness, but precisely because of it.

But let us be precise. I said a moment ago that it is easy to doubt the faith, especially living in the postmodern world. However, we know that this is not yet speaking accurately enough. As we said above in light of Hebrews 11:1, describing faith as the "evidence" (*argumentum*) of things hoped for distinguishes it from opinion (*opinio*) and doubt (*dubitatio*). An important difference is that, unlike faith, these two do not cause the intellect to adhere to anything firmly, because it remains unconvinced. In doubt, one does not find there to be more evidence for one side than for the other for a given proposition, whereas in opinion, one assents, but with fear that the opposite might be true, and thus that the faith might be false. Faith, however, depends on the authority of the one in whom we place our trust. If there is certainty in the reliability of this figure and no fear of the opposite side, we have faith.[26] Aquinas is definitely no postmodern "doubting Thomas."

---

[25] *ST* I, q. 1, a. 5, ad 1, citing Aristotle, *Metaphysics* 2.1.

[26] *ST* II-II, q. 1, a. 4. See also *Super Heb* 11, lec. 1 (no. 558), and *Super Rom* 1, lec. 6 (no. 104), in *Commentary on the Letter of St. Paul to the Romans*, trans. F. R. Larcher (Lander, WY: Aquinas Institute for the Study of Sacred Doctrine, 2018).

Perhaps some insight into this question can be garnered from *ST* II-II, q. 4, a. 8, in the treatise on faith. This article interacts with a series of biblical texts. In the first objection, faith's certitude is challenged on the basis that doubt is opposed to certitude, yet "the believer may sometimes suffer a movement of doubt, and doubt about matters of faith" ("credens autem interdum potest pati motum dubitationis et dubitare de his quae sunt fidei"). In objection 2, we are reminded that sight is more certain than hearing, and yet St. Paul tells us that faith—in contrast with science and understanding—is through hearing (Rom 10:17). Objection 3, meanwhile, has recourse to the Septuagint (LXX) of Isaiah 7:9: "Unless you believe, you will not understand" (ἐὰν μὴ πιστεύσητε, οὐδὲ μὴ συνῆτε; *ean mē pisteusēte, oude mē synēte*). Understanding must be more perfect, the argument thus goes, since faith is the way to understanding.[27]

In the *sed contra* of article 8, Thomas's argument from authority is drawn from 1 Thessalonians 2:13: "When you received the word of God which you heard from us, you accepted it not as the word of men but as what it really is, the word of God." Since nothing is more certain than the word of God, it follows that neither science nor anything else is more certain than faith. In his reply, Aquinas then draws the distinction that certitude can be looked at in two ways. Faith is more certain than other knowledge when considered with respect to its cause, God. However, if considered with respect to the subject, man's intellect, then "faith is less certain, because matters of faith are above the human intellect." Accordingly, the bottom line is that "faith is more certain simply, while the others are more certain relatively, i.e., for us."[28]

What of the objections? As to the first, it is interesting that Thomas does not deny that a believer may indeed have a "movement of doubt" (*motum dubitationis*). We find something similar stated in *De veritate*, when he acknowledges that "a movement directly opposite [*motus de contrario*] to what the believer holds most firmly [*firmissime*] can arise in him, although this cannot happen to one

---

[27] *ST* II-II, q. 4, a. 8, obj. 1–3. The verb συνῆτε (*synēte*), from συνίημι (*syniēmi*), is employed frequently in biblical wisdom literature to denote revealed insight, a faculty that not everyone possesses. For a helpful entry on this word, see *New International Dictionary of New Testament Theology and Exegesis*, ed. Moisés Silva (Grand Rapids, MI: Zondervan, 2014), 407–8.

[28] *ST* II-II, q. 4, a. 8.

who understands or has scientific knowledge."[29] At first glance, this seems to stand somewhat in tension with his contention elsewhere that doubt is opposed to certitude.

I suspect that the path to resolve this apparent discrepancy is to consider what Thomas means in saying back in the *Summa* that doubt is intrinsically opposed to certitude *if we consider it on the side of the cause of faith, God*. If we are unconvinced that God really knows what he is about and we thereby withdraw our will from assent to his goodness—in other words, if doubt arises "on the side of the cause of faith"—then this is opposed to the virtue of faith. However, Aquinas then immediately proceeds to acknowledge that doubts regarding particular matters of faith do sometimes exist "on our side, in so far as we do not fully grasp matters of faith with our intellect."[30] As a result, when faced with these doubts, he says that our intellect "still thinks discursively and inquires about the things which it believes, even though its assent to them is unwavering [*firmissime*]."[31] Here, then, Aquinas seems to allow for the presence of certain doubts, or movements of doubt, in the soul of a believer. However, these are

---

[29] *De veritate*, q. 14, a. 1.

[30] *ST* II-II, q. 4, a. 8, ad 1.

[31] *De veritate*, q. 14, a. 1. I think that a further distinction still may prove helpful on this point. Although faith assents firmly to all the articles of faith even in the face of movements of doubt, my experience is that one may continue to maintain a vibrant faith even while wondering whether *a particular interpretation* of a given doctrine is correct, even if said interpretation is longstanding. For example, a hundred years ago, one may have entertained doubts concerning the veracity of the traditional interpretation of *extra ecclesiam nulla salus* to the effect that all non-Christians will be damned. Today, we know that this interpretation stood in need of emendation, as it indeed received in the twentieth century. The same applies historically to the Church's grappling with the issues of religious freedom, heliocentrism, evolution, and the like. The way I would put it is that, while the person of faith unrelentingly assents to the truth revealed by Christ, he may have difficulties in regard to particular conclusions that have commonly been drawn in connection with the Church's dogmas. Thus, as Benedict XVI says, there is need to distinguish within dogma between the essential and the accidental, the contingent and the permanent. For extended treatments of this distinction in light of two separate issues that the Church has had to emend her stance on over the ages, see Matthew Ramage, "*Extra Ecclesiam Nulla Salus* and the Substance of Catholic Doctrine: Towards a Realization of Benedict XVI's 'Hermeneutic of Reform,'" *Nova et Vetera* (English) 14, no. 1 (2016): 295–330, and Ramage, "Benedict XVI's Hermeneutic of Reform: Toward a Rapprochement of the Magisterium and Modern Biblical Criticism," *Nova et Vetera* (English) 14, no. 3 (2016): 879–917.

not full-fledged doubts, since the believer's assent to them is still said to be most firm. Quite distinct from a decision to reject the truth claims of the Church, they belong to what you might call the psychological experience of anxiety that goes by the name of "doubt," what Josef Pieper calls "mental unrest" or perhaps what John Henry Newman calls "difficulties."[32]

As to the second objection based on Romans 10:17, Aquinas replies that, for most things, it is true that the certitude of that which comes through hearing is inferior to that which comes through seeing. If, however, the authority of the person from whom we hear surpasses that of our sight, then hearing is more certain than sight. This is true even in ordinary human affairs when a man of little science attains greater certitude about what he hears from an expert on the subject than he would by virtue of exercising his intellect alone. All the more so is this man certain about what he hears from God, who can neither deceive nor be deceived.[33]

Finally, in response to objection 3 of article 8, Aquinas admits that a certain sort of understanding—the Holy Spirit's gift—is indeed more perfect than faith due to its greater clarity (though it does not bring about greater adhesion). In this respect, it can be indeed said with Isaiah 7:9 that faith leads to understanding, which is in some way superior to it. But as for the science and understanding which are the real target of the objection, these cannot be said to be more certain than faith because they "are based upon the natural light of reason, which falls short of the certitude of God's word on which faith is founded."[34]

In his full commentary on Isaiah, Thomas gives further nuance to Isaiah 7:9: Whereas the LXX renders the verse, "Unless you believe, you will not understand" (ἐὰν μὴ πιστεύσητε, οὐδὲ μὴ συνῆτε; *ean*

---

[32] Josef Pieper, *Faith, Hope, Love* (San Francisco: Ignatius Press, 1997), 49–54. Pieper's text contains such lines as these: "The curious coexistence of certainty and uncertainty . . . not only describes but actually constitutes the psychological experience of the believer. . . . It is astonishing to see with what outspoken candor a theologian such as Thomas Aquinas describes this element of uncertainty in the act of belief" (52, 54). For Newman's contrasting of "difficulties" and "doubt," see his *Apologia*, ch. 5, in which he famously says: "Ten thousand difficulties do not make one doubt" (John Henry Newman, *Apologia Pro Vita Sua and Six Sermons* [New Haven, CT: Yale University Press, 2008], 321).

[33] *ST* II-II, q. 4, a. 8, ad 2.

[34] *ST* II-II, q. 4, a. 8, ad 3.

mē pisteusēte, oude mē synēte), Aquinas's Vulgate translates it, "Unless you believe, you shall not continue" ("Si non credideritis, non permanebitis"). I bring this up not so much for its relation to the question of certitude, but rather to show that Aquinas is aware of and attentive to the text's literal and spiritual senses. First there is the literal:

> "If you will not believe the promises of the Lord, even you shall not remain in your land [*non permanebitis in terra vestra*], but will be taken captive." . . . And he says this because Ahaz did not put his trust in prophecy and invoked the help of Tiglathpeleser, the king of the Assyrians, that he might help them.[35]

This reference to captivity evinces remarkable attention to Isaiah's original thrust, as I suppose one would expect, given that it is a literal commentary on Isaiah (*expositio super Isaiam ad litteram*). All the same, I am always impressed at just how attentive Thomas is to the literal sense in his Isaiah commentary.

Yet I also find myself edified by how he attends not just to external events but also to the spiritual sense in this commentary.[36] In the present case, he immediately follows up by observing: "Behold, he that is unbelieving, his soul shall not be right in himself." This is a reference to Habakkuk 2:4—"Behold, he whose soul is not upright in him shall fail, but the righteous shall live by his faith." In other words, if you refuse to believe, you will be exiled (you will not "continue," per the Vulgate), and you will cease being upright in your own soul (you will not "understand," per the LXX).

On the Need to Affirm the Whole Faith

Having surveyed Aquinas's definition of faith, his position on the

---

[35] *Super Isa* 1, lec. 7, in *Commentary on Isaiah* (Lander, WY: Aquinas Institute for the Study of Sacred Doctrine, 2017). Having discussed the Vulgate and LXX here, we will discuss the Hebrew further below in Benedict's treatment of this text.

[36] For another fine example of how Aquinas attends to the literal and spiritual sense of restoration from exile in Isa 26:19, see Aquinas, *Super Isa* 26 and Ramage, *Dark Passages*, 221.

power of the soul in which faith resides, and the issue of how much certitude the virtue enjoys, I would like to explore briefly a final point in his biblical account of faith that concerns the necessity of affirming the entire deposit of faith.

A good place to begin is Thomas's commentary on 1 Corinthians 13:7, where Paul says that "love . . . believes all things." Referencing Genesis 15:6, in which we are told that "Abraham believed the Lord, and he reckoned it to him as righteousness," the Angelic Doctor understands Paul as saying that love believes not all things absolutely, but rather "all things, namely, which are divinely revealed" ("omnia credit, scilicet quae divinitus traduntur").[37] Now, to believe everything said by men would be light-headedness (*levitatis*), as it says in Sirach 19:4: "One who trusts others too quickly is light-minded." On the other hand, to believe everything revealed by God—who can neither deceive nor be deceived—is eminently rational. All this makes perfect theological sense, though I suspect Aquinas is reading into Paul more than the apostle himself had in mind in order to avoid having him commit an error. I will comment more on this point further below.

Turning now from Aquinas's biblical commentary back to the *Summa*, Thomas poses the important question of whether a man who disbelieves one article of faith can have faith in the other articles. In reply, he makes an illuminating comparison: just as mortal sin is contrary to charity, so disbelief in one article of faith is contrary to faith. Accordingly, for Aquinas, neither living nor lifeless faith remains in a heretic who disbelieves even one article of faith. His reasoning merits to be quoted at some length:

> Now it is manifest that he who adheres to the teaching of the Church, as to an infallible rule, assents to whatever the Church teaches; otherwise, if, of the things taught by the Church, he holds what he chooses to hold, and rejects what he chooses to reject, he no longer adheres to the teaching of the Church as to an infallible rule, but to his own will. Hence it is evident that a heretic who obstinately disbelieves one article of faith, is not prepared to follow the teaching of

---

[37] *Super I Cor* 13, lec. 2 (no. 785), in *Commentary on the Letters of Saint Paul to the Corinthians*, trans. F. R. Larcher (Lander, WY: Aquinas Institute for the Study of Sacred Doctrine, 2012).

the Church in all things. . . . Therefore it is clear that such a heretic with regard to one article has no faith in the other articles, but only a kind of opinion in accordance with his own will.[38]

Thomas's reply to objection 3 of this same article is also very informative. The challenge he faces is that "a man can obey some commandments, and disobey others," and that therefore it would seem that he ought to be able to "believe some articles, and disbelieve others." Aquinas's reply in this case is that: "The various precepts of the Law may be referred either to their respective proximate motives, and thus one can be kept without another; or to their primary motive, which is perfect obedience to God, in which a man fails whenever he breaks one commandment."[39] In other words, it may happen that one will have to disobey a particular law if following it in a particular instance would violate the higher-order principle of love of God. When it comes to the articles of faith revealed by God, however, such a distinction does not apply: one cannot choose to reject any of them, because there no situation exists in which doing so would be for the sake of following some higher-order principle. Thomas grounds this teaching biblically in James 2:10, in which we read that "whoever keeps the whole law but fails in one point has become guilty of all of it." By analogy, then, a person who fails to affirm the faith in only one point has thereby rejected its totality by dismissing its very ground, the trustworthiness of the First Truth, God himself, to whom faith is ultimately directed.

BENEDICT'S BIBLICAL ACCOUNT OF FAITH

Turning now to Benedict XVI's biblical account of the virtue of faith, I will compare and contrast the emeritus Pontiff's approach with that of the Angelic Doctor on the same key points discussed above.

---

[38] *ST* II-II, q. 5, a. 3.
[39] *ST* II-II, q. 5, a. 3, ad 3.

What Is the Virtue of Faith, and Where Does It Reside?

In the attempt to arrive at a definition of what it fundamentally means to say *credo*, Ratzinger writes the following in his extensive treatment of the question that we find in his *Introduction to Christianity*:

> The little word *credo* contains *a basic option vis-à-vis reality* as such; it signifies, not the observation of this or that fact, but *a fundamental mode of behavior toward being*, toward existence, toward one's own sector of reality, and toward reality as a whole. . . .
>
> *It is a human way of taking up a stand in the totality of reality, a way that cannot be reduced to knowledge.*[40]

Right from the start, it is clear that, in contrast with Aquinas, Ratzinger does not think of belief primarily as an intellectual virtue. As he puts it in another place, when we proclaim, "I believe in God," we are telling our Lord not just that we are accepting the truth claims of divine revelation, but moreover that we are "founding our entire life on him."[41] Ratzinger's words would seem to indicate that he views faith as residing primarily elsewhere than in the intellect, as it does in Aquinas.

In a couple of key places throughout his corpus, Benedict appeals to the Hebrew verb behind the English "to believe" (אָמַן; *'āman*) to drive home his above point regarding the holistic nature of belief. For instance, he makes much of the prophet Isaiah's warning to King Ahaz that we discussed also in Aquinas above: "If you do not believe [תַאֲמִינוּ; *ta'ămînû*], then you will not be established [וְנֶאֱמַתְ; *te"āmênû*]" (Isa 7:9). There is a delightful word play in this passage in the original Hebrew. The first instance of *'āman* occurs in the hiphil stem, in which the verb means either (1) "to stand firm" or (2) "to believe or put trust [in]." However, the second instance occurs in the niphal stem, in which it has meanings including (1) "to be carried by a nurse," (2) "to be made firm, sure, lasting," (3)

---

[40] Cardinal Joseph Ratzinger, *Introduction to Christianity* (San Francisco: Ignatius Press, 1990), 50–51, 72–73 (emphasis added).

[41] Benedict XVI, General Audience of January 23, 2013.

"to be confirmed, established, sure," (4) "to be verified, confirmed," and (5) "to be reliable, faithful, trusty."[42] Although Benedict himself does not comment on these finer points of the Hebrew verb ʼāman, he does take the opportunity to discuss its various shades of meaning. On a material level, he notes, it denotes firmness, firm ground, or a foothold. By extension, it denotes a person's steadfastness or faithfulness, his firmness in adherence to the Lord. It also denotes truth itself, that which holds firm always. Cast in covenantal terms, it refers to God's fidelity and to man's faith, which is to say the firm mutual commitment to upholding their familial bond. For Ratzinger, "essentially, [belief] is entrusting oneself to that which has not been made by oneself."[43] Of course, this is by no means to say that Ratzinger's approach to faith is anti-intellectual or is deprived of noetic content, but it is elaborated with a different emphasis than we find in Aquinas.[44]

---

[42] Francis Brown, Samuel Rolles Driver, and Charles Augustus Briggs, *Enhanced Brown-Driver-Briggs Hebrew and English Lexicon* (Oxford: Clarendon, 1977), 53. Although not employed in this passage, ʼāman also occurs in the qal stem, in which it can refer to a support person such as a foster parent or a nurse, the supports or pillars of a door, or the action of supporting and nourishing. For further analysis of the Hebrew and Greek of this verb, with the indication that its occurrence in the plural results from being spoken to both King Ahaz and his advisors, see John D. W. Watts, *Isaiah 1–33*, rev. ed., Word Biblical Commentary 24 (Nashville, TN: Thomas Nelson, 2005), 131–32.

[43] Ratzinger/Benedict, *Introduction*, 70. See also the very similar discussion of ʼāman in Francis, *Lumen Fidei* (2013), §10. Although Francis officially promulgated this document, I will be attributing sections of it to Benedict because, after comparing the encyclical's motifs and vocabulary to Benedict's corpus as a whole, I have confidence that the sections I am excerpting from it were penned by Benedict.

[44] Francis/Benedict, *Lumen Fidei*, §23–24. See also Ratzinger/Benedict, *Introduction*, 69–70. That Christian belief necessarily involves an intellectual component can be seen in Benedict's fascinating exegesis of Isa 7:9, a text we discussed extensively above in light of Aquinas. Ratzinger/Benedict observes as we did above that the LXX renders this verse, "Unless you believe, you will not understand [συνῆτε; *synēte*]." While it might seem that the Greek translation has profoundly altered the sense of the original Hebrew discussed above (wherein belief is said to lead not to understanding but to being established), he makes the case that the later version preserves the essential meaning of the original. Standing, he observes, certainly has something to do with under-standing: "We need knowledge, we need truth, because without these we cannot stand firm. . . . Faith without truth does not save."

The Certitude of Faith

And what of faith's certitude in relation to the reality of doubt? Somewhat unexpectedly, Benedict signals the life of "doubting" St. Thomas as a model for how to deal with uncertainty in our faith life. Thomas is known well for his skepticism about the truth of Jesus's resurrection (John 20:25). However, Thomas's frank willingness here to confront the Lord is actually put forward by Benedict as a model for "he shows us that every doubt can lead to an outcome brighter than any uncertainty."[45]

As we see here, for Benedict, doubt is a psychological state of uncertainty. It is not an unequivocally negative defect of the will, but rather a reality that can lead to a great good if confronted with sincerity and humility. In this, Benedict's work has a different nuance from that of Aquinas, for whom doubt or fear that an opposing position might be true is incompatible with faith, a state Aquinas would describe as "opinion" rather than faith. That said, we did see that the Angelic Doctor appears to allow for certain "movements" of doubt within the believer which cause him to seek out deeper understanding of his faith as he continues to remain firm in his assent. Given this point of contact between the two theologians and the clear need to distinguish the decision of doubt from the experience of mental unrest, a helpful way forward may consist in continuing to refer to Aquinas's "doubt" as "doubt" while replacing our culture's typical usage of the word "doubt" with Newman's "difficulties." Or perhaps we may retain the current English usage and continue referring to the common understanding of doubt as a psychological experience with the word "doubt" while employing a more technical word like *dubitum* to capture the specific meaning Aquinas attaches to the word.

Other biblical models of faith whom Benedict engages include such figures as Jacob and Job. I would just mention a pair of lines that he has to say on the latter, whose desperate, even impious, pleas to God Benedict considers to be a model for how we are to relate to the divine mystery. First, there is the observation that God's answer to Job explains nothing; rather, it reminds us that "faith is not a light which scatters all our darkness, but a lamp which guides our steps

---

[45] Benedict XVI, General Audience of December 19, 2012: "The Virgin Mary, Icon of Obedient Faith."

in the night and suffices for the journey."[46] To this Benedict adds, "Faith [is] a confident entrustment to a 'You,' who is God, who gives me a different certitude, but no less solid than that which comes from precise calculation or from science."[47] In these lines, we find a different emphasis but a profound continuity with the thought of Aquinas. Both authors admit that movements of doubt (Aquinas) or darkness (Benedict) can remain in our lives even as we steadfastly walk the path of faith. Both authors affirm faith's eminent certitude, but they spell it out differently.

On the Need to Affirm the Whole Faith

In addition to affirming the eminent certitude of faith, both Aquinas and the emeritus Pontiff emphasize that this certitude applies to the whole faith, which must be accepted in its totality. Reflecting on how the magisterium of the Catholic Church is the same authority that both gave us the Bible centuries ago and continues to ensure its proper interpretation today, Benedict draws a crucial implication of the magisterium's role in faith. Reflecting on the meaning of St. Leo the Great's saying, "If faith is not one, then it is not faith," he writes:

> Since faith is one, it must be professed in all its purity and integrity. Precisely because all the articles of faith are inter-connected, to deny one of them, even of those that seem least important, is tantamount to distorting the whole [Quando-quidem nempe omnes fidei articuli in unum coalescunt, si unus eorum negatur, etiamsi quidam ex iisdem minoris mo-menti videantur, idem est ac si eorum complexus deleatur]. . . . To subtract something from the faith is to subtract something from the veracity of communion.[48]

In order to understand why this so, it is helpful to pause for a moment to mention how Benedict develops his theology of the virtue of faith by way of commenting on Hebrews 11:1 in the encyclical *Spe*

---

[46] Ratzinger/Benedict, *Introduction*, 26.
[47] Benedict, General Audience of October 24, 2012: "What Is Faith?"
[48] Francis/Benedict, *Lumen Fidei*, §48; St. Leo the Great, Sermon 24 [*In Nativitate Domini*, sermon 4], no. 6.

Salvi. Following the Vulgate, Benedict translates this verse, "Faith is the 'substance' of things hoped for; the proof of things not seen." Benedict's translation squares with the version of the text taken up by Aquinas and discussed above. The term "substance" used here is a translation of the Latin *substantia* and the original Greek ὑπόστασις (*hypostasis*). Benedict indicates that this word choice is important because it emphasizes something about the nature of the faith that other translations fail to convey. Unlike translations which translate Hebrews 11:1 so as to define faith as the mere "assurance" of things hoped for (as the RSV has it), *substantia*, or "substance," implies that the Christian faith is an organism with a distinct and perduring identity.[49] This organism is composed of different *articuli* or subject matters (literally, "joints"), each one of which designates a fundamental revealed truth, from the Trinity to the Incarnation of Christ to the resurrection of the dead—in short, all the truths we profess in the Nicene Creed. These are the principles upon which the entirety of Christian theology rests, and to reject one is tantamount to—in Benedict's words—"distorting the whole." Unlike Aquinas, the Vatican translation of Benedict's words does not go quite so far as to say that a heretic with regard to one article of faith has no faith in the other articles, but I think that the sense he wishes to convey is close to the same. I think that this is especially seen if we consider the Latin referenced above. In this version, we read that, if even one article of the faith is denied ("si unus eorum negatur"), it is as if the whole faith were erased or destroyed ("idem est ac si eorum complexus deleatur").

The above discussion has important practical ramifications for the Church today. As Benedict indicates, contemporary man finds it hard to conceive of a unity in truth under the umbrella of the magisterium. We tend to fear that assent and obedience to the Church will lead to the destruction of our freedom. In reality, however, it turns out that this is precisely the Church's genius, part of the Gospel's paradoxical path to freedom. Ironically, if we choose not to follow the path of total obedience to the magisterium, we end up locked within the boundary of our own ego with no faith at all. In other words, what we call "faith"

---

[49] "Now faith is the assurance of things hoped for, the conviction of things not seen" (RSV). The other rendition of the term ὑπόστασις (*hypostasis*) as "standing firm" in one's faith appears in the Einheitsübersetzung, the ecumenical translation of the Bible approved by the German Catholic bishops. For more on Benedict's understanding of Heb 11:1 in dialogue with Aquinas, see Ramage, *Dark Passages*, 93–104.

is really just a ratification at every turn of what we had already thought to be true beforehand through the light of our own reason.[50]

Faith's Truth Is Seen with the Heart

Having surveyed the thought of Aquinas and Benedict on the issues of what faith is, where it resides, what kind of certainty it enjoys, and why it is necessary to affirm its totality, I would like to address a final crucial tenet of Benedict's theology of faith which is important in that it adds an additional nuance to Aquinas's approach that Benedict is able to achieve precisely because he is standing on the shoulders of giants. As he has contended for decades, Benedict is emphatic that the certitude of faith cannot be grasped from the outside. Or, in keeping with the LXX of Isaiah 7:9, one can "understand" only within the context of *lived belief*. When celebrating Mass in St. Patrick's Cathedral in New York in 2008, the emeritus Pontiff gave a fascinating homily in which he described the great building as an allegory of faith. As with any Gothic cathedral, from the outside, the church's windows appear dark and dreary. But, once one enters the church, these same windows suddenly come alive with resplendent light. This is the allegory he draws: "It is only from the inside, from the experience of faith and ecclesial life, that we see the Church as she truly is: flooded with grace, resplendent in beauty, adorned by the manifold gifts of the Spirit."[51]

Ratzinger develops this notion of the faith as experiment at length in his *Introduction to Christianity*. As is frequently the case in his writings, he makes an appeal to the sciences for an analogy: "We know today that in a physical experiment the observer himself enters into the experiment and only by doing so can arrive at a physical experience. . . . There is no such thing as a mere observer. There is no such thing as pure objectivity."[52]

---

[50] For a more in-depth discussion of this reality, including a contribution to the discussion based on John Henry Newman's theology of assent, see my article "Benedict XVI on Freedom in Obedience to the Truth: A Key for the New Evangelization," *Homiletic and Pastoral Review*, May 12, 2014, hprweb.com/2014/05/benedict-xvi-on-freedom-in-obedience-to-the-truth-a-key-for-the-new-evangelization/.

[51] Benedict XVI, Homily for Votive Mass for the Universal Church, April 19, 2008.

[52] Ratzinger/Benedict, *Introduction*, 175.

In Benedict's view, pure objectivity is impossible because, as he is keen to highlight, Paul teaches us that man "believes with his heart" (Rom 10:10). Biblically speaking, the heart represents "the core of the human person, where all his or her different dimensions intersect."[53] As he puts it concisely in his commentary on the Beatitudes, "the organ for seeing God is the heart—the intellect alone is not enough."[54] Accordingly, for Benedict, what distinguishes a true assent of faith is that it is expressed through a love that is open to deep transformation and living in conformity with the demands of the truth.[55]

In its own turn, says Benedict, this very love brings its own form of enlightenment, transforming us inwardly and enabling us to see reality with new eyes. "One who loves," writes Benedict, "realizes that love is an experience of truth, that it opens our eyes to see reality in a new way, in union with the beloved."[56] Citing St. Gregory the Great, the emeritus Pontiff thus writes that "amor ipse notitia est"—love is itself a source of knowledge possessed of its own logic.[57] Again, we discern here a different emphasis from that present in Aquinas, although both emphasize the necessity of love or affectivity in our quest to possess faith more perfectly. Indeed, as we already heard Thomas saying in his commentary on Galatians 5:6, faith is not perfectly possessed unless the love which it hopes for is also possessed.[58]

On Benedict's Sources and Why His Approach Differs from That of Aquinas

Although he eventually developed a deep appreciation of the Angelic Doctor, from the start of his career, Joseph Ratzinger always had

---

[53] Francis/Benedict, *Lumen Fidei*, §26.

[54] Benedict XVI, *Jesus of Nazareth: From the Baptism in the Jordan to the Transfiguration* (New York: Doubleday, 2007), 92. See also Joseph Ratzinger, "The Dignity of the Human Person, Commentary on *Gaudium et Spes*," in *Commentary on the Documents of Vatican II*, ed. Herbert Vorgrimler (New York: Herder and Herder, 1969), 2:155.

[55] While Benedict does not cite him explicitly on this point, Newman's distinction between "notional" and "real" assent offers a valuable parallel to the Pontiff's understanding of what constitutes belief. See John Henry Newman, *An Essay in Aid of a Grammar of Assent* (Garden City, NY: Image, 1955), 49–92.

[56] Francis/Benedict, *Lumen Fidei*, §27.

[57] Francis/Benedict, *Lumen Fidei*, §28.

[58] *Super Gal* 5, lec. 2 (no. 286).

a predilection for the theology of the Seraphic Doctor, St. Bonaventure. This reality helps to explain why his approach differs from that of Aquinas, and why he so privileges the role of love within the life of faith. This can be seen throughout his corpus, but his Wednesday audiences on the Seraphic Doctor serve particularly well to illuminate the source of his outlook. As summarized by Benedict, for Bonaventure, "the fundamental intention of theology" is to be better acquainted with the beloved, and thus, in the end, "for St. Bonaventure, the primacy of love is crucial."[59] Along these lines, Benedict summarizes the difference between the two medieval doctors by saying that the loftiest category for St. Thomas is the true, whereas for St. Bonaventure, it is the good. As the Seraphic Doctor himself says of the contemplation of the bride in the Song of Songs, "No one can grasp [the correct path to contemplation] except him who receives, since it is more a matter of affective experience than rational consideration."[60]

As I have been contending throughout the present exploration, however, it would be mistaken to see a contradiction in the thought of these two medieval masters. In the words of Benedict:

> For both of them the true is also the good, and the good is also the true; to see God is to love and to love is to see. Hence it was a question of their different interpretation of a fundamentally shared vision. Both emphases have given shape to different traditions and different spiritualities and have thus shown the fruitfulness of the faith: one, in the diversity of its expressions.[61]

As for Bonaventure, adds Benedict, his emphasis on the will in faith and theology is best explained on the basis of the Franciscan charism—that the *poverello* of Assisi had shown the primacy of love throughout his whole life.[62]

Ultimately, however, the primacy of love in Bonaventure and the "general suspicion which he seems to have thrown upon all the achievements of human reason," as Étienne Gilson puts it, are even

---

[59] Benedict XVI, General Audience of March 17, 2010.
[60] Bonaventure, *The Soul's Journey into God* (New York: Paulist, 1978), 89.
[61] Benedict XVI, General Audience of March 17, 2010.
[62] Benedict XVI, General Audience of March 17, 2010.

further grasped by taking a step further back and considering the influence of another thinker upon the Seraphic Doctor.[63] This theologian is Pseudo-Dionysius the Areopagite, whom Benedict describes as having been "virtually rediscovered" above all by Bonaventure in the thirteenth century.[64] Given the influence of this sixth-century Syrian theologian upon the Seraphic Doctor, we can say that, if Benedict is dependent on Bonaventure, then he is also dependent on Dionysius.[65]

As in the case of Bonaventure, a good place to gain understanding of Benedict's dependence on Dionysius can be found in his catechetical address on the figure. In this brief but rich text, Benedict reminds us of several truths dear to himself that he locates in the thought of this great patristic theologian: that faith can be rightly lived only in the humility of ecclesiality; that God is found above all in praising him through liturgical worship; that the liturgy itself has been received as a gift from God; that the path of Christian sanctity necessarily involves the darkness of knowing God only by what he is not; and that the experience of love is a real mode of knowledge which transcends the power of reason and illumines it. Like Bonaventure, Pseudo-Dionysius ultimately reveals the reality that, in our ascent toward God, there comes a point at which reason no longer sees. And yet, Benedict insists, in the night of the intellect, love sees what is inaccessible to reason. The gift of love outpoured when we join Jesus on the Cross goes beyond reason, and thereby enters more profoundly into God's mystery.[66] All of these points of contact, which center around divine "experience" (a word deployed

[63] Étienne Gilson, *The Philosophy of St. Bonaventure* (Paterson, NJ: St. Anthony Guild, 1965), 349.

[64] Benedict XVI, General Audience of May 14, 2008.

[65] Of course, we should remember that Dionysius also plays a crucial role in Aquinas's thought—he is Aquinas's second-most-cited Eastern Father after Chrysostom. Aquinas's Dionysian apophaticism can be seen, for example, in his writing that "the highest modality of our knowing here below" and the "summit of our knowledge of God in this life" consist not in knowing what God is, but what he is not. Or, as Thomas articulates elsewhere, in this life "we know God as unknown" and we "do not know what he is, but we know nonetheless *that* he is" (*De veritate*, q. 8, a. 1, ad 8; *Summa contra gentiles* III, ch. 39, no. 2270; *Super Boethius de Trinitate*, q. 2, a. 2, ad 1). For an outstanding discussion of apophaticism in Aquinas, see Jean-Pierre Torrell, O.P., *St. Thomas Aquinas: Spiritual Master* (Washington, DC: Catholic University of America Press, 2005), 25–52.

[66] Benedict XVI, General Audience of March 17, 2010.

by Benedict nine times in this short catechesis), are particularly conducive to his project of helping contemporary Christians to deal with lack of intellectual certitude that comes from living in today's "secular" context.[67]

CONCLUSION

In this essay, I have sought to lay out the meaning of biblical faith as articulated in the respective theological visions of Thomas Aquinas and Benedict XVI. Aquinas sees faith as an act of the intellect moved at the command of the will, which nevertheless does not reach perfection unless accompanied by love. Benedict's account of the faith, meanwhile, takes its inspiration from different sources, and thereby envisions faith more as an existential reality that, while not above all an intellectual virtue, nevertheless depends upon the truths of divine revelation. In all of this, I have endeavored to show that we stand to benefit from both the *ressourcement* of the ancient and engagement with the modern—from the approaches of both Aquinas and Benedict—in the effort to understand the nature of biblical faith.

In the end, I hope that this essay has cast a little light on the deep harmony that unites the thought of these two master biblical theologians, emphasizing that each author has something profound to say to those of us who experience the "secular" condition of doubt and contestability in our faith lives. Each author provides us the grounding we need to walk forward day by day along the Way of Jesus Christ, believing in him in order that we might understand and one day know him as we are known by him.

---

[67] Benedict XVI, General Audience of May 14, 2008.

Lectio Scripturae at the Heart of Aquinas's Theology and Preaching*

Michael G. Sirilla
Franciscan University of Steubenville

Biblical Thomism has a great relevance for contemporary theology. The way that theology was conducted in the thirteenth century can serve as a beacon or a model for us, perhaps, to imitate, approximate, or recover via *ressourcement* because it was ecclesial—that is, not severed from or set against the Church and her teaching. It was Christological, spiritual, prayerful, and eschatological insofar as theology was understood and conducted as a peculiar participation in the salvific mission of Christ and His mystical body the Church, the mission to bring about the knowledge of Christ by faith, an increase of holiness, and ultimately everlasting life consisting in the vision of the Triune God, and all this for the good of souls and the extrinsic glory of God. And this was done by a deep study of Scripture aided by the dialectics of disputed questions that arose in the masters' Scripture commentaries, finally arriving at treasures of doctrine through this contemplation and bringing the divine mysteries contemplated to the faithful by preaching for their conversion, sanctifi-

* Adapted from Michael Sirilla, *The Ideal Bishop: Aquinas's Commentaries on the Pastoral Epistles*, Thomistic Ressourcement 8 (Washington, DC: Catholic University of America Press, 2017) and "The Theological and Pastoral Purposes of Aquinas's Biblical Commentaries," *Biblica et Patristica Thoruniensia* 10, no. 3 (2017): 375–87.

cation, and salvation. As such, biblical Thomism has much to offer to the contemporary Catholic theologian and, indeed, to the Church.

The Structure and Method of Aquinas's Biblical Commentaries

In a recent essay on St. Thomas's approach to biblical interpretation, Thomist theologian John F. Boyle notes: "Throughout his commentaries, Thomas is thoroughly theological; that is, he is first and always concerned with deepening his understanding of the revealed truths of the faith. Scripture always speaks to that faith."[1] Why, then, have his biblical commentaries been so often ignored in theological and biblical studies for much of the twentieth century? There are at least two reasons.

First, in the wake of the specific aims of Pope Leo XIII's Scholastic revival, some twentieth-century Thomists did not find Aquinas's biblical commentaries to be useful in their task of adapting and applying his thought for the correction of contemporary philosophical errors that hampered sound theology. Concerned primarily with the apologetic, epistemological, and metaphysical problems of their day, Aquinas's commentaries on Scripture perhaps appeared to them as less relevant than his systematic works. But in overlooking his commentaries, they left untouched a rich strand of theological reflection. Polish theologian and bishop Wacław Świerzawski remarks, "almost all of the theology called neo-scholastic which was based on Thomas omits from consideration what he had provided in his biblical commentaries."[2] Though their contributions to Christian theology and philosophy are unquestionably of great value, neo-Thomists too often neglected the biblical foundations of Aquinas's theology.[3]

---

[1] John F. Boyle, "St. Thomas Aquinas and Sacred Scripture," *Pro Ecclesia* 4 (1996): 102.

[2] Wacław Świerzawski, "L'exégèse biblique et la théologie spéculative de s. Thomas d'Aquin," *Divinitas* 18 (1974): 138. All translations are mine unless otherwise noted.

[3] Offering a corrective to this problem, Marie-Dominique Chenu noted that St. Thomas's *Summa theologiae* [*ST*], "despite its technical methodology, can only be understood properly as a living emanation from the *pagina sacra* (the sacred page of the Bible)" (*Aquinas and His Role in Theology*, trans. Paul Philibert [Col-

Second, many twentieth-century Catholic biblical scholars employing historical-critical methods did not find Aquinas's commentaries adequate as exegetical works precisely because they are *not* strictly and exclusively "exegetical" according to admittedly questionable standards. Roland Murphy, for example, issues this warning regarding patristic and medieval allegorical exegesis: "If historical-critical methodology is not brought into play, there is nothing to serve as a control on the reading of the text by Christian imagination."[4] Since his method of interpretation was judged "pre-critical" (a claim contradicted by a survey of twelfth- and thirteenth-century critical tools), Thomas Aquinas's collection of biblical commentaries, comprising almost one third of the entire corpus of his published works, remained largely unexamined by biblical scholars as well.[5]

Both groups failed either to recognize or to accept the theological aims of thirteenth-century biblical exegesis. Neo-Thomists often did not recognize Aquinas as principally a biblical commentator, rather than as a philosopher or systematic theologian. For their part, many historical-critical scholars rejected the theological purpose of his (or of any) biblical commentaries. And for both parties, their neglect of the overriding theological concerns of the medieval university commentator on Scripture led them to mistaken judgments on the relevance and worth of Aquinas's biblical commentaries. Thomas Prügl cautions contemporary scholars to be "mindful of the unified character of medieval theology in approaching Aquinas's interpretation of Scripture, shaped as we are by a rather different, modern, and more specialist understanding of exegesis and biblical theology."[6]

---

legeville, MN: Liturgical Press, 2002], 21; originally published in French in 1959 as *Saint Thomas d'Aquin et la théologie*). See also Étienne Gilson, *The Christian Philosophy of St. Thomas*, trans. L. K. Shook (New York: Random House, 1956), 13.

4 Roland Murphy, "Patristic and Medieval Exegesis—Help or Hindrance?," *Catholic Biblical Quarterly* 43 (1981): 515.

5 For a recent survey of the critical tools used by Aquinas and his contemporaries in the study of Scripture, see Sirilla, *Ideal Bishop*, 77–82.

6 Thomas Prügl, "Thomas Aquinas as Interpreter of Scripture," in *The Theology of Thomas Aquinas*, ed. Joseph Wawrykow and Rik van Nieuwenhove (Notre Dame, IN: University of Notre Dame Press, 2005), 386. For all that, contemporary critical exegesis need not be seen as excluding traditional biblical commentaries, as Boyle notes: "The traditional exegesis and the modern critical methods need not be necessarily contradictory. But when one considers Thomas one sees how much more there is to the interpretations of Scripture, beyond that which is the focus

The Theological and Pastoral Purpose of Aquinas's Biblical Commentaries

Thomas Aquinas was, by profession, a biblical commentator. Lecturing on Scripture was the chief occupation of his academic life. Heinrich Denifle demonstrated that the primary theology textbook used by Aquinas and the other thirteenth-century *magistri* at the University of Paris was the Bible.[7] Boyle underscores this fact, noting that two of the *principal* duties of a thirteenth-century master of theology were "to hold periodic public disputations throughout the course of the academic term and to lecture on sacred Scripture":

> Although Thomas wrote a dozen commentaries on various works of Aristotle, he never taught Aristotle in the classroom. Likewise, the two great summas, the *Summa contra gentiles* and the *Summa theologiae*, were private works of the study; Thomas never taught them. What Thomas taught in his classroom as a master of theology was Scripture.[8]

Aquinas's official title during his two regencies at the University of Paris was *Magister in Sacra Pagina*. Throughout his entire career, he expressed a keen awareness of the privileged place of Scripture in the theological discipline. On receiving their office, newly minted Parisian *magistri* delivered an inaugural lecture, setting the tone for their entire regency. In his inaugural lecture, *De commendatione Sacrae Scripturae*, Aquinas shows that the foundation of the master's teaching is the *sacra doctrina* revealed in the canonical Scriptures.[9] Likewise, in his mature work, in *Summa theologiae [ST]* I, q. 1, a. 8, ad 2, he claims that, in the science of theology, the authority of Scripture alone provides *proper* arguments from authority furnishing *necessary* conclusions. In this text, Thomas contrasts Scripture's authority with arguments from authority appealing to philosophical

---

of the critical methods" ("St. Thomas Aquinas," 104).

[7] Heinrich Denifle, "Quel livre servait de base à l'enseignment des Maîtres en Théologie dans l'Université de Paris?," *Revue thomiste* 2 (1894): 129–61.

[8] Boyle, "St. Thomas Aquinas," 94.

[9] Thomas's *De Commendatione Sacrae Scripturae* is the *Breve Principium*, that is, the shorter second part of his *Principia*, or inaugural lectures. It may be found in *Opuscula theologica*, ed. R. A. Verardo and Raimondo Spiazzi (Turin: Marietti, 1954), 1:441–43 (see esp. 1:442).

sources that remain extrinsic to theology, and therefore cannot provide *proper*, but only *probable*, argumentation for theology.[10] In this same article of *ST*, he argues that the articles of faith, revealed in Scripture, constitute the first principles of the science of theology. These principles are self-evident to God and the blessed, but accepted by the faith of the Church on earth. In practice, Thomas devoted his academic career to the interpretation and explanation of Scripture as the means by which *sacra doctrina* is revealed and understood.

The medieval theological approach to the exegesis of Scripture did not obviate ascertaining the literal sense of the text, but rather mandated it. Medieval historian Beryl Smalley (1905–1984) underscored the importance of this mandate for Aquinas.[11] However, Aquinas sought the literal sense of the text in order to discern its deeper meaning or doctrine—to attain a theological insight. The Dominican biblical scholar Ceslas Spicq observes: "If he applies himself to drawing out the true literal sense, this is only to the degree that these efforts are necessary and fruitful in order to elaborate a biblical theology as a source for his scholastic theology. A master of theology, commenting on Scripture, Saint Thomas perceived exegesis as a science subordinate to theology."[12]

Aquinas's ultimate aim in commenting on Scripture was not

---

[10] *ST* I, q. 1, a. 8, ad 2: "Sacra doctrina huiusmodi [viz., philosophical] auctoritatibus utitur quasi extraneis argumentis, et probabilibus. Auctoritatibus autem canonicae Scripturae utitur proprie, ex necessitate argumentando" ("Sacred doctrine uses authorities of this kind as extrinsic and probable arguments. But it properly uses the authority of the canonical Scriptures as an argument from necessity"). Thomas is not saying that philosophical arguments *as such* cannot conclude with necessity in theology; he is merely saying that philosophical arguments *from authority* cannot be used in this way. In this assertion, Thomas argues for the privileged place of the canonical Scriptures in scientific theology. For a basic study of the role of Scripture in Thomas's theology, see P. E. Persson, *Sacra Doctrina: Reason and Revelation in Aquinas* (Oxford: Blackwell, 1970).

[11] Beryl Smalley, *The Study of the Bible in the Middle Ages* (Oxford: Blackwell, 1952), 300. However, she later came to appreciate the importance of the spiritual senses for Aquinas; see her book *The Gospels in the Schools* (London: Hambledon, 1985), 265–66.

[12] "S'il s'applique à dégager le vrai sens littéral, c'est uniquement dans la mesure où ces efforts sont nécessaires et féconds pour élaborer une théologie biblique source de sa théologie scholastique. Maître en théologie, commentant l'Écriture, saint Thomas voit dans l'exégèse une science annexe de la théologie" (Ceslas Spicq, "Saint Thomas d'Aquin Exégète," in *Dictionnaire de théologie catholique*, ed. Alfred Vacant et. al. [Paris: Letouzey et Ané, 1908–1950], vol. 15.1, col. 718).

merely to discover its literal sense, but to arrive at a theological under-standing of the literal meaning of revealed doctrine and, ultimately, to provide the fruits of these insights as material for preaching. The literal sense of the text was the foundation for the edifice of Aqui-nas's theology, for he understood that Scripture itself is theological and that it provides the basis for further theological argumentation and elaboration. In his treatment of the nature and extent of sacred doctrine in the *prima pars* of his *ST*, Thomas argues that Scripture provides the first principles, or sources, of scientific theology, and he insists that all theological argumentation must be drawn from the literal sense of Scripture.[13] In the commentary tradition of the medieval schools that he inherited, we see a firm correlation between the interpretation of the sacred page and the theological inquiry and pastoral preaching that emerge in the very process of discovering its literal meaning.

The theological aim of medieval exegesis was pursued by system-atically probing the text to uncover its presuppositions and to develop its further implications, conclusions, or moral imperatives—includ-ing even those about which the human author, it would seem, could not have been aware. This systematic examination most often took the form of *quaestiones*: dialectical questioning and rational demon-stration used by the master to penetrate the biblical text, producing commentaries that are distinctively theological in tone and purpose. With few exceptions, in the thirteenth century, hard divisions be-tween the various branches of theology had not yet developed, so this activity—freely moving between literal exegesis and theological argumentation—enjoyed an unfettered expression in the scriptural commentaries of this period.[14]

An example of this type of theological commentary may be found in St. Thomas's remarks on 1 Timothy 1:1, where Paul greets Timothy with wishes for "grace, mercy, and peace." Thomas asks why three gifts are mentioned here, while in his other epistles Paul

---

[13] See *ST* I, q. 1, aa. 2–3 and 8, where Thomas argues that Scripture provides the first principles of the science of theology, and a. 10, ad 1, on the literal sense of Scripture as the basis for all theological argumentation.

[14] The most notable exception to the absence of distinct branches of specialization in theology is the somewhat autonomous development of the study of ecclesial law and its magisterial interpretation by medieval canonists such as Gratian. Yet even their undertakings were not envisaged as entirely distinct from the task of the medieval theologians.

wishes only two gifts to the recipients: grace and peace. Why would Paul wish Timothy mercy as well? Thomas answers simply that, due to the grave demands of their office, "prelates need more."[15] He then proceeds to interpret "grace" and "mercy" in terms of the needs of bishops and their flocks, providing two alternate theological elaborations. First, *mercy* could signify the remission of the bishop's personal sins and *grace* "the gift of graces that prelates need" to minister to the faithful.[16] Alternately, *grace* could signify sanctifying grace personally needed by the bishop and *mercy*, "the divine office that raises him to spiritual charisms."[17] In this short theological amplification, Thomas suggests that the greeting in 1 Timothy reveals the greater needs of prelates. A bishop—represented in this passage by Timothy, bishop of Ephesus—personally needs the divine gifts of the forgiveness of his sins and sanctifying grace so that he may be enabled to minister to the faithful by means of spiritual charisms.

There is a contemporary perspective that would view scriptural interpretations like this as overstepping the bounds of legitimate exegesis by assuming presuppositions and drawing conclusions not directly found in the words of the scriptural text itself. To address this concern, it is necessary to understand the historical development of the thirteenth-century theological lecture on Scripture.[18] As masters of Scripture, Thomas and his colleagues at Paris were strictly bound by university statute to perform three primary and interrelated duties: *legere, disputare,* and *praedicare*—to read, to dispute, and to preach.[19]

---

15 "Praelati pluribus indigent" (*Super I Tim* 1, lect. 1 [no. 6] [Turin: Marietti, 1952], 2:213).

16 "Gratia vero pro munere gratiarum, quo indigent praelati" (*Super I Tim* 1, lect. 1, [no. 6; p. 2:213]).

17 "Munere divino in spiritualibus charismatibus exaltante" (*Super I Tim* 1, lect. 1, [no. 6; p. 2:213]).

18 The studies of Denifle and Smalley, among others, facilitated the appreciation of the historical context of Aquinas's theology and stimulated research on Thomas's scriptural commentaries and his use of Scripture in his theological syntheses. See also: P. Glorieux, "Essai sur les commentaires scripturaires de saint Thomas et leur chronologie," *Recherches de théologie ancienne et médiévale* 17 (1950): 237–66; T. Domanyi, *Der Römerbriefkommentar des Thomas von Aquin* (Bern: Peter Lang, 1979); Wilhelmus G. B. M. Valkenberg, *Words of the Living God: Place and Function of Holy Scripture in the Theology of St. Thomas Aquinas* (Leuven, BE: Peeters, 2000).

19 These three labors of the master in theology "were announced at the end of the twelfth century by Peter Cantor and later confirmed in the statutes of the theol-

Legere meant more than merely "to read" a given text. It signified a sequential, line-by-line reading of a biblical text accompanied by the careful, magisterial commentary of the lecturer. Jean-Pierre Torrell writes, "'to read' Scripture was the first task for the master in theology, and therefore also for Thomas."[20] The charter of the University of Paris makes it clear that the magisterial lecture on Scripture was the first and, by far, the most important lecture of the day.[21]

These three magisterial duties at Paris—to lecture, to dispute, and to preach—resulted from the transformation in the twelfth century of the monastic *lectio divina*, a prayerful reading of Scripture aimed at promoting spiritual growth. Smalley traces the reception and development of the *lectio divina* by the Victorines, especially Hugh of St. Victor (1096–1141), who was greatly influenced by the rules enumerated by Augustine in *De doctrina christiana* for interpreting and teaching Scripture.[22] In his *Didascalicon*, Hugh of St. Victor designs a program of scriptural hermeneutics that entails ascertaining the "letter," its meaning, and its *sententia*—that is, its deeper meaning or doctrine.[23] The Dominican theologian Otto H. Pesch summarizes this heuristic model:

> An exposition contains three things: letter, meaning, doctrine. The letter means the fitting order of the words, which we also call construction. The meaning is the obvious and open significance which the letter evidences outwardly. The doctrine is the more profound insight, which is only found through exposition and interpretation. In these three things

---

ogy faculty [of the University of Paris]" (Jean-Pierre Torrell, *Saint Thomas Aquinas*, vol. 1, *The Person and His Work*, trans. Robert Royal, rev. ed. [Washington, DC: Catholic University of America, 2005], 54).

[20] Torrell, *Saint Thomas*, 1:55. *Legere* may also be construed as "to lecture."

[21] Denifle cites this charter in "Quel livre," 150. See also James R. Ginther, "There is a Text in this Classroom: The Bible and Theology in the Medieval University," in *Essays in Medieval Philosophy and Theology in Memory of Walter H. Principe, C.S.B.: Fortresses and Launching Pads*, ed. J. R. Ginther and C. N. Still (Aldershot, UK: Ashgate, 2005), 31–51.

[22] Smalley, *The Study*, 196. M.-D. Chenu also describes the evolution of exegetical methodology from the twelfth century to the thirteenth in *Toward Understanding St. Thomas*, trans. A. M. Landry and D. Hughes (Chicago: Henry Regnery, 1964), 58–69 and 249–59.

[23] Hugh of St. Victor, *The Didascalicon of Hugh of St. Victor*, trans. Jerome Taylor (New York: Columbia University Press, 1991), 6, 8–12, and 147–50.

there is an order, following which first of all the letter, then the meaning, and then the doctrine should be investigated; when that is done, the exposition is completed.[24]

To discover first the "letter" or "construction" of the text, the commentator "divides" or analyzes it into its constituent parts. By means of this *divisio textus*, he clarifies the mutual relations of the parts, thus uncovering the "literal sense"—that is, the sense or meaning directly signified by the letter. This often spontaneously leads him to uncover the reasons behind what is said in the text and to discover the conclusions that follow from the text. To achieve this purpose, the medieval commentator would integrate *quaestiones* or small systematic chapters into his biblical commentary.[25] By this method, a doctrinal reformulation of the text is produced in which the literal sense is not abandoned, but rather is elaborated and built upon by an identification of its presuppositions and further implications.

Hugh's approach to scriptural interpretation was further refined and transmitted by the great twelfth-century Parisian masters: Peter Comestor (d. 1178), Peter the Chanter (d. 1197), and Stephen Langton (1155/56–1228). These three masters established the agenda of medieval Scholastic biblical commentary: *legere, disputare,* and *praedicare.* This program found its definitive historical form in the academic life of the theologates in the thirteenth century. Thus was standardized the dialectical and logical *disputatio,* following upon the *lectio,* as the ordinary means to arrive at the deeper meaning of a text. By means of the disputation, the text is worked over with questions until it yields its meaning and the doctrine is discerned. Retaining and amplifying the spiritual purpose of the monastic *lectio divina,* the scriptural doctrine discovered by the *disputatio* must then be applied pastorally for spiritual growth through *praedicatio,* preaching, which was considered an integral task of exposition or academic biblical study. The duty of preaching has become somewhat foreign to contemporary academic theology, but it was an essential component that crowned and completed the work of the theologian in the thirteenth-century academy. Thus, the interpretation of divine revelation was both an academic and an ecclesial task directed

---

[24] Otto Herman Pesch, "Paul as Professor of Theology: The Image of the Apostle in St. Thomas' Theology," *The Thomist* 38 (1974): 591.

[25] Pesch, "Paul as Professor," 592–93.

toward a pastoral end for the good of souls. In his *Verbum abbreviatum*, Peter the Chanter employs the image of constructing an edifice of study in order to describe the interrelation of the commentator's three labors: *lectio, disputatio,* and *praedicatio*:

> The practice of Bible study consists in three things: reading, disputation, preaching. . . . Reading is, as it were, the foundation and basement for what follows, for through it the rest is achieved. Disputation is the wall in this building of study, for nothing is fully understood or faithfully preached if it is not first chewed by the tooth of disputation. Preaching, which is supported by the former, is the roof, sheltering the faithful from the heat and from the whirlwind of vices. We should preach after, not before, the reading of Holy Scripture and the investigation of doubtful matters by disputation.[26]

The action of "chewing" the text by scholarly disputation exemplifies Peter's transformation of the monastic *lectio divina's* "mastication"—repeatedly turning over the text of Scripture in the mind to discern its deeper meaning—into a twelfth-century academic endeavor. Disputation analyzes the text by means of questions posed in such a way as to extract the frequently hidden substance. For Peter, the text itself provokes these questions, and thus the disputation emerges naturally and organically in the course of a commentary.

Despite the fundamental continuity in this historical development from private monastic contemplation to public academic dispu-

---

[26] Peter the Chanter, *Verbum abbreviatum*: "In tribus igitur consistit exercitium sacrae Scripturae: circa lectionem, disputationem et praedicationem. . . . Lectio autem est quasi fundamentum, et substratorium sequentium; quia per eam caeterae utilitates comparantur. Disputatio quasi paries est in hoc exercitio et aedificio; quia nihil plene intelligitur, fideliterve praedicatur, nisi prius dente disputationis frangatur. Praedicatio vero, cui subserviunt priora, quasi tectum est tegens fideles ab aestu, et a turbine vitiorum. Post lectionem igitur sacrae Scripturae, et dubitabilium, per disputationem, inquisitionem, et non prius, praedicandum est." (*PL*, 205:25A–B; cited and translated by Smalley, *The Study*, 208). Note that the metaphor of "chewing" (a means of breaking down) does not, in this instance, signify the destruction of the edifice (i.e., the biblical text); rather, it indicates that distinctions are made by way of analysis ultimately for the sake of organic growth into a unified understanding of divine revelation. The purpose of making distinctions is not to separate the components of the biblical text, but rather to discern their unity and meaning in order to foster growth to spiritual maturity.

tation, several significant monastics—most famously St. Bernard of Clairvaux—strongly resisted the use of Scholastic disputation in biblical commentary. Yet Peter the Chanter and the other twelfth-century masters did their part to preserve the medieval academy from an excessive rationalism. These masters viewed human arts and sciences as ordered to knowing Christ, worshiping him, and leading others to the same knowledge and love. Thus, they proposed a scholastic, systematic, and dialectical approach to the interpretation of Scripture with the theological end of arriving at its meaning and doctrine. But they subordinated this theological end to a pastoral one: communicating what has been understood to others by preaching and teaching. The *ratio* of the Dominican order itself reflects this aim. The order has been called "apostolic," since its charism is to bring the fruits of contemplation to others through preaching—hence, the Order of Preachers.

St. Thomas Aquinas and his contemporaries inherited this exegetical approach, and thus they sought to develop a systematic, theological understanding of the biblical text with the explicit purpose of preaching for the salvation of souls and the glory of God. The tasks of the lecture, the disputation, and the university sermon were eventually standardized as official academic duties by the theology faculty at the University of Paris in their statutes.[27] In his inaugural address, *De commendatione Sacrae Scripturae*, St. Thomas correlates the university mandate of these duties with the command in Titus 1:9 to instruct in sound doctrine and refute those who contradict it.[28] Although these three obligations were not always viewed as distinct in the twelfth century, by the thirteenth century, they were clarified and distinguished. The theological disputations that were formerly incorporated into the lectures on Scripture were shortened, since at that time, the disputations themselves began to take on a life of their own in the newly emerging genres of the *quaestiones disputatae* and the *quaestiones de quolibet*.[29] Smalley writes, "after this change

---

[27] Torrell cites the charter of the University of Paris to this effect (*Chartul.* II, no. 1185) in *Saint Thomas*, 1:54.

[28] Aquinas, *De commendatione Sacrae Scripturae* (also called his *Breve principium*), originally 1213, in Verardo and Spiazzi, *Opuscula theologica*, 1:442).

[29] Pesch notes: "The ordinary professor, the so-called 'magister,' was alone concerned with continuous commentary on the Holy Scriptures. Only in public debate, the so-called 'quaestiones disputatae,' did the magister teach as systematician. And these 'quaestiones disputatae' had also been developed from the

in the syllabus, questions in the lecture [on Scripture] are short and arise directly from the text."[30] The *quaestiones* that continued to be incorporated into the lecture represent a *via media* between literal exegesis, on the one hand, and the various forms of extended disputation more or less remote from the biblical text, on the other.[31] Having a distinct and independent venue for extended disputations, the thirteenth-century biblical commentator was at liberty to keep his *quaestiones* directly focused on the biblical passage in his lectures, producing integrated disputations that did not stray too far from the text itself.[32]

The integration of these medieval disputations into the biblical commentary developed organically as the ordinary means of achieving a deeper understanding of Scripture for spiritual edification. Fr. Torrell describes them as "active pedagogy where one proceeded by objections and responses on a given theme."[33] In fact, as with an article in an independent collection of disputed questions or in a theological synthesis like *ST*, they were often distinguished by the standard phrases: *videtur quod*, *sed contra*, and *respondeo quod*. Raising and responding to the difficulties elicited by the text itself, the disputations frequently developed argumentation with scriptural premises and theological conclusions. Such disputations, or as Pesch calls them, "short systematical chapters," are incorporated throughout Aquinas's biblical commentaries.[34] By thus systematically scrutiniz-

---

commentary on the Scriptures, both as an academic exercise and as literary form. For in the text of the biblical commentary it had long been customary to deal with 'questions' which arose in the context of the text in the form of a systematic excursus. Thus, the 'magister in sacra theologia' has been produced by the 'magister in sacra pagina,' and not vice versa. . . . But, except for the debates, his daily courses were concerned with the interpretation of the Holy Scriptures" ("Paul as Professor," 587–88).

[30] Smalley, *The Study*, 209–10.

[31] See Torrell, *Saint Thomas*, 1:60.

[32] Theologian Thomas Ryan notes that, besides theological *quaestiones*, Aquinas also includes in his commentaries historical questions and even conundrums regarding apparent scriptural contradictions (*Thomas Aquinas as Reader of the Psalms* [Notre Dame, IN: University of Notre Dame Press, 2000], 27).

[33] Torrell, *Saint Thomas*, 1:59.

[34] Pesch, "Paul as Professor," 592–93. Conversely, short biblical commentaries are found in portions of his systematic works. For example, in *ST*, see: I, qq. 65–74, on the six days of creation; I-II, qq. 98–105, on the Mosaic law; and III, qq. 27–59, on the life of Christ narrated in the Gospels.

ing the biblical text, Thomas consistently develops a theology—or a set of theological reflections—in the course of his scriptural commentaries.[35]

Biblical scholar C. Clifton Black discovers in Aquinas's biblical writings "a thoroughgoing theological commentary, . . . an exegesis whose motive power is *fides quaerens intellectum*."[36] This motive imbues the medieval biblical commentary with a distinctively theological character. It also distinguishes the medieval commentary from contemporary exegesis, since the medieval heuristic goal proceeds well beyond uncovering the human author's immediate intention, and thus is not limited merely to an interpretation of the direct meaning of the words, even while it is inclusive of it. Though Aquinas moves beyond the text, uncovering its presuppositions and developing further conclusions, he intends to do so without violating the literal meaning. When executed correctly, this procedure in fact illuminates the literal sense.[37] Thus, if Aquinas's biblical commentaries are to be appreciated properly, they should be seen as the *union* of exegesis and theological reflection. Theologian Christopher Baglow sees this fusion as "an extremely valuable exegetical trademark of St. Thomas Aquinas."[38] He likens Thomas to a molder "who works with a pre-existing frame or mesh upon which final materials (such as plaster . . .) are applied": "A new model (in the case of Thomas, a new theological model) has emerged from the molder's labors, one which

---

[35] A. Paretsky notes that the medieval theological examination of the biblical text aimed at doctrinal formulations: "The twelfth and thirteenth centuries reveal the growing tendency of Scripture commentators to insert theological questions into their commentaries, the chief purpose being to extract from the text those teachings relevant to . . . theology" ("The Influence of Thomas the Exegete on Thomas the Theologian: The Tract on Law (Ia-IIae, qq. 98–108) as a Test Case," *Angelicum* 71 [1994]: 549).

[36] C. Clifton Black, "St. Thomas' Commentary on the Johannine Prologue: Some Reflections on Its Character and Implications," *Catholic Biblical Quarterly* 48 (1986): 694.

[37] Brevard Childs explains the enduring value of Aquinas's Scripture commentaries: "As a master theologian, Thomas struggled in his way with most of the major problems which still confront a serious theological reflection on the Bible" (*Biblical Theology of the Old and New Testaments* [Minneapolis, MN: Fortress, 1992], 41).

[38] Christopher T. Baglow, *"Modus Et Forma": A New Approach to the Exegesis of Saint Thomas Aquinas with an Application to the Lectura Super Epistolam Ad Ephesios* (Rome: Pontifical Biblical Institute, 2002), 112.

arises out of the fusion of the work of the two artisans. We can therefore speak of the theology of a particular Thomistic commentary as distinct from Thomas' theology in general."[39] Thus, Thomas's biblical commentaries can and should be examined for their own theological value independent of their possible role as a basis and support for his systematic works.[40] As such, they constitute an indispensable theological source, and investigations of his theological work that fail to consider them remain incomplete.

The Prologue and the *Divisio Textus*

Aquinas customarily introduces his Scripture commentaries with a prologue headed by a passage selected from another book of Scripture. He deploys this passage, often interpreted allegorically, to introduce his reader or auditor to the primary subject matter and purpose of the main text.[41] For this reason, this pericope is called the *accessus*, since it provides a point of entry to the main themes or "synchronic categories" by which the rest of the commentary is to be understood.[42] Thomas Ryan, following A. J. Minnis, calls this a "sermon type of prologue."[43] In light of this initial biblical citation, Aquinas proceeds in the body of the prologue to identify the principal elements of the main text, often by structuring his analysis according to the four Aristotelian causes: efficient (the text's author), material (its content or subject matter), formal (its literary mode or genre), and final (its purpose or usefulness). Aquinas, however, did not inflexibly adhere to this model, as he ordered his prologues with some variety.[44] In

---

[39] Baglow, *"Modus Et Forma,"* 69.

[40] See Pesch, "Paul as Professor," 599, and Baglow, *"Modus Et Forma,"* 78.

[41] See *ST* I, q. 1, a. 10, where he says, speaking of the spiritual senses that are founded on the literal sense, that the "allegorical sense" (*sensus allegoricus*) is constituted by the things of the Old Law signifying the things of the New. In his commentaries on Paul, Aquinas more often than not employs an Old Testament passage as the *accessus* interpreted in its allegorical sense.

[42] See Ryan, *Thomas Aquinas*, 17.

[43] See Ryan, *Thomas Aquinas*, starting on page 13, and Alastair J. Minnis, *Medieval Theory of Authorship* (London: Scolar Press, 1984), 6, 64. The Catholic liturgical tradition manifests this approach in the selection of Old Testament readings that adumbrate or illuminate the New Testament readings.

[44] According to Fr. Matthew Lamb, sometimes, "he borrowed the introductory pro-

any event, the method of procedure in the prologue is a synchronic (as opposed to a diachronic) identification of the principal themes, ideas, or arguments of the main text.

In the body of a medieval textual commentary, the principal methodological tool employed is the *divisio textus*—an analysis of the text into its component parts in order to elucidate their interrelationship and unity. This method examines the text's meaning diachronically, following the sequential order of the text itself, explaining its structure and coherence.[45] Aquinas employed this method, according to the late Father Matthew Lamb, in order "to define the main theme of a book and then relate each of its parts to this unifying center."[46] The *divisio* was not to be an artificial and extrinsic manipulation of the text. Rather, it was used as a means to discover and express the structure, distinctions, and unity already present in the text itself. Were these divisions merely imposed arbitrarily by the commentator, he would have failed to employ *divisio textus* properly.

The *divisio* identifies the text's component parts from the most general to the most particular: the arguments or great themes are constituted by sets of propositions or statements, which are in turn constituted by individual terms and notions. Thus, Thomas often divides the text down to the level of the individual words themselves. This method evidently presupposes a theory of scriptural inspiration that discerns meaning in every part of the text. According to Pesch:

> The text is divided into large, small, and miniscule units, in order to clarify its inner structure, the exact sequence and the connection of the ideas. Nobody at that time was afraid to drain the text of its original vividness and the particular trait of its author. God is a god of order, also in his written word. Therefore, nothing in the text can be by accident or without intention. Analysis, therefore, has to investigate each word right to the last letter.[47]

---

cedure of the grammarians and speaks of the matter, intention, and utility of the book" ("Introduction," in *Commentary on St. Paul's Epistle to the Ephesians by St. Thomas Aquinas* [Albany, NY: Magi, 1966], 22).

[45] "The *divisio textus* method, which highlights thematic *development* . . . represents a diachronic approach" (Ryan, *Thomas Aquinas*, 17).

[46] Lamb, "Introduction," 26.

[47] Pesch, "Paul as Professor," 589–90. In response to criticisms that this process is merely tedious and artificial, Lamb contends, "modern scholarship renders

But the analysis achieved by the *divisio* was not an end in itself. It enabled the commentator to perceive and communicate with great precision the sequence of thought and argumentation in the text that leads to its conclusions and, ultimately, to its rational and literary unity. The highly analytical *divisio*, then, is ordered to an ultimate synthesis. The text's distinct components are identified in order to appreciate their relation and resolution in an organic unity.

It is in this way that a meticulous *divisio* is employed in order to arrive at a theological or doctrinal insight for the ultimate pastoral end of the edification of souls through preaching.[48] By this method, the exegete begins with a consideration of the text word by word to discover its immediate meaning. After determining the literal sense of the text, he then seeks to ascertain the presuppositions and reasons for what the author says.[49] Uncovering these reasons is a source of theological insight, and when extended argumentation is warranted, a theological excursus or *quaestio* is incorporated into the commentary itself as mentioned above.[50]

In terms of methodology, then, the medieval master's lecture on Scripture begins with a synchronic prologue that determines the subject matter and principal themes of the text. The commentary itself proceeds diachronically to discover the inner structure of the text and uncover both the presuppositions of the literal meaning and the conclusions that follow from it. St. Thomas employs this method masterfully in his biblical commentaries, most notably on the fourteen Pauline epistles. He views them as an integral whole, united by a common theme, specifically, the name (or the grace) of Christ. He sustains this perspective throughout his lectures on the Pauline corpus.

---

justice to many of Thomas' precisions" ("Introduction," 26). According to Boyle: "The genius of the commentaries [of Aquinas] is often in the division of the text. It is this division that sets every passage in a context, or perhaps better, in a set of nested contexts" ("St. Thomas Aquinas," 100–101).

[48] Pesch describes the process of the *divisio* as follows: "To follow the text word for word and to rise to the 'sententia,' to the doctrine, only on the basis of the 'littera' and the 'sensus,' on the letter and the immediate meaning of the words" ("Paul as Professor," 590–91).

[49] Pesch explains the rationale for this: "The biblical author *must* have reasons in his mind, if in the Scriptures nothing exists by accident" ("Paul as Professor," 591).

[50] On these "small systematical chapters," Pesch remarks: "In an extreme case we meet within the commentary the structure of an 'article' customary in systematic works, i.e., objections, counter-objections, systematic statement, and answers to objections" ("Paul as Professor," 592–93).

As both Spicq and Torrell indicate, Aquinas consistently displays great skills as an exegete and even as a historian. Belying allegations of philological and critical-historical weaknesses, Thomas incorporates the best of prior exegesis—both patristic and early medieval. He conducts a sustained evaluation of the literal sense, and he builds his theology directly upon it. As such, he is an eminently reliable interpreter of Scripture, serving as a model for contemporary theologians who are recovering his integrated approach to biblical commentary and theological insights for the good of souls.

Dividing in Order to Unite: Thomas's *Resumptio* Address at Paris, *Hic est Liber*, and the Thirteenth-Century *Divisiones Textus* of the Books of the Bible

Randall Smith
University of St. Thomas

Modern scholarship suggests that one of the required steps in a master's inception ceremony at the University of Paris was the *principium in aula*, a sermon in praise of Sacred Scripture given before the assembled masters. Four disputed questions also had to be resolved and a second "commendation of Sacred Scripture," sometimes called the *resumptio* address, had to be given several days later.[1] Both Father James Weiheipl and Father Jean-Pierre Torrell suggest that Thomas delivered his *resumptio* address, *Hic est liber*, on the first

---

[1] For more on the circumstances surrounding Thomas's inception, see James Weisheipl, O.P., *Friar Thomas d'Aquino: His Life, Thought, and Works* (Washington, DC: Catholic University of America Press, 1974; repr. 1983), 93–97. For what is still the best treatment of these thirteenth-century inception addresses at the University of Paris, see the unpublished dissertation by Nancy Spatz, "*Principia*: A Study and Edition of Inception Speeches Delivered before the Faculty of Theology at the University of Paris, ca. 1180–1286" (PhD diss., Cornell University, 1992). Both Weisheipl and Spatz are depending upon the earliest account we have of the inception ceremony *secundum usum Parisienem*, which is contained in a Bologna manuscript published in *Chartularium Universitatis Parisiensis*, ed. H. Denifle, O.P., and E. Chatelian, vol. 2 (Paris: Delanian, 1891), no. 1188 (pp. 691–95).

day of classes after his inception—an address that contained, as university statutes dictated, a commendation of Sacred Scripture and a *divisio textus* of all the books of the Bible.[2]

HIC EST LIBER: A LAW THAT GIVES LIFE

Thomas took the *thema* verse for this sermon from Baruch 4:1, which begins: "This is the book of the commandments of God, and the law, that is forever: all they that keep it, shall come to life: but they that have forsaken it, to death."[3] This was the same verse the Franciscan John of La Rochelle had chosen when he incepted in 1238, a little over twenty years before Thomas. It was also the verse chosen by secular master Henry of Ghent when he incepted in 1275, nearly twenty years after St. Thomas. This was *not* the verse revealed to Thomas by an aged man in a white garment who came to him in a dream, however.[4] That was the verse from Psalm 103:13, which begins *rigans*

---

[2] See Weisheipl, *Friar Thomas*, 96–110, and Jean-Pierre Torrell, O.P., *Saint Thomas Aquinas*, vol. 1, *The Person and His Work*, trans. Robert Royal (Washington, DC: Catholic University of America Press, 1996), 53 (following Weisheipl on this point).

[3] Throughout, I have quoted the Latin text from the best modern critical edition of *Hic est liber*, which can be found in volume 1 of *Opuscula Theologica*, ed. R. A. Verardo and Raimondo Spiazzi (Turin: Marietti, 1954). All English translations in this article are mine, but a good English translation of the whole address is "The Inaugural Sermons," trans. Ralph McInerny, in *Thomas Aquinas: Selected Writings* (Harmondsworth, UK: Penguin, 1998), 5–17.

[4] See, for example, Weisheipl, *Friar Thomas*, 96. The story, told by Thomas's medieval biographer, Bernardo Gui, is that, "with tears," Thomas begged "for inspiration as to the theme he should choose for his inaugural lecture." Afterward, he fell asleep and seems to have had a very clear dream in which, according to Bernardo Gui, he seemed to see an old man, white-haired and clothed in the Dominican habit, who came and said to him: "Brother Thomas, why are you praying and weeping?" "Because," answered Thomas, "they are making me take the degree of master, and I do not think I am fully competent. Moreover, I cannot think what theme to take for my inaugural lecture." To this, the old man replied: "Do not fear: God will help you to bear the burden of being a master. And as for the lecture, take this text, 'Thou waterest the hills from thy upper rooms: the earth shall be filled with the fruit of thy works [*Rigans montes de suprioribus suis; de fructu operum tuorum satiabitur terra*]." Then he vanished, and Thomas awoke and thanked God for having so quickly come to his aid. There are three sources for this story, reports Fr. Torrell, all of which can with confidence be traced back

montes—"Watering the mountains from the heights above, the earth shall be filled with the fruit of your works"—the verse he used as the basis of his *principium in aula* address.[5]

Using Old Testament passages praising the law seems to have been common among thirteenth-century masters. Thomas's teacher Albert the Great used the passage from Ecclesiasticus 24:33: "Moses commanded a law in the precepts of justice, and an inheritance to the house of Jacob, and the promises to Israel."[6] The Franciscan Matthew Aquasparta, who incepted in 1277/1278, used the passage from Psalm 93 (94):12: "Blessed is the man whom you shall instruct, O Lord: and shall teach him out of your law." Of the seven surviving *resumptio* addresses we have from the thirteenth century delivered at the University of Paris, five began by praising Sacred Scripture as a book of *law*: Albert, Mathew of Aquasparta, Thomas Aquinas, Henry of Ghent, and John of La Rochelle.

THE *DIVISO TEXTUS* OF THE SACRED SCRIPTURES

The *resumptio* address of any new master was by university regulation to contain a "commendation and partition of the sacred Scripture" (*Scripturae sacrae commendationem et particionem*).[7] By "partition," this regulation meant doing a *divisio textus* of all the books of the Bible. And indeed, when we look over these *resumptio* addresses, one of the characteristic features shared by them is the inclusion of a long list cataloguing all the books of the Bible.

Reading through these lists of biblical books can be a laborious task. For this reason, many readers skip over them in frustration the

---

to Thomas himself (*Saint Thomas*, 1:51).

[5] For an English translation of the *principium* and a good discussion of it, see *Albert and Thomas: Selected Writings*, trans. and ed. Simon Tugwell, Classics of Western Spirituality (Mahwah, NJ: Paulist Press, 1988), 268–70, 353–62.

[6] See "Principium Biblicum Alberti Magni," ed. Albert Fries, C.SS.R., based on Cod. Vat. Lat. 4245, fols. 22va–24ra, in *Studia Albertina: Festschrift für Bernhard Geyer*, ed. H. Ostlender (Münster: Aschendorf, 1952), 128–47. See also A. Fries, "Eine Vorlesung Alberts des Grossen über den biblischen Kanon," *Divus Thomas* 28 (February 1950): 195–213, and "Der Schriftkanon bei Albert der Grossen," *Divus Thomas* 29 (February 1951): 3–4.

[7] Denifle and Chatelian, *Chartularium*, vol. 2, no. 1188 (p. 694). Note that this is the requirement for *biblici*, not *baccalarii*.

way students skip over the "catalogue of ships" in Homer's *Iliad* and the genealogies in the Gospels of Matthew and Luke.[8] They are long lists filled with dozens of names, the importance of which is not always clear. Let me suggest, however, that these *divisiones* provide important information and give us important clues as to how these medieval masters conceived of the Scriptures.

THE THEOLOGICAL CHARACTER OF THE SCHOLASTIC *DIVISIO TEXTUS*

Though some find these lists labored and dull, John Boyle has argued that crafting a suitable *divisio textus* was a way of ordering the mind to prepare it for reading by viewing the parts in relation to the whole. According to Professor Boyle:

> For a theologian such as Saint Thomas who understands the theological enterprise as the articulation of the ways in which revealed truths—indeed all truths—stand in relation one to another the scholastic division provides a way in which such a theological task can be undertaken in the very reading of scripture itself. It is not merely a matter of breaking the text down into component bits, but of seeing how its parts stand in relation one to another.[9]

For the scholastics, says Boyle, "the division of the text is precisely a means to arrive at ways of seeing the fundamental unity of revealed truth."[10]

---

[8] The catalogue of ships can be found in *Iliad* 2.494–759. The genealogies of Matthew and Luke can be found in Matt 1:1–17 and Luke 3:23–38, respectively.

[9] See John Boyle, "The Theological Character of the Scholastic 'Division of Text' with Particular Reference to the Commentaries of Saint Thomas Aquinas," in *With Reverence for the Word: Medieval Exegesis in Judaism, Christianity, and Islam*, ed. J. McAuliffe, B. Walfish, and J. Goering (Oxford: Oxford University Press, 2003), 276–83, at 277. See also Boyle, "Authorial Intention and the *Divisio Textus*," in *Reading John with St. Thomas Aquinas*, ed. Matthew Levering and Michael Dauphinais (Washington, DC: Catholic University of America Press, 2005), 3–8.

[10] Boyle, "Theological Character," 277.

Modern biblical exegetes might not always agree with the validity of the "themes" by which these medieval theologians associated and distinguished the books of the Old Testament and New Testament, whether it was the distinction between "law" (Old Testament) and "grace" (New Testament), as in Thomas's *divisio*, or "signs" (Old Testament) and "things" (New Testament), as in Henry of Ghent's *divisio*, but the medieval goal was one we should still be able to appreciate: the attempt to identify a unity of divine purpose rich enough to express itself in a variety of approaches, genres, and texts. It is for this reason that I think Professor Boyle is right to describe the creation of the *divisio textus* as a properly "theological" project.[11]

THE MASTER'S *DIVISIO*: A UNIQUE VISION

Providing a *divisio textus* of all the books of the Bible was a required part of the inception ceremony for decades, but no two were quite the same. There is not one ideal division to which they all conformed. Although one can find similarities, it appears that each master was supposed to come up with his own distinctive *divisio*.

To give the reader a sense of the similarities and differences, I have provided outlines of four of the *divisiones*, from the *resumptio* addresses of four medieval masters who incepted at Paris over a roughly forty-year period, between 1238 and 1278. In addition to Thomas's, there are outlines of the *divisiones textus* done by the Franciscan John of La Rochelle, who incepted in 1238, the secular master Henry of Ghent, who incepted in 1275 or 1276; and Matthew of Aquasparta, another Franciscan and a personal pupil of Bonaventure's, who incepted in 1277 or 1278.[12] Thomas's inception in 1256

---

[11] Boyle, "Theological Character," 277.

[12] For John of La Rochelle's text, see "Deux leçons d'ouverture de Cours Biblique données par Jean de La Rochelle," ed. Delorme, O.F.M., *La France Franciscaine* 16 (1933): 345–60. The text of interest for our purposes is the second of the two, which is presumably the one John gave as his *resumptio* address. For Henry's text, see Henry of Ghent (Henrico de Gandavo), *Lectura Ordinaria Super Sacram Scripturam*, ed. Raymond Macken, in *Opera Omnia*, vol. 36 (Leuven: Leuven University Press, 1980), 5–27. The first lecture would presumably have been Henry's *principium in aula*. The second was likely Henry's *resumptio* and contains Henry's *divisio textus* of the Bible. For Matthew of Aquasparta's text, see *Quaestiones*

falls roughly in the middle of the span.

Leaving aside Aquinas's *divisio* for the moment, we can sum-
marize the basic characteristics of the *divisiones* of the other three
masters under five general headings: (1) the most basic division is
that between the Old and New Testaments, but the masters treat it in
various ways; (2) all three masters use "law," of various types, as a key
component in their concerted efforts to correlate the Old Testament
with the New; (3) much more effort is expended on partitioning the
Old Testament than the New; (4) even when the three masters use
the same divisions, they usually create their own subdivisions and
descriptions; (5) many of these *divisiones* were likely crafted with an
eye toward (a) memory and (b) their usefulness as aids to preaching.

Old Testament and New Testament

Not surprisingly, the most basic division each master makes is between the Old Testament and the New, but they establish the distinction in a variety of ways. The most common account given by
these masters to explain what distinguishes the Old Testament from
the New is one that can be traced back to Augustine's *De doctrina
christiana* on the difference between "signs" and "things."[13] Henry's
text is clearest in this regard: "Since, therefore, according to Augustine, in the first book of *On Christian Doctrine*, 'every doctrine
is either of signs or of things,' and Sacred Scripture is a doctrine, it
contains both things and signs: signs in the Old Testament, things
in the New." This *divisio* is a creative synthesis of St. Augustine's
distinction between "signs" and "things" in the *De doctrina christiana*
and his famous affirmation that "what lies hidden in the Old Testament is made manifest in the new."[14]

And yet, this division according to "sign" and "thing" is merely
one of a series of distinctions thirteenth-century masters used to distinguish the Old Testament from the New. Others included the distinctions between: judgment (OT) and mercy (NT); severity (OT)

Disputatae Selectae (Florence: Quaracchi, 1903), 16–22.

[13] See Augustine, *De doctrina christiana*, esp. 2.1–3.

[14] See Augustine, *Quaestiones in heptateuchum* 2.72: "Et in Vetere Novum lateat,
et in Novo Vetus pateat" ("the New lies hidden in the Old, and the Old is made
manifest in the New").

and piety (NT); labor (OT) and rest (NT); onerous burdens (OT) and light ones (NT); lessening evil deeds (OT) and helping men to do good (NT); temporal goods (OT) and eternal goods (NT); and finally, for Thomas, law (OT) and grace (NT).

Types of Law

All three masters contrast the Old and the New Testaments as types of "law." What this allows them to do, moreover, is to associate books and sections of the Old Testament with books and sections of the New. So, for example, it is common to subdivide the books of the Old Testament into: first, the laws set forth in the five books of the Pentateuch; second, the *exempla* or "moral examples" found in the historical books; third, the admonitions and exhortations to wisdom found in the sapiential or wisdom literature; and finally, the prophecies in the books of the prophets. So, in the New Testament, we find: "the Lord's precepts" in the four Gospels corresponding to the books of the Mosaic Law; the historical *exempla* in the Acts of the Apostles corresponding to the *exempla* in the Old Testament historical books; the Pauline and canonical epistles corresponding to the sapiential books of the Old Testament; and finally, the Book of Revelation corresponding to the Old Testament prophetic books. These associations may seem odd to us at first, but they make more sense if we understand them as aids to preaching. More on that in a moment.

Greater Attention to the Old Testament than to the New

Although a chief concern for all three masters is to show how the Old Testament is a prefiguration of the New, oddly enough, all three devote much more space to dividing and subdividing the books of the Old Testament than they do for those in the New. This will be true of Aquinas as well.

The Old Testament is admittedly much larger than the New, with a greater number and variety of books, but this alone does not explain the different treatments. While these masters supply exhaustive categories and subcategories to account for each book of the Old Testament, when it comes to the New Testament, after listing the four Gospels, they lump all the remaining books into large categories such as "Pauline epistles" and "canonical epistles" without listing each individual book.

Unique Subdivisions and Descriptions Even with Shared Main Divisions

Although they wrote over a roughly forty-year spread, several of the basic categories they use remain remarkably constant—the categories of law, *exempla*, and prophets figure in all three treatments of the Old Testament—but arrangement varies. For instance, John of La Rochelle and Henry of Ghent place *exempla* as a subcategory under "law," whereas Matthew of Aquasparta gives it its own separate category at the same level as "law."

Another complication is what to do with the wisdom literature and the Psalms. John and Henry, taking their cue from Christ's words in Luke 24:44 ("Everything must be fulfilled that is written about me in the Law of Moses, the Prophets and the Psalms"), make the threefold *divisio* into law, prophets, and Psalms foundational. Matthew takes a different approach and includes the Psalms as a species of prophecy. And whereas Matthew separates the wisdom books into their own separate category, John and Henry include them under *exempla*, categorizing them as "paternal" admonitions delivered in words, rather than examples in deeds such as we find in the historical books.

The most numerous and complicated series of divisions and subdivisions are always to be found among the Old Testament *exempla*, with the second place going to law. Clearly, the effort to categorize all the books of the Old Testament from Joshua, Judges, Kings, and Chronicles up to Job, Tobit, Judith, and Esther was no small task: there are many books of varying genres, and the relationships among them is not obvious, unlike those among the five books of the Pentateuch, which have a much clearer unity. And yet, even the five books of the Pentateuch were subjected to divisions and subdivisions. John and Henry both made divisions among these five in order to account for various elements of the natural and Mosaic laws.

It had become a commonplace by the thirteenth century to distinguish the four Major Prophets—Isaiah, Jeremiah, Ezekiel, and Daniel—from the twelve so-called Minor Prophets. This division was made centuries earlier, likely for purely utilitarian reasons, "major" and "minor" being designations of size of book, not importance of author. Matthew of Aquasparta testifies to the fact that, even in his day, the twelve books known collectively as the Minor Prophets were bound together in one volume, as were the four books of the Major Prophets. The latter were then associated with the four authors of the four Gospels—Matthew, Mark, Luke, and John—and the eponymous prophets of the former with the twelve apostles, suggesting that a certain *theological* significance was by this time being attached to what had earlier been a simple decision about binding and bookmaking. These associations would not be immediately apparent to us, but they were to these medieval masters, which brings me to my fifth point.

Aids for Memory and Preaching

We might ask about all these odd categories and attempts to associate the books of the Old Testament with the books of the New—"Why all the fuss?" Why was so much time and energy spent creating these divisions and associations? This was not just the pastime of a single scholar, but a mandatory exhibition of skill required of every incoming master at the University of Paris.

We would appreciate these division practices better, I suggest, if we understood them, first, as a reflection of the "memory culture" that characterized the high Middle Ages and, second, as expressions of the special concern to foster better preaching which arose in the wake of the Fourth Lateran Council.[15]

I have argued in more detail in my book on the sermons of Aquinas that the *divisiones* in the *sermo modernus*-style sermon were mnemonic devices meant to help listeners recall the major points of the sermon by bringing to mind the words of the opening biblical *thema*

---

[15] Mary Carruthers, *The Book of Memory: A Study of Memory in Medieval Culture*, 2nd ed. (Cambridge: Cambridge University Press, 1990, 2008). For the important influence of the Fourth Lateran Council on the nature of the founding of the University of Paris, see Ian P. Wei, *The Intellectual Culture in Medieval Paris: Theologians and the University, c. 1100–1330* (Cambridge: Cambridge University Press, 2012), esp. 92–105. I have found no other book as clear or as valuable a guide to the history and culture of the founding years of the University of Paris as this superb volume.

verse.[16] This was especially helpful for providing continuity during the break between the morning's sermon and the evening's continuation at vespers that University regulation required masters to preach using the same *thema* verse as assigned for the morning.[17] In both the thirteenth-century "modern sermon" and the *divisio textus*, the goal was to divide a large mass of material into smaller, more-easily-grasped memory "cells" or "units" and then associate each of these with the parts of something easily memorized, like a single Bible verse.

As much as these *divisiones* owe to the memory culture of the medieval university, they also owe much to the thirteenth-century renewal of preaching. Take, for example, what may seem an odd set of associations we find for the Major Prophets in Thomas, Matthew, and Henry: Isaiah and the Incarnation, Jeremiah and the passion, Ezekiel and the resurrection, and Daniel and the final judgment. We can make sense of it both as a memory aid—four and four—and as a preaching aid. If the topic is the Incarnation, where can the dedicated preacher go in the Old Testament to search for figures prefiguring Christ's Incarnation? If he remembered his master's *divisio*, he would start in the book of Isaiah.

Consider as well John's and Henry's subcategories under *exempla*. Both subdivide Kings, Chronicles, Ezra, and Nehemiah into books dealing with the active life (Kings and Nehemiah) and those concerning the contemplative life (Chronicles and Ezra). Nehemiah is associated with the active life because he undertook to repair the city; Ezra with the contemplative life because he repaired the temple. These are precisely the sort of images a preacher would use in preaching.

---

[16] Randall B. Smith, *Reading the Sermons of Thomas Aquinas: A Beginner's Guide* (Steubenville, OH: Emmaus Academic, 2016).

[17] Denifle and Chatelian, *Chartularium*, vol. 2, no. 1188 (p. 692); see esp. item 17: "Item, nota, quod quando unus prelatus vel unus magister in theologia facit sermonem de mane in Universitate in aliquot festo in aliqua domo Mendicantium vel alibi: tunc ille qui facit collationem post prandium, debet accipere illud thema in collatione, quod assumptum fuit per prelatum vel per magistrum, qui fecit sermonem eadem die" ("Again, note that, when a priest or a master in theology preaches a sermon in the morning at the university during some feast in some house of the mendicants or elsewhere, then he who delivers the collation in the afternoon ought to use that same *thema* in the collation which was selected by the priest or master who delivered the sermon on the same day").

THOMAS AQUINAS'S *DIVISIO TEXTUS*

We turn now briefly to Thomas Aquinas's *divisio*. In line with the approach taken by his fellow masters, Thomas sees the Old Testament primarily in "legal" terms. So, for example, he divides the Old Testament according to the various types of precepts it contains, the basic division being between those precepts that *bind* and those that merely *warn*. According to Thomas, the binding precepts are to be understood as analogous to "the commands of a king who can punish transgressors," while those that "merely warn" are analogous to "the precepts of a father who must teach." This distinction between "commanding" (such as done by a king) and "warning" or "admonishing" (such as is done by a father) was common. But Thomas further subdivides this first category into two, suggesting that the precepts of a king are of two kinds: one that establishes the laws and another that induces to observance of the law, which is customarily done through his heralds and ambassadors. The result is a division of the Old Testament into three basic parts: books containing royal commandments; books containing heraldic inducements to obey the commandments; and books containing fatherly warnings to act justly. This threefold distinction replaces the more common division into law, *exempla*, and prophets.

And yet, Thomas's threefold division into *commandments*, *inducements*, and *admonitions* is an echo of John of La Rochelle's division into *precepts* such as we find in the Pentateuch, *exempla* such as we find in the historical books, and *admonitions* such as we find in the wisdom books. Thomas tucks the prophets under "heralds who induce observance of the law," while John had put them into their own separate category.

Although some of the terms are the same, Thomas crafts his own unique set of categories and subdivisions. So, for example, the division of some historical books into one category ("heralds who induce the observance of the law") and some into another ("precepts of a father who teaches—by deed") is unique to Thomas.

John of La Rochelle had suggested that the four Major Prophets speak about the head, Christ, while the twelve Minor Prophets speak about the body, the Church. Thomas affirms, by contrast, that the Major Prophets were those who "were sent to the whole people and called for observance of the whole law," while the Minor Prophets were sent to particular tribes of Israel, each for different reasons.

Thomas is, in fact, the only master who mentions any of the Minor Prophets by name, listing Hosea and Jonah as two who imparted edicts of the law "for special reasons to special tribes." Thomas does say elsewhere (echoing John of La Rochelle) that the Major Prophets speak about Christ, with Isaiah foretelling the Incarnation, Jeremiah the passion, and Ezekiel the resurrection, but he differs from John by making no mention of the Minor Prophets speaking about "the body," the Church.

Thomas—unlike John, Henry, and Matthew—does not use the term *exempla*. Rather, he uniquely associates books of the Old Testament with the four cardinal virtues: justice with Chronicles, temperance with Judith, fortitude with Maccabees and Tobit, and prudence with Ezra-Nehemiah and Esther. Further on, he associates three of the "sapiential" books—Proverbs, Ecclesiastes, and the Song of Songs—with the three categories of virtue listed by Plotinus: political virtues, which involve the use of this world, he associates with Proverbs; purgative virtues, which involve contempt for worldly goods, he associates with Ecclesiastes; and finally, the virtues of the purged soul wholly cleansed from worldly cares and given over to contemplation alone he associates with the Song of Songs.

Interestingly, although Thomas is renowned as one of the prime expositors of the natural law, he does not follow John of La Rochelle's lead in associating the natural law with the book of Genesis.

Whereas John of La Rochelle divides the New Testament into two parts, the *evangelical*, dealing with Christ, and the *apostolic*, which is further divided into *origins* (Acts of the Apostles), *doctrine* (epistles), and *consummation* of the Church (John's Apocalypse), Thomas divides the New Testament into *the origin of grace* (the Gospels), *the power of grace* (the Pauline epistles), and *the execution of the power of grace* in the progress of the Church, in whose development there are three stages: the beginning of the Church, treated in the Acts of the Apostles; the progress of the Church, treated in the canonical epistles; and the end of the Church, which we find in the Apocalypse.

Indeed, this theme of Christ as the origin and power of grace is unique to Thomas's account. The other masters stress the New Testament as the locus of laws, teachings, and moral *exempla*. What no one but Thomas mentions is the centrality of grace. Significantly, when Thomas finally, many years later, crafted a *divisio textus* of the Pauline epistles (an outline of which I have inserted into his *divisio*), he did so precisely in terms of the various modes and categories of grace, as he had suggested years before at his inception.[18]

Thomas's *divisio* has fewer explicit associations between the Old Testament and the New than do those of John, Henry, and Matthew, but he puts more emphasis on the grace of Christ as a unique gift enabling us (a) to live in accord with the precepts and admonitions of the Old Law and (b) to develop the virtues exemplified in the Old Testament books.

CONCLUSION

Thomas's *divisio* was both elegant and simple; it does some things better than do those of his peers, but given the complexity of the Scriptures, it could not do everything perfectly. A *divisio* of this sort was not meant to be "the last word." If this had been the goal, university officials would not have asked for a new one from each incepting master. These *divisiones* of the books of the Bible were meant, rather, as a "first word": a beginning task by which the newly incepted master could demonstrate his ability to lay out a beginning lecture and a beginning outline for his incoming students. In years to come, Thomas would be expected to lecture on whatever books of the Bible the needs of the students dictated. In those circumstances, his first task would be to give a *principium*, a prologue lecture in the *sermo modernus* style, as part of which he would lay out for his students a *divisio textus* to aid them in their reading and to give them a road map of the lectures to come. In his *principium*, *resumptio*, and *divisio textus*, Thomas demonstrated not only the skills necessary for inception as a master theologian, but also the skills of laying out an admirably clear outline for his students, the hallmark of the great and marvelously lucid teacher he would become.

---

[18] Compare the *divisio textus* of the Pauline epistles in *Hic est liber* with the more thoroughly worked-out *divisio* of the Pauline epistles in Thomas's prologue to his *Commentary on Romans*.

91

OUTLINES OF THE *DIVISIONES TEXTUS* OF THE BOOKS OF THE BIBLE FROM THE INCEPTION *RESUMPTIO* ADDRESSES OF FOUR THIRTEENTH-CENTURY MASTERS

John of La Rochelle's *Divisio Textus* of the Books of the Bible

I. Old Testament (signs; wrapped in obscurities and veiled figures)— three parts:

A) Law: Christ is shown as mediator of precepts, which pertains to power

- what ought to be done

1. Teaching of precepts: five books of Moses

a) unwritten: **Genesis** (proemium of the Law)

i. before sin

α) nature

α1) conservation of the individual: eat of every tree

α2) conservation of the species: increase and multiply

β) discipline: do not eat of the tree of the knowledge of good and evil

ii. after the fall—3 ages:

α) Adam to Noah: resist concupiscence (given to Cain) [moral precept]

β) Noah to Abraham: do not eat meat with blood: abhor letting blood (to Noah) [judicial precept]

γ) Abraham to Moses and prophets: circumcision [ceremonial precept]

b) written:

i. First edition—3 states of man:

      α) beginners: receding from evil, approaching good: precepts in **Exodus**

      β) progressing in the desert (moral, ceremonial, judicial): **Leviticus**

      γ) perfection: prepare to enter land of promise (signifying the perfection of contemplatives and actives): **Numbers**

  ii. Second (explanation): **Deuteronomy** (recap of the Law)

      α) Love the Lord your God (affirmative precepts)

      β) Fear God (negative precepts)

2. Teaching of exempla (deeds): ten books: Joshua, Judges, Kings, Chronicles, Ezra, Esther, Judith, Tobit, Job, Maccabees—threefold state:

  a) acting (in accord with the Law), in state of prosperity: Joshua, Judges, Kings, Chronicles, Ezra, Nehemiah

    i. exempla of perfection to the good (before captivity):

      α) beginning (entering land): **Joshua**

      β) progress (in land, people tested): **Judges**

      γ) consummation:

         γ1) exempla for actives: regal power: **Kings**

         γ2) exempla for contemplatives: priestly: **Chronicles**

    ii. exempla of reparation to the good after the captivity: Ezra, Nehemiah

      α) contemplative (repair of the temple): **Ezra**

      β) active (repair of the city): **Nehemiah**

  b) sustaining in state of adversity: Esther, Tobit, Job, Judith

    i. personal adversity: **Job, Tobit**

  ii. general adversity:

    α) through hidden machination: **Esther**

    β) through open violence: **Judith**

  c) persevering (in both): **Maccabees**

3. Teaching of admonitions (words): Proverbs, Ecclesiastes, Songs, Wisdom, Ecclesiasticus

  a) general admonition: **Proverbs**

  b) special admonitions:

    i. contempt for commutable goods: **Ecclesiastes**

    ii. conversion to incommutable good: **Song of Songs**

    iii. to justice: **Wisdom**

    iv. to the benefits of mercy: **Ecclesiasticus**

B) Prophets: Christ is shown as mediator of revelation, which pertains to truth

- what ought to be believed (both affections and intellect)

1. Concerning the Head (Christ): four Major Prophets → four Gospels: Christ is God-man

  a) focus on divinity: **Isaiah** (Immanuel) and John (the Word)

  b) focus on humanity—dignity of Christ; union of:

    i. power (king): **Daniel** (Dan 7: Son of Man) and **Matthew** (prologue; Sermon on the Mount)

    ii. wisdom (preaching): **Jeremiah** (preaches to Jews) and **Mark** (begins preaching after baptism by John, focus on preaching)

    iii. goodness (priest): **Ezekiel** (was a priest) and **Luke** (begins with Zechariah; true priesthood in passion)

2. Concerning the Body (the Church): **twelve Minor Prophets** → twelve apostles

C) **Psalms:** Christ is shown as mediator of prayers, which pertains to goodness

- seeking the grace of perseverance in prayers to God: divided into three parts in accord with three rules or *regula* [not specified]

II. Teaching of the New Testament—two parts

A) Evangelical Teaching: four **Gospels** (treat of the Head, Christ) [see above]

B) Apostolic Teaching: Acts, epistles, Apocalypse (treat of the Body, the Church)

- three states:

1. beginning: **Acts**

2. growth: **Epistles**

3. culmination: **Apocalypse**

MATTHEW OF AQUASPARTA'S *DIVISIO TEXTUS* OF THE BOOKS OF THE BIBLE

Old Testament: four parts

I. Legal precepts: provide ruling precepts

A) **Genesis**: treats of multiplication of the people and election, to which the Law was given

B) **Exodus**: treats of the legislation

C) **Leviticus**: treats of rites of sacrifice and divine cult

D) **Numbers**: treats of the progress and order of that people

E) **Deuteronomy**: recapitulation of the Law

II. Examples (exempla) of the fathers: provide moving examples from history

A) the common state of the whole people

1. **Joshua**: entry into the promised land and distribution of it

2. **Judges**: progress of the people, multiplication in variety of states

3. **Kings**: promotion and exaltation of a king

4. **Chronicles**: exaltation of the priesthood

5. **Ezra-Nehemiah**: reparation after ruin (temple and city)

B) the state of notable singular persons

1. **Job**: example of patience under the natural law

2. **Tobit**: example of the same patience under the written Law

3. **Judith**: example of purity and chastity (merited cutting off the head of Holofernes)

4. **Esther**: example of clemency and mercy as queen, not elevated by pride

5. **Maccabees**: example of constancy to the laws of the fathers even to death (prefiguring the martyrs of the Church)

III. Sapiential literature: provide directing warnings and information [ed., this is a switch from his opening]

    A) special information

        1. **Proverbs**: information concerning the exercise and progress of virtue

        2. **Ecclesiastes**: contempt of vanity, preparing the mind for the love expressed in the Song of Songs

        3. **Song of Songs**: the embrace of love

        4. **Wisdom**: the contemplation of truth

    B) universal information (all higher things): **Ecclesiasticus**

IV. Oracles of the prophets: provide illustrating oracles

    A) through the medium of prayer (by which the light of grace is obtained by entreaty)

        - **Psalms**: because of the truth of the grace of the Spirit

    B) through the medium of preaching (by which the truth is manifested)

        1. **Isaiah**: principally predicts the mystery of the Incarnation (Advent readings)

        2. **Jeremiah**: principally predicts the remedy of the passion (Lamentations: prefigures the passion of the Lord)

        3. **Ezekiel**: principally predicts the resurrection (rededication of the temple)

        4. **Daniel**: principally predicts the judgment (Son of Man coming on the clouds)

    C) through the medium of testifying: **twelve Minor Prophets** = twelve apostles [bound in one volume]

New Testament

I. Lord's precepts (correspond to books of the Law)

    - Christ is God-man, king and priest

    A) **Matthew**: treats of his humanity

B) **Mark**: treats of his regal power

C) **Luke**: treats of his priestly dignity

D) **John**: treats of his divinity

II. Apostolic exempla (correspond to historical books)

- **Acts of the Apostles**: unity of the mystical body and bond of charity commended

III. Canonical literature (correspond to sapiential books)

A) special information for the churches and persons to whom they are directed:

- **Pauline epistles**

B) general information, thus common name retained

- **Canonical epistles**

IV. Prophetic Oracle (corresponding to prophetic books)

- **Apocalypse**: deals with the final state of the Church, in which is rest and consummation

HENRY OF GHENT'S *DIVISIO TEXTUS* OF THE BOOKS OF THE BIBLE

Augustine: "signs" and "things"

I. Old Testament: (sign; mystical senses; figural with respect to the New)

A) Law: what ought to be done (to be expounded principally with tropological sense)

1. Preceptive (what ought to be done): five books of Moses

(Genesis as prologue: rejected)

(Genesis provides creation of creatures; other books provide the law for them: rejected because Genesis not part of law; instead:)

a) remembrance of natural law (not only word, but deeds in history; man was made in natural law; patriarchs observed it; corrupted by sinners; shown by deeds): **Genesis**

b) coercion to observe the natural law: precepts of written law

    i. Law promulgated:

        α) moral precepts (man ordered in relation to himself): **Exodus**

            - pertains to beginners (beginning good): describes the people exiting from Egypt, hastening to sea of baptism and to mountain of divine law

        β) sacramental (man ordered in relation to God): **Leviticus**

            - pertains to those progressing and the increase of good: describes the people progressing through the desert of this world to the promised land

        γ) judicial (man ordered in relation to neighbor): **Numbers**

            - pertains to the perfect and the consummation of good: describes the people preparing themselves to enter and possess the promised land

    ii. Law explained: **Deuteronomy**

2. Directive (how it ought to be done):

    a) exempla through just deeds: historical books

        i. of doing the good of justice

            α) entry (beginning): **Joshua**

            β) progress (against temptation; progress in virtue): **Judges**

                - annexed: time under one judge: **Ruth**

            γ) perfect consummation: justice of divine cult

                γ1) active life (kings and princes): **Kings**

γ2) contemplative life (ministers; spiritual matters): **Chronicles**

δ) reparation for lost justice—twofold:

δ1) in the spiritual regimen of the contemplative life: **Ezra** (temple)

δ2) in the temporal regimen of the active life: **Nehemiah** (city)

ii. of sustaining the evil of punishment

α) personal:

α1) pain of loss: **Tobit** (struck with blindness)

α2) pain of sense: **Job** (struck with the worst boils: sustained the Cross)

β) communal

β1) through open violence: **Judith**

β2) through hidden machinations: **Esther**

iii. of persevering in both doing the good of justice and in enduring the evil of punishment: **Maccabees**

b) exhortation through words: books of Solomon

i. dissuading from doing evil

α) flee iniquity: **Proverbs**

β) not to love vanity: **Ecclesiastes**

ii. persuading to do good

α) to the contemplative life: **Song of Songs**

β) to the conservation of the republic: **Wisdom**

γ) by an invocation to divine mercy: **Ecclesiasticus**

B) Prophets: what ought to be believed (principally with allegorical)

1. Twelve Minor Prophets: concern the mystic body, the Church

2. Four Major Prophets: concern the head, Christ

   a) nativity and Incarnation: **Isaiah** (Virgin will conceive)

   b) passion and death: **Jeremiah**

   c) resurrection and ascension: **Ezekiel**

   d) advent to judgment: **Daniel**

C) Psalms: for what we ought to hope (principally with anagogical): most excellent, preeminent prophet (less involved with images and coverings of words; dreams; more directly inspired by Holy Spirit)

II. New Testament: (New Law divided as was the Old)

A) Law (what ought to be done from charity)

1. Preceptive: Evangelical doctrine, concerning Christ per se

   a) principally divinity: **John**

   b) principally humanity:

     i. his entry into the world and things pertaining to human generation and birth: **Matthew**

     ii. his progress in the world and things pertaining to things foretold of him: **Mark**

     iii. his exit from the world and things pertaining to his passion: **Luke**

2. Directive: Apostolic doctrine, concerning Christ through the apostles and his disciples

   a) through the example of the just: **Acts**

   b) through the instruction of words: epistles of Apostles

     i. for informing the faithful in the time of prosperity: **Pauline epistles** (Grace to you and peace)

     ii. for consoling the afflicted in the time of adversity: **Canonical epistles** ("Count it joy when you fall into various temptations" [James 1:1])

B) Prophets (how it ought to be done fruitfully): **Apocalypse**

Thomas Aquinas's *Divisio Textus* of the Books of the Bible

The Sacred Scriptures lead to eternal life—and this in two ways:

I. By commanding:

(Old Testament)

    A) Binding: command of a king who punishes

        1. King who establishes the law

            a) private: **Genesis** (Adam, Eve, Abraham, etc.)

            b) public:

                i. Law from LORD to mediator: three ways people need to be ordered:

                    α) equity of judgments: **Exodus**

                    β) establishment of worship: **Leviticus**

                    γ) establishment of offices for community: **Numbers**

                ii. Law from mediator to people: **Deuteronomy**

        2. Heralds who induce its observance (prophets)

            a) manifest beneficence of the king

                i. effect of heredity: **Joshua** [see also under B.1 below, "Warning: By deed"]

                ii. in destruction of armies: **Judges**

                iii. exultation of the people

                    α) private: **Ruth**

                    β) whole people: **Kings**

            b) declare the edict of the law

                i. to the whole people for observance of the whole law (Major Prophets)

                    α) by cajoling: **Isaiah** (also foretells Incarnation, read during Advent) β) by warning: **Jeremiah** (foretells passion, read during Passiontide)

γ) arguing, scolding: **Ezekiel** (foretells resurrection: raising of bones)

δ) **Daniel** spoke of the divinity of Christ

  ii. for special reasons to special tribes (**Minor Prophets**), e.g.:

α) to the ten tribes: **Hosea**

β) to the Ninevites: **Jonah**

B) Warning: precept of a father who teaches

  1. By deed

    a) warning about future: **Joshua** (see St. Jerome)

    b) teaches virtues from past

      i. Justice: **Paralipomenon (Chronicles)**

      ii. Temperance: **Judith**

      iii. Fortitude

α) to attack: **Maccabees**

β) to endure: **Tobit**

      iv. Prudence:

α) to build city and temple while enemies plot: **Ezra–Nehemiah**

β) to repel the violent: **Esther**

  2. By word

    a) asking for gift of wisdom: **Psalms**

    b) teaching wisdom:

      i. expose the liar: driving out errors by disputation: **Job**

      ii. not to lie about what is known:

α) wisdom is commended to us: **Wisdom**

β) precepts of wisdom (and virtue) are proposed

-three grades of virtue (see Poltinus)

β1) political virtues (use things of the world): **Proverbs**

β2) purgative virtues (contempt of the world): **Ecclesiastes**

β3) virtues of purged soul (wholly cleansed from worldly care; contemplation alone): **Song of Songs**

3. By word and deed: **Ecclesiasticus**

II. By helping with gifts of grace:

(New Testament)

A) Origin of Grace: Jesus Christ (divine and human: priest, prophet, king)

1. Divine nature: esp. **John** (eagle)

2. Human nature: Synoptics

a) king: **Matthew** (Incarnation: man)

b) prophet: **Mark** (resurrection: lion)

c) priest: **Luke** (passion: bull)

B) Power of Grace: Pauline epistles:

[missing from the *resumptio*; the divisiones of the Pauline epistles has been taken from the prologue to Thomas's Commentary on Romans]

---

1. As it is in the Head—namely, Christ: **Hebrews**

2. As it is found in the chief members of the Mystical Body: the letters to the prelates, both spiritual and temporal:

a) spiritual prelates instructed about:

i. establishing, preserving, and governing ecclesial unity: **I Timothy**

ii. resistance against persecutors: **II Timothy**

iii. defense against heretics: **Titus**

b) temporal lord instructed: **Philemon**

3. As it is found in the Mystical Body itself, that is, the Church: the letters to the Gentiles:

a) as it is in the Church itself: **Romans**

b) as it exists in the sacraments of grace:

i. nature of the sacraments: **I Corinthians**

ii. dignity of the minister: **II Corinthians**

iii. superfluous sacraments rejected against those who wanted to join old sacraments to the new: **Galatians**

c) with regard to the effect of the unity it produces in the Church:

i. establishment of ecclesial unity: **Ephesians**

ii. consolidation and progress of unity: **Philippians**

iii. defense against certain errors: **Colossians**

iv. unity during existing persecutions: **I Thessalonians**

v. during persecutions to come, especially in time of the anti-Christ: **II Thessalonians**

C) Execution of Power of Grace: progress of the Church

1. Beginning: **Acts of the Apostles**

2. Progress: **Canonical epistles** (James; 1 and 2 Peter; 1, 2, and 3 John; and Jude)

3. End: **Apocalypse**

"ITS LAMPS ARE LAMPS OF FIRE AND FLAMES": THOMAS AQUINAS ON THE SONG OF SONGS

DARIA SPEZZANO
Providence College

William of Tocco claims that St. Thomas, on his deathbed, gave a brief commentary on the Song of Songs to the Cistercians of Fossanova, although no written record of these words exists.[1] Denys Turner, among others, considers this implausible; in his view, "the *Song* is not Thomas's style," for Aquinas chooses the love of friendship over *eros* as a model for Christian love, unlike the majority of medieval theologians.[2] Nevertheless, Thomas refers to texts from the Song of Songs in a number of places throughout his works, especially in the context of discussions about charity, the Church, Christ, the Holy Spirit, and the Eucharist. Whether or not Thomas actually gave his deathbed commentary, it is worth asking what he might have said about this Scripture that reportedly so occupied his last

---

[1] William of Tocco, *Ystoria Sancti Thome de Aquino* 58, in *Ystoria sancti Thome de Aquino de Guillaume de Tocco (1323): Édition critique, introduction et notes*, ed. C. Le Brun-Gouanvic, Studies and Texts 127 (Toronto: Pontifical Institute of Medieval Studies, 1996), 197–98. James Weisheipl, O.P., notes that, although "all the early catalogues of Thomas's writings list a *Super Cantica*," none has yet been found; two attributed to him in the Vulgate editions are spurious, one belonging to Haimo of Auxerre and the other to Giles of Rome (*Friar Thomas D'Aquino: His Life, Thought and Works* [Garden City, NY: Doubleday, 1974], 369).

[2] Denys Turner, *Thomas Aquinas: A Portrait* (New Haven, CT: Yale University Press, 2013), 147.

thoughts, and to what extent the Song contributed to his theology of charity. Through a contextual analysis of Thomas's citations of the Song, I will argue that it was in fact a significant text for him, introducing an element of distinctively Dominican spiritual *eros* into his view of divine love.

Thomas Aquinas is rightly noted for his original analysis of charity as a kind of friendship with God, in which he draws from both the Johannine Scriptures and Aristotle's *Nicomachean Ethics*.[3] Indeed, Thomas is sometimes presented as an exception to the rule of medieval reflection on Christian love shaped, Denys Turner has argued, by an allegorized language of *eros*, drawn from the long tradition of commentary on the Song of Songs. Turner comments that Aquinas "appears not to share the otherwise almost universal medieval preference for the *Song of Songs* as a biblical source for his doctrine of Christian love."[4] In *Eros and Allegory*, Turner argues that medieval monastic exegetes were drawn to the Song's "exuberant celebration of *eros*,"[5] understanding it allegorically as a love dialogue between God or Christ and the Church, Mary, or the individual soul.[6] This exegetical tradition is complemented by the influence of Pseudo-Dionysian Neoplatonism, with its paradoxical language of divine *eros*, in which God and his creation can be said to ecstatically yearn toward each other, though God remains transcendent.[7] Keith Egan, too, argues that Thomas's approach stands in tension with an

---

[3] On this, see Anthony Keaty, "Thomas's Authority for Identifying Charity as Friendship: Aristotle or John 15?" *The Thomist* 62 (1998): 581–601.

[4] Turner, *Thomas Aquinas*, 148.

[5] That is, precisely because it seemed to them that "the natural, spontaneous . . . human model for divine love is love in its erotic expression" (Denys Turner, *Eros and Allegory: Medieval Exegesis of the Song of Songs* [Kalamazoo, MI: Cistercian, 1995], 41). Gregory the Great, for instance, writes of the Song that: "In this book we find the words of bodily love, so that the soul, its numbness caressed into warmth by familiar words, through the words of a lower love is excited to a higher" (translation in Turner, *Eros and Allegory*, 217).

[6] Turner, *Eros and Allegory*, 155. For this tradition, "the reality of *eros* is found in the inversion of its own significance, that is, in celibacy" (156). Turner proposes that Aquinas's commitment to the literal sense, had he written a commentary on the Song, would have allowed him to argue for "the historical veracity of the love affair" as a real foreshadowing of the "love story between Christ and the Church through the prophetic love between Israel and Yahweh" (138).

[7] Turner, *Eros and Allegory*, 67. That is, God transcends both unity and difference between God and creatures, a concept congenial to mystical spirituality, and Neoplatonism provides a "logic and metaphysics" for this language (63).

erotic spirituality,[8] that he "did not engage in any significant way the Song tradition,"[9] and that, since Thomas "only infrequently cites the Song," he seems to show a "reluctance" to use it in his works.[10] The predominant Western spiritual tradition of commentary on the Song of Songs is erotic, then, in that it celebrates the yearning desire for union with God or Christ, whether by the Church or the individual soul. And with this tradition, it seems, Thomas's treatment of charity as friendship with God has little to do.

Fergus Kerr argues that this was actually an important theological advance for Thomas. According to Kerr, through his study of the *Nicomachean Ethics*, Thomas "dramatically" revised his understanding of charity between the *Scriptum* on Lombard's *Sentences* and the *Summa theologiae*.[11] In doing so, he moved away from an account of the Song of Songs in the *Scriptum* that, "if it does not exactly reek of sublimated eroticism, nevertheless has a certain neo-Platonic redolence."[12] In the *Scriptum*, Thomas encompasses in his definition of charity as friendship multiple terms from the tradition, including *dilectio, concupiscentia* (or desire), and *amor* (translating *eros*).[13] Kerr notes that Thomas introduces here the notion of *amatio*, "adding to *amor* a certain *intensio* and *fervor* (straining and burning)."[14] Kerr contrasts this with Thomas's simpler definition of charity in the *Summa* as a "kind of friendship of man for God" based on the communication of God's happiness to us through fellowship with the Son.[15] Kerr argues that, by comparison with the *Scriptum*'s anal-

---

8   Keith Egan, "Eros, Friendship and Love: The Future of Bridal Mysticism," in *Studies in Spirituality* 16 (2006): 131–50, at 141–42.

9   Egan, "Eros, Friendship and Love," 141.

10   Egan remarks that Thomas's texts "have none of the explicit passion of the Song" ("Eros, Friendship and Love," 135, 141). Egan relies on the *Indices auctoritatem omniumque rerum notabilium occurrentium in Summa theologiae et in Summa contra gentiles*, Leonine ed. 16 (Rome: Leonine Commission, 1948), a source that provides citations only in the two *Summae*.

11   Fergus Kerr, "Charity as Friendship," in *Language, Meaning and God*, ed. Brian Davies (London: Chapman, 1987), 1–23, at 3.

12   Kerr, "Charity as Friendship," 17–18.

13   These terms are drawn from Peter Lombard, Augustine, and Dionysius respectively.

14   Kerr, "Charity as Friendship," 5. This is Kerr's translation; he refers to *In III sent.*, d. 27, q. 2, a. 1.

15   *Summa theologiae* [*ST*] II–II, q. 23, a. 1. All citations of *ST* are from *S. Thomae Aquinatis Doctoris Angelici Opera Omnia Iussu impensaque Leonis XIII P. M. edita*,

ysis, the *Summa* is "sure-footed, elegant and condensed": "The atmosphere is . . . cleared of the imagery of longing and yearning, of being hot and sticky. It is as if the mutual absorption of two lovers in one another had been abandoned in favor of the model of colleagues engaged in a common adventure."[16]

AQUINAS'S USE OF THE SONG

In spite of this common opinion, however, Thomas does make significant references to the Song in his treatments of charity, Christ, the Eucharist, and other topics; in some cases, I will argue, his use of Song texts even seems to approach the traditionally "hot and sticky." Thomas's *partitio* of the Bible in his inaugural lecture, *Hic est liber,* shows that he saw the Song as the spiritual culmination of the three books of Solomon (Proverbs, Ecclesiastes, and the Song of Songs) in the Old Testament's wisdom literature. Thomas draws from Plotinus's *Enneads* to categorize these books according to three steps of virtue. While Proverbs treats political (or ethical) virtue and Ecclesiastes has to do with purgative virtues by which one leaves behind worldly things in contempt, the Song deals with "the virtues of the purified soul, whereby one, having entirely trampled down worldly

---

vols. 4–12 (Rome: Leonine Commission, 1888–1906). All translations from Latin in this essay are my own unless otherwise noted.

[16] Kerr, "Charity as Friendship," 6. Kerr also remarks that "notions like *amor, concupiscentia,* etc., have been, or are to be, redistributed to other places in the *secunda pars,* thus lightening the argument" (6). Kerr concludes that Thomas's mature view of charity as friendship with God, without being impersonal at all, escapes the temptation to view union with God as any kind of infatuation or self-annihilation, although later Dominican mystics would subvert his idea of being a friend of God into the notion of a "solitary merging of the individual with the absolute" that Thomas himself would reject (22). It should be noted that Thomas's "redistribution" of notions like *amor* to other parts of the *Summa* does not mean that Thomas dissociates them from his understanding of charity. Peter Kwasniewski notes the fluidity of Thomas's vocabulary for love and charity in all of his works; see "Brief Introduction," in *On Love and Charity: Readings from the Commentary on the Sentences of Peter Lombard,* ed. Peter Kwasniewski, Thomas Bolin, and Joseph Bolin (Washington, DC: Catholic University of America Press, 2008), xxiii. This includes the *Summa,* where Thomas himself says that *amor, dilectio, caritas,* and *amicitia* are "four words that refer, in a way, to the same thing" (*ST* II-II, q. 26, a. 3).

cares, delights in the contemplation of wisdom alone."[17] Thomas's division of Scripture in the inaugural lecture draws an implicit parallel between the Song in the Old Testament and the Book of Revelation in the New.[18] The latter, Thomas says, describes the end of the Church: "[Revelation] concludes the whole of sacred Scripture until the entrance of the bride into the wedding-chamber of Christ, to share in his life of glory."[19] As Thomas begins his division in *Hic est liber*, he refers to the Song to frame all of Scripture as a life-giving gift to those who keep it: "All fruits, new and old, my beloved, I have kept for you" (Song 7:13). From the beginning of his teaching as a master of the sacred page, Thomas gives the Song a privileged place in Scripture: it describes the delights of wisdom given by Christ to his beloved bride, the Church, in anticipation of her union with him in glory.

The goal of the present project, then, was to collect every reference to the Song in Thomas's works in order: first, to find out where and how often he cites the Song; second, to evaluate whether, by arranging the material in order of the verses cited, it would be possible to construct some elements of a commentary by a kind of reverse engineering, based on the citations in their contexts; and finally, to find out to what extent his use of the Song introduces an element of spiritual *eros*—of yearning desire, intensity, and fervor—into his thought on charity and related matters.[20] The search,

---

[17] Aquinas, *Hic est liber* 2. The Latin text (online at corpusthomisticum.org/ptc. html) is taken from: Michael Estler, *"Rigans montes" (Ps. 104, 13): Die Antrittsvorlesung des Thomas von Aquin in Paris 1256*, Stuttgarter biblische Beiträge 73 (Stuttgart: Katholisches Bibelwerk, 2015), 83–91. Notably, Gregory the Great, in his commentary on the Song, constructs a similar "ladder that leads to contemplation of God" from these three books, noting that "the Greeks" refer to these three stages of life as "ethical, physical, and theoretical" (*Expositio in Cantica Canticorum* 9, in *CCSL* 144:12–13; see translation in Richard A. Norris Jr., *The Song of Songs: Interpreted by Early Christian and Medieval Commentators*, The Church's Bible Series [Grand Rapids, MI: Eerdmans, 2003], 10).

[18] I am indebted to Michael Waldstein for this observation in an unpublished (as of yet) essay.

[19] Aquinas, *Hic est liber* 2.

[20] One day before this paper was presented, a short book was published by Fr. Serge-Thomas Bonino, O.P., in which he undertakes a remarkably similar project: *Saint Thomas d'Aquin, lecteur du Cantique des cantiques* (Paris: Cerf, 2019). Although our results overlap at many points, it seems worthwhile to present this essay nevertheless, as we focus on somewhat different aspects of the texts. It is recommended that the reader consult Bonino's work for a comprehensive and

using the online Index Thomisticus, included explicit references to the Song, as well as significant words and phrases in the Vulgate text to which Thomas alludes without citation.[21] My underlying premise, of course, is that quotation is a kind of interpretation: the choice of a particular Scripture text to demonstrate an idea or gloss another Scripture text depends on the meaning attributed to the text cited, and each text imports its own set of associations, acting as a place marker for a complex of related ideas.

The results show that Thomas refers to the text of the Song over three hundred times, mostly in his Scripture commentaries (Egan, for instance, refers only to Thomas's two *Summae*). Thomas also cites at least some part of most verses of the Song (but not all verses) at least once, and some noticeably more than others. Song texts appear more often in his mid- to late-career works, in particular the commentaries on Matthew (thirty-four times), John (forty-two times), and the Psalms (thirty-six times), as well as in numerous Pauline epistles, with some key references also in his systematic works.[22] His earlier commentary on Isaiah, though, has sixty-two Song quotations, including what were originally his marginal collations, in which the Song is the most frequently quoted book after the Psalms, Proverbs, and Isaiah itself.[23] These collations are Thomas's own handwritten assemblies of Scripture quotations that reveal the spiritual, and especially Christological, associations he makes with the more literal

---

insightful treatment of this seldom-examined aspect of Thomas's scriptural exegesis.

[21] I am grateful for the assistance of the online Corpus Thomisticum website (corpusthomisticum.org) edited by Enrique Alarcón, S.J., for the Fundación Tomás de Aquino, incorporating the *Index Thomisticus: Sancti Thomae Aquinatis operum omnium indices et concordantiae*, ed. Roberto Busa, S.J., 50 vols. (Stuttgart: Frommann-Holzboog, 1974–1980).

[22] The commentaries on John and the Psalms are probably dated after 1270; Jean-Pierre Torrell, O.P., considers it highly probable that the *reportatio* on Matthew is dated to Thomas's second Parisian period, during 1269–1270 (*Saint Thomas Aquinas*, vol. 1, *The Person and His Work*, trans. Robert Royal [Washington, DC: Catholic University of America Press, 2003], 339). However, Weisheipl dates it as "most likely," though not certainly, from his first Parisian period, 1256–1259 (*Friar Thomas D'Aquino*, 121, 371). My original count for Song references in these works underestimated the number and has been adjusted in accord with Bonino; for further detailed statistics, see Bonino, *Saint Thomas d'Aquin*, 14–15.

[23] Torrell, *Saint Thomas Aquinas*, 1:34.

exegesis of his commentary,[24] and which were likely memory aids for preaching.[25] So, it is not surprising to find also over twenty Song citations in his sermons, four of which are in one short passage of the vespers sermon of *Germinet terra*, in the midst of a discussion of the "fruit-bearing tree, the Cross of our Lord."[26]

Here, as in *Hic est liber*, Thomas quotes Song of Songs 7:13, importing associations with wisdom and the union of Christ and his beloved Church, as he explains that the tree of the Cross is loaded with "all fruits, old and new." The old fruits are prefigured by the ancient fathers, while the new are fruits of heaven, of sun and moon, and of the eternal hills.[27] In his discussion of each of these new fruits, he places a quote from the Song to explain how the Cross is bountifully adorned by both Christ and his bride. The fruits of heaven are Christ's members: "The Cross was adorned with the members of Christ, just as a tree is adorned with fruits; not only with the corporeal members of Christ's body, but with those of his mystical body," who are crucified with him. "About these fruits it is said in the Song (5:1): 'May my beloved enter his garden, to eat the yield of his fruits.'"[28] The fruits of sun and moon are examples of the virtues Christ shows on the Cross—love, humility, obedience, and patience: "These are the fruits of the enclosed valleys, of which we read in the Song of Songs (6:11), 'I have come down into my garden, to see the fruit of the enclosed valleys.'"[29] The fruits of the eternal hills are the writings of wise teachers, especially Christ on the Cross, who teach-

---

[24] Torrell, *Thomas Aquinas, vol. 1*, 30. See Jean-Pierre Torrell, O.P. and Denise Bouthillier, "Quand saint Thomas méditait sur le prophète Isaïe," *Revue Thomiste* 90 (1):5–47 (1990). For a helpful discussion of the collations see Joseph Wawrykow, "Aquinas on Isaiah," in *Aquinas on Scripture: An Introduction to His Biblical Commentaries*, edited by Thomas Weinandy, Daniel A. Keating, John Yocum (New York: T&T Clark International, 2005), 43–72, 50–53.

[25] On Thomas's method of scriptural word associations as mnemonic devices for preaching, see Randall Smith, "How to Read a Sermon by Thomas Aquinas," *Nova et Vetera* (English) 10, no. 3 (2012): 775–803.

[26] Aquinas, *Germinet terra collatio in sero* 2, sermon 18 in *Thomas Aquinas: The Academic Sermons*, trans. Mark-Robin Hoogland, C.P., CCCM 11 (Washington, DC: Catholic University of America Press, 2010), 277.

[27] Thomas refers here to Moses's threefold blessing of the tribe of Joseph in Deut 33:13–15.

[28] Aquinas, *Germinet terra collatio in sero* 2.1 (Hoogland trans., 277–78; trans. slightly modified).

[29] Aquinas, *Germinet terra collatio in sero* 2.3 (Hoogland trans., 278).

es hope, patience, and devotion: "These are the fruits of the eternal hills mentioned in the Song (4:13): 'The things you bring forth are a paradise-garden of pomegranate trees bearing fruits.'"[30] In his prologue to the *Scriptum*, illustrating Sirach's (24:40–42) description of wisdom watering her garden, Thomas unfolds the Song's fruitful metaphor further: "The garden is the Church, of which the Song of Songs (4:12) says, 'My sister, my spouse, is a garden enclosed,' in which there are diverse plants according to the diverse order of the saints." Christ waters this garden by the sacraments and brings forth the faithful as his fruit: "The fruits of this bringing forth are the saints who are in glory, of which fruit the Song of Songs (5:1) says: 'Let my beloved come into his garden and eat the fruit of his apple trees.'"[31] Christ crucified is the beloved, the Church his bride and fecund garden, and the faithful, ripened in glory, are his fruit.

THE BRIDEGROOM AND THE BRIDE

Thomas's allusions in the texts above to Christ and his bride the Church are examples of the generally traditional approach Thomas takes to the Song, perhaps because he was aware of the glosses or Song commentaries of Origen, Ambrose, Gregory the Great, and Bernard of Clairvaux, referring to them all, as well as to the *Glossa ordinaria*.[32] Thomas also likely drew from some glosses without ci-

---

[30] Aquinas, *Germinet terra collatio in sero* 2.3 (Hoogland trans., 279).

[31] *In* I *Sent.*, prol. Citations from the *Scriptum* are based on *S. Thomae Aquinatis, Scriptum super libros Sententiarum magistri Petri Lombardi episcopi Parisiensis*, vols. 1–4, ed. P. Mandonnet (Paris: P. Lethielleux, 1929).

[32] For Origen: *In* IV *sent.*, d. 49, q. 4, a. 4, sc 1. For Bernard: *In* II *sent.*, d. 43, q. 1, a. 5, obj. 1; *In* IV *sent.*, d. 50, q. 2, a. 1, qa. 2, corp. 1; *De spiritualibus creaturis*, a. 5, obj. 3; *ST* I, q. 51, a. 1, obj. 1; *Contra impugnantes*, pars 2, ch. 3, obj. 2. For Gregory: *Contra impugnantes*, pars 5, ch. 1, corp.; *Super Matt* 20, lec. 1 (*reportatio* Leodegarii Bissuntini); *ST* I, q. 8, a. 3. For Ambrose: *In* III *sent.*, d. 29, q. 1, a. 6, corp. For the *Glossa ordinaria*: *In* IV *sent.*, d. 49, q. 4, a. 4, obj. 1; d. 49, q. 5, a. 3, qa. 3, sc; *ST* II-II, q. 108, a. 1, obj. 2; *Contra impugnantes*, pars 4, ch. 4, corp.; *Super Matt* 9, lec. 2 (*reportatio* Leodegarii Bissuntini); *Super I Cor* 5, lec. 2.; *Super Psalmos* 44[Hebrew=45], no. 3. Thomas's knowledge of the gloss from Ambrose may provide a further hint that he drew from Cistercian sources, since Ann Matter notes: "Ambrose actually wrote no commentary on the Song of Songs, but cited the text frequently in his writings, always with a spiritual or (admittedly going

tation.[33] For Thomas, the literal sense of this text—the intent of its divine author—is in effect its allegorical meaning: the marriage of Christ and his members.[34] Perhaps the clearest evidence of this is found in his commentary on Psalm 44[45], the title of which reads in part, "a song for the beloved." As Thomas introduces the Psalm, he notes that it is an "epithalamium," a wedding song in praise of a bridegroom and bride.[35] "Therefore, the subject matter of this Psalm is the same as that of the book called the Song of Songs, . . . the espousal of Christ and the Church, which was begun when the Son of God united himself to a human nature in the virginal womb."[36]

As the commentary on this wedding psalm unfolds, Thomas weaves in lines from the Song (among many other Scripture texts)

---

beyond Origen) a mariological interpretation. Ambrose's comments on verses of the Song of Songs were widely diffused through a systematic catena put together by the twelfth-century Cistercian, William of Saint-Thierry"; see E. Ann Matter, *The Voice of My Beloved: The Song of Songs in Western Medieval Christianity* (Philadelphia: University of Pennsylvania Press, 1992), 74.

[33] For instance, Thomas may be drawing from the *Glossa ordinaria* for Song 5:1 in the passage from his prologue to the *Scriptum* just cited above. A standard gloss taken from Alcuin on this text likewise identifies the "fruit of his apple trees" as Christ's saints in the garden of his Church, providing a possible source for Thomas's somewhat unusual image; see *The Glossa Ordinaria on the Song of Songs*, ed. Mary Dove (Kalamazoo, MI: Medieval Institute Publications, 2004), 95, 104.

[34] As Matter points out: "There is no 'non-allegorical' Latin tradition of Song of Songs commentary. . . . Even Nicholas of Lyra, champion of the historical sense of the Bible, argued that the Song of Songs has no literal sense" (*The Voice of My Beloved*, 42). See Thomas's prologue to his commentary on the Psalms: "Blessed Jerome therefore expounding on Ezekiel passed on to us a rule that we will observe in the Psalms; namely, that events are to be expounded as prefiguring something about Christ or the Church. As indeed it says in 1 Cor 10: 'Everything happened to them as a prefigurement'" (*Super Psalmos*, prol.). The Latin edition for all of Thomas's Psalms commentaries (*Super Psalmos*) is *In psalmos Davidis expositio*, vol. 14 in *Opera Omnia* (Parma: Typis Petri Fiaccadori, 1863), 148–312. Where the Latin/English numbering of psalms differs from the Hebrew, the Hebrew follows in brackets.

[35] *Super Psalmos* 44[45], no. 1. Augustine says this also in his commentary on this psalm: *Ennarationes in psalmos* 44.3, in *S. Aurelii Augustini Opera Omnia* [PL 36], as do Origen and William of St. Thierry in the prefaces to their commentaries on the Song. Parts of Origen's *Commentarium in Canticum Canticorum* and William of St. Thierry's *Expositio in Cantica Canticorum* are translated in Norris, *Song of Songs*; the two prefaces begin on pages 2 and 10, respectively.

[36] *Super Psalmos* 44[45], no. 1.

with his Christological exegesis. For instance, concerning Psalm 44:3—"You are beautiful beyond the sons of men and graciousness is poured upon your lips"—Thomas says that Christ was beautiful both to sight and hearing, for "it says in the Song 2: 'show me your face, let your voice sound in my ears, for your voice is sweet and your face is lovely.'" Christ's beauty was not only on account of his divinity and virtues, but was even bodily, according to the Song 1: "Behold, you are beautiful, my beloved."[37] Later, Thomas comments that the "oil of gladness" (Ps 44:8) anointing Christ is the Holy Spirit. The Spirit, like oil, is excellent, sweet, and diffusive; oil also kindles fire and heat, and the Holy Spirit warms and nourishes the heat of love in us, as it says in Song of Songs 8: "his lamps are lamps of fire."[38] The psalm goes on to describe the queen, who is Christ's spouse the Church, or the Blessed Virgin (Ps 44:10). The Church is clothed in the shining gold of the two testaments, resplendent with the divine wisdom of doctrine, and covered too with the gold of charity's virtuous works. This can also describe the Blessed Virgin, who "stands above all the choirs in golden robes, that is the gold of divinity; not because she is God, but because she is the Mother of God."[39] On Psalm 44:15—"virgins shall be drawn to the king after her"—Thomas comments that the Church draws the faithful to Christ with her doctrine; or as the Blessed Virgin, she draws her virgin companions after her to preserve chastity and to the exercise of other virtues; "They are drawn," he says, "because they cannot come by themselves: John 6:44, 'no one comes to me unless the Father draws him'; and likewise, from the Song 1:3: 'draw me after you.'"[40]

In this Psalm commentary are some of the three or four Song texts Thomas quotes most often, texts that I think one can say are central bearers of the Song's meaning for him. One is Song of Songs 1:3:

---

[37] *Super Psalmos* 44[45], no. 2

[38] *Super Psalmos* 44[45], no. 5.

[39] *Super Psalmos* 44[45], no. 7.

[40] *Super Psalmos* 44[45], no. 10. Thomas ends by tying each section of the psalm to the reason why it is sung on particular liturgical feast days: "And this psalm is sung on the feast of the Lord's birth because it mentions the praise of the bridegroom. Likewise it is sung on the feasts of the Virgin, because it praises her. In the former case, where it says, 'You are beautiful.' In the latter, where it says, 'The queen stands.' It is also sung on the feasts of virgins, because 'they are drawn.' And it is sung on the feasts of the apostles, 'in place of your fathers'" (*Super Psalmos* 44[45], no. 11).

"Draw me after you, we will run in the odor of your perfumes. The king led me into his storerooms; we shall exult and rejoice in you." As in the passage above, this text has a special connection with John 6:44, "no one can come to me unless the Father draw him."[41] Thomas perhaps follows Augustine, who quotes Song of Songs 1:3 in his own exegesis of John 6:44; Augustine's text appears in Thomas's *Catena on John* on this passage.[42] In Thomas's own *Commentary on John*, he pairs these texts three times, giving the bride in the Song as an example of one who is drawn to Christ by a "wonderful joy and love of the truth," moved by the *instinctus* of the Holy Spirit, and whose request to be "drawn" is fulfilled as Christ is lifted up in love on the Cross for her salvation.[43] As we will see below, Thomas often associates texts from the Song with the notion of being urged on by the love of God in the Holy Spirit. In his commentary on Matthew, Thomas adds an eschatological dimension to this divine attraction, associating the bride's ultimate entrance into the king's storerooms with the spiritual goods that come from entrance into the kingdom of heaven (Matt 7:21) and the joy of the Lord (Matt 25:23).[44]

The sinlessness of the Blessed Virgin Mary is often associated by Thomas with Song of Songs 4:7: "You are all beautiful, my beloved, and there is no stain in you." This can be said of her because the wisdom of God entered not only her soul, like other saints, but also her

[41] Bonino also notes the frequency of Thomas's use of Song 1:3 and its association with John 6:44, remarking that love for God, on the part of creatures, "is always a response to the call and to the divine attraction that manifest themselves in particular in and through Christ" (*Saint Thomas d'Aquin*, 58; my translation).

[42] Aquinas, *Catena on John* 6, lec. 6. The Latin edition of all texts from the *Catena aurea* is *Catena aurea in quatuor Evangelia*, vols. 1–2, ed. A. Guarenti, 2nd ed. (Turin: Marietti, 1953).

[43] *Super Ioan* 6, lec. 5 (Marietti no. 935). Also see *Super Ioan* 12, lec. 5 (Marietti no. 1673), and 15, lec. 5 (Marietti no. 2055). All citations of the *Commentary on John* are based on *S. Thomae Aquinatis Super Evangelium S. Ioannis lectura*, ed., R. Cai, 6th ed. (Turin: Marietti, 1972). Thomas draws from Augustine extensively in this commentary; in *Super Ioan* 6, lec. 5, he clearly refers to the passage from Augustine's *Tractatus in Ioan* 26, included in the *Catena on John* 6, lec. 6: "If each of us is drawn by his own pleasure, how much more strongly ought we to be drawn to Christ if we find our pleasure in truth, happiness, justice, eternal life, all of which Christ is!"

[44] *Super Matt* 7, lec. 2 (Marietti no. 655); 25, lec. 2 (Marietti no. 2054). All citations of the *Commentary on Matthew* are based on *S. Thomae Aquinatis Super Evangelium S. Matthaei lectura* (*reportatio* Leodegarii Bissuntini), ed. R. Cai, 5th ed. (Turin: Marietti, 1951), nos. 583–602, 611–2469.

body, by taking flesh from her.[45] Unlike other saints, the Blessed Virgin never sinned even venially;[46] in her, "nothing was disordered, neither in action nor in affection, nor did she have the first movements leading to sin. Hence it says in Song 4:7: 'You are totally beautiful, my friend, and no stain is in you.'"[47] The Virgin was "all beautiful," as in the Song, because "in the womb," she was "cleansed by a special privilege even from original sin."[48] In question 27 of the *Summa*'s *tertia pars*, Thomas cites Song of Songs 4:7 in three consecutive articles discussing exactly how the Virgin Mary was sanctified in the womb. In article 2, he quotes Anselm's *De conceptu virginalis*, where Anselm himself refers to this verse to argue that "the purity of the Virgin would have been greater had she never been stained by original sin."[49] While Thomas famously refutes this claim, he nevertheless goes on in article 3 to place Song of Songs 4:7 in the *sed contra* and to argue that the *fomes* of sin was "bound" in the Virgin until the time that she conceived Christ, when she was completely freed from stain.[50] In article 4, he quotes the verse again as he concludes that "it is simply to be confessed that the Blessed Virgin committed no actual sin, neither mortal nor venial, so that what is said in Song 4 is fulfilled: 'You are all beautiful, my beloved, and no stain is found in you.'"[51]

Another text frequently cited by Thomas is Song of Songs 6:8: "One is my dove, my perfect one." Thomas consistently relates this text to the Church made one by the unity of charity—for instance, with reference to Christ's baptism in his commentary on John 1:32 ("I saw the Spirit coming down, as a dove from heaven"). He explains that the Holy Spirit appeared in the form of a dove "because of the unity of charity, for the dove burns with much love; 'one is my dove' (Song 6:8). So, in order to show the unity of the Church, the Holy Spirit appears in the form of a dove."[52] In the *Summa*, too, Thomas

---

[45] *In* III *sent.*, d. 3, q. 1, a. 2, qa. 2, sc 2.

[46] *Super Psalmos* 45[46], no. 4; *ST* III, q. 27, a. 4; *Comp. theol.* 1, ch. 224; *Super Matt* 12, lec. 4; *Super Ave Maria*, a. 1.

[47] *Germinet terra collatio in sero* 2.2 (Hoogland trans., 267–68).

[48] *Comp. theol.* 1, ch. 224; *Super Ave Maria*, a. 1. Citation of both are based on texts at the Corpus Thomisticum website. Both appear to be drawn from: *S. Thomae Aquinatis Opuscula theologica*, ed. R. M. Spiazzi, 2nd ed. (Turin: Marietti, 1954).

[49] *ST* III, q. 27, a. 2, obj. 2.

[50] *ST* III, q. 27, a. 3, sc.

[51] *ST* III, q. 27, a. 4.

[52] *Super Ioan* 1, lec. 14 (Marietti no. 272).

argues that it was fitting for the Holy Spirit to descend on Christ in the form of a dove, "which is both loving and gregarious," to signify the common effect of baptism, "the building up of the unity of the Church."[53] In the *Summa contra gentiles*, Thomas introduces Song of Songs 6:8 into a beautiful passage on the sacrament of matrimony as a sign of the unbreakable union of love between Christ and the one Church:

> Because, through the conjoining of husband and wife, the conjoining of Christ and the Church is designated, the fig-ure must correspond to the signified. Now, the conjoining of Christ and the Church is that of one to one to be held forever. For there is one Church, according to the Song (6:8): "One is my dove, my perfect one"; nor will Christ ever be separated from his Church, for he himself says: "Behold I am with you all days even to the consummation of the world" (Matt 28:20); and, further: "we shall be always with the Lord," as it says in 1 Thess 4:16. Necessarily, then, matrimony as a sacrament of the Church is [a union of] one to one that is indivisible, and this pertains to the faith by which the man and wife are bound to each other.[54]

So far, it seems, Thomas has a fairly standard view of the Song as a wedding song about Christ and the Church, Mary, or the individual soul; but does his exegesis ever display a tone of spiritual *eros*—of yearning desire, intensity and fervor?

SONG OF SONGS 5:1

Two of Thomas's favorite Song of Songs texts do begin to raise the spiritual temperature. One is Song of Songs 5:1, and Thomas most often quotes the last part of this verse: "Eat, friends, and drink, and

---

[53] *ST* III, q. 39, a. 6, ad 4. This connection between Song 6:8 and the Church's unity is present in a text on Christ's baptism attributed to Jerome in the *Catena on Mark* 1, lec. 4.

[54] *Summa contra gentiles* [*SCG*] IV, ch. 78, no. 5. Citations from the *SCG* are based on *Liber de veritate catholicae Fidei contra errores infidelium seu Summa contra gentiles*, ed. P. Marc, C. Pera, and P. Caramello (Turin: Marietti, 1961).

be inebriated, dearest ones." Figure 1 shows just a sampling of passages from works in which Thomas employs this text, presented as his glosses on the Bible verse. In his commentary on Isaiah 25 (gloss 1), Thomas associates this verse with the spiritual intoxication of the saints enjoying the *convivium* of heaven;[55] they are inebriated by the provocation of love (*amor*; gloss 2, on Isaiah 28).[56] As we have already seen, the same eschatological reference is in the prologue to the *Scriptum* (gloss 3), where Thomas refers the first part of the Song verse to the saints in glory ("let my beloved come into my garden and eat the fruit of his apple trees").[57] In his commentary on John 2 (gloss 4), Thomas explains with two quotes from Song of Songs 5:1 that the wine at the wedding of Cana symbolizes the charity brought by Christ: "Wine inebriates: Song 5:1, 'drink, friends, and be inebriated, dearest ones,' and according to this charity is called wine: Song 5:1, 'I will drink my wine with my milk.' And charity is also called wine by reason of its heat." Christ "converted the water of fear into the wine of charity, when 'he gave the spirit of adoption of sons' (Rom 8:15), and when 'the charity of God was poured into our hearts (Rom 5:5).'"[58]

The heat and inebriation of charity even causes spiritual ecstasy. In the commentary on Psalm 22[23] (gloss 5), Thomas is interpreting the words "how excellent is my chalice that inebriates me":

> This chalice is the gift of divine love which inebriates. For the drunk person is not in himself, nor does he speak according to himself, but according to the impulse of the wine; so the one who is filled with divine love speaks according to God: for he has been made ecstatic [*in extasim factus*]. Song 5:1: "eat, friends, and drink, and be inebriated."[59]

Thomas refers to the same idea of ecstasy or being taken out of oneself, now by the inebriation of love in heaven, in his commentary on Psalm 35[36] (gloss 6):

---

[55] *Super Isa* 25. All citations from Thomas's commentary on Isaiah are based on *Expositio super Isaiam ad litteram*, Leonine ed. 28 (Rome: Leonine Commission, 1974).

[56] *Super Isa* 28.

[57] *In* I *sent.*, prol.

[58] *Super Ioan* 2, lec. 1 (Marietti no. 347).

[59] *Super Psalmos* 22[23], no. 2.

"They [the saints] shall be inebriated [with the plenty of your house]," insofar as their desire will be fulfilled above all measure of merit, for drunkenness is a kind of excess. Isaiah 64: "The eye has not seen [O God, what you have in store for those who love you]"; and Song of Songs 5: "be inebriated, dearest ones." And those who are drunk are not in themselves, but outside of themselves.[60]

He goes on in this commentary to explain that, when the psalmist says, "you shall make them drink of the torrent of your pleasure," "this is the love of the Holy Spirit, which makes an impetus in the soul, like a torrent," producing pleasure and sweetness. "Just as those who would hold their mouths to a fountain of wine would become inebriated, so, those who hold their mouth, that is, their desire, to the fountain of life and sweetness, are inebriated."[61] Likewise, commenting on the Second Letter to the Corinthians 5:13 ("if we are transported in mind it is to God, if we are sober, it is for you"), Thomas writes that it is the Holy Spirit who makes one drunk with the love of God, and "snatches one up to divine things" (gloss 7).[62]

As Peter Kwasniewski notes, when Thomas discusses the effects of love in the *Summa*, he draws from the Dionysian tradition known to him from his commentary on the *Divine Names* to include effects that "seem to belong more in a treatise on erotic love or mystical prayer than in a summa of theology." Among these are *extasis*, or being taken out of oneself.[63] While a lower love of concupiscence, as for actual wine, can debase the soul, the higher love of friendship for

[60] *Super Psalmos* 35[36], no. 4.
[61] *Super Psalmos* 35[36], no. 4.
[62] *Super II Cor* 5, lec. 3 (Marietti no. 179). All citations from Thomas's commentaries on the Pauline letters are based on: *S. Thomae Aquinatis Super Epistolas S. Pauli lectura*, vols. 1–2, ed., R. Cai, 8th ed. (Turin: Marietti, 1953).
[63] Peter Kwasniewski, "St. Thomas, *Extasis*, and Union with the Beloved," in *The Thomist* 61, no. 4 (1997): 587–603. See *ST* I-II, q. 28. Kwasniewski notes that *ST* I-II, q. 28, is especially interesting: "Thomas chooses to include discussions of certain effects that his predecessors, particularly Dionysius the Areopagite, had traditionally ascribed to love, even when at first glance these phenomena seem to bear little resemblance to the doctrine outlined in previous questions of the Summa. Three of these effects—mutual indwelling, ecstasy, and 'passion that wounds the lover' (*mutua inhaesio, extasis, passio laesiva amantis*)—attract our attention by their very names, which seem to belong more in a treatise on erotic love or mystical prayer than in a summa of theology" (587).

neighbor or God perfects the soul by raising one up to higher things, making the lover dwell intently on the beloved and will their good, impelled by a desire for union.[64] Remarkably, in an article on whether love is a passion that wounds the lover, Thomas places a different quote from the Song in each of the three objections, which all argue that love is corruptive because it causes weakness ("I languish with love"; Song 2:5), it melts ("my soul melted when my beloved spoke"; Song 5:6), and it burns ("its lamps are lamps of fire and flames"; Song 8:6). But he responds that these effects of love, softening one's heart and intensifying one's desire, work for the good when one is being perfected and bettered by the love of God.[65] Thomas's allusions to all these Song texts help us to see that, for him, charity as friendship with God by a communication of God's own happiness is not only a "collegial" relationship; it should make one melt, burn, and even be ecstatically drunk with the Holy Spirit, the Love of God through whom "the road to beatitude is opened to us."[66]

Not surprisingly, Thomas refers to Song of Songs 5:1 multiple times in connection with preparation for and reception of the Eucharist, which is the sacrament of charity and a foretaste of heaven.[67] For instance, in his sermon *Homo quidam fecit cenam magnam*, where he describes the threefold spiritual refreshment offered by Christ in the Eucharist, the intellect, and the affections, he says that Christ "prepares for us a banquet of the affections; so in the Song: 'eat, my friends,' namely, here by grace, 'and be drunk, dearest ones,' namely, in the future by glory" (gloss 8).[68] In the words of institution in Matthew 26:26, Christ invites us to receive him in faith and love by eating him, "not only spiritually, but also sacramentally; Song 5:1: 'eat, friends, and drink'" (gloss 9).[69] Thomas refers again to Song of Songs

---

[64] *ST* I-II, q. 28, a. 3; see Kwasniewski, "St. Thomas, *Extasis*, and Union with the Beloved,"603.

[65] *ST* I-II, q. 28, a. 5. Cf., *In* III *sent.*, d. 27, q. 1, a. 1, ad 4.

[66] *SCG* IV, ch. 21, no. 8.

[67] In the *Summa*, Thomas teaches that the Eucharist is called the sacrament of charity because it perfects one "in union with Christ who suffered"; it both signifies and enkindles charity and bestows the grace that leads to eternal life. See: *ST* III, q. 73, a. 3, ad 3; q. 78, a. 3, ad 6; I, q. 12, a. 6.

[68] Aquinas, *Homo quidam fecit cenam magnam* 2. The Latin edition is found in L.-J. Bataillon, "Le sermon inédit de Saint Thomas *Homo quidam fecit cenam magnam*, Introduction et edition." *Revue des sciences philosophiques et théologiques* 67 (1983): 353–68.

[69] *Super Matt* 26, lec. 3 (Marietti no. 2180).

5:1 in the *Summa* (gloss 10) as he explains that, in the Eucharist:

> Not only are the *habitus* of grace and virtues conferred, but they are also excited into act, as in 2 Cor 5:14, "the charity of Christ urges us." And so, by the power of the sacrament the soul is spiritually refreshed in being delighted and in a certain manner inebriated with the sweetness of the divine goodness, according to Song 5, "eat, friends, and drink; and be inebriated, dearest ones."[70]

Song of Songs 5:1, for Thomas, refers to Christ's invitation to his dear friends to eat and drink him in a loving and inebriating union, an invitation that is ultimately consummated in the ecstasy of heaven.

SONG 8:6–7

The Song text that is perhaps most often cited by Thomas brings out even more what might be called an element of spiritual *eros*—a yearning, burning, and urging dimension in his teaching on divine love. The text is from Song of Songs 8:6–7: "Strong as death is love, jealousy as unyielding as the netherworld; its lamps are lamps of fire and flames. Many waters cannot extinguish charity, nor floods overwhelm it" (see Figure 2).

Thomas refers to this text a number of times in his *Commentary on Romans*, where he treats Paul's climactic rhetorical question at the end of Romans 8—"Who then shall separate us from the love of Christ?"—and his fervent answer that nothing, "neither death, nor

---

[70] *ST* III, q. 79, a. 1, ad 2. Torrell notes that, in Thomas's composition of the Office for Corpus Christi, "we can confirm a new cognizance of the affective element in the eucharistic communion. While it is hardly emphasized in the *Sentences*, the words *suavitas* and *dulcedo* return in the lessons of the *Sacerdos*, and in the *Summa* Thomas will emphasize that though venial sins or distractions do not hinder a fruitful reception of the Eucharist, whoever receives communion in that state deprives himself of the sweetness of a certain spiritual repast" (*Saint Thomas Aquinas*, 1:136). In *ST* III, q. 79, a. 8, Thomas draws from John Damascene to argue that, as the Eucharist excites charity into act, it can be compared to a burning coal communicating the fire of divinity and enkindling the heat of holy desire in us.

life, nor angels, nor principalities, nor powers, nor present things,
nor future things, nor might, nor height, nor depth, nor any other
creature, will be able to separate us from the love of God, which is in
Christ Jesus our Lord."[71] Thomas comments that "God bestows great
benefits on his holy ones, and when we consider them, such love of
Christ burns in our hearts that nothing can quench it: 'many waters
cannot quench love' (Song 8:7)" (Fig. 2, gloss 1).[72] He explains that
Paul means, "'no might,' that is, no strong creature can separate me
from Christ, neither strong fire nor water, because 'love is as strong
as death'" (gloss 2).[73] This citation of Song of Songs 8:6 follows a
remarkable passage on the strength of Paul's love for Christ, a love
that impels him to preach:

> He speaks this way to show how great is the power in him
> of divine love, and to lay everything out before our eyes. For
> this is the way of lovers, that they cannot hide their love in
> silence but assert and reveal it to their close friends and to
> their beloved, and they cannot confine the flames within
> their heart. They speak of them frequently, so that by con-
> stantly telling about their love they may gain some solace,
> and obtain some cooling of their immense ardor.[74]

This passionate declaration gives insight into Thomas's own mo-
tivation as a preacher and teacher. The fire of charity not only burns
within but also impels the lover of Christ to greater love and service of
God and neighbor; its flames are always active. And so, Thomas says in
the *Summa* (gloss 3) that charity cannot diminish, because according
to the Song, it is like fire: "'its lamps,' that is, the lamps of charity, 'are
lamps of fire and flames.' Therefore, as long as charity remains, it always mounts upwards."[75] Indeed, even when one carries great burdens
for the sake of God, "love itself is not destroyed, but rather, grows
greater; Song 8:7: 'many waters,' that is, many tribulations, 'cannot

---

[71] Rom 8:35 and 38–39; in the Vulgate text: "neque mors, neque vita, neque angeli, neque principatus, neque virtutes, neque instantia, neque futura, neque fortitudo, neque altitudo, neque profundum, neque creatura alia poterit nos separare a caritate Dei, quæ est in Christo Jesu Domino nostro."
[72] *Super Rom* 8, lec. 7 (Marietti no. 722).
[73] *Super Rom* 8, lec. 7 (Marietti no. 730).
[74] *Super Rom* 8, lec. 7 (Marietti no. 728).
[75] *ST* II-II, q. 24, a. 10.

quench charity, nor floods overwhelm it'" (gloss 4).[76]

In his *Commentary on John*, Thomas quotes the Song several times in connection with this active and inflammatory quality of charity. Concerning John 5:35, Thomas explains that John the Baptist was "a lamp, burning and blazing brightly" because he was inflamed with the ardor of charity. Thomas says that the blazing of fire "signifies love for three reasons" (gloss 5):

> First, because fire is the most active of all bodies; so too is the warmth of charity, so much so that nothing can withstand its impetus: "the charity of Christ urges us" (2 Cor 5:14). Secondly, because just as fire, being most volatile, causes great unrest, so also this love of charity makes a person restless until he achieves his objective: "Its lamps are lamps of fire and flames" (Song 8:6). Thirdly, just as fire is inclined to move upward, so too is charity; so much so that it joins us to God: "He who abides in love abides in God, and God in him" (1 John 4:16).[77]

On John 14:23, Thomas explains that it is charity that makes one obedient to God, "conjoining" the soul to God, causing one to abide in God, and God in him, by keeping God's word.[78] This obedience arises from an urgent restlessness to be united to God and to see God: "A person does not rest until he does those things which will bring him to his intended end, especially if it is intensely desired." And so, Thomas continues (gloss 6):

> When a person's will is intent on God, who is its end, it moves all the powers to do the things that lead to him. The will is made intent in this way by charity; and so charity is what makes us keep the commandments: 2 Cor 5:14: "the charity of Christ urges us"; Song 8:6: "its lamps are lamps of fire." And through obedience, one is made fit to see God.[79]

---

[76] Aquinas, *Collationes de decem praeceptis,* prol. The Latin edition found on the Corpus Thomisticum website, from which the text is drawn, is based on *S. Thomae Aquinatis Opuscula theologica,* ed. R. M. Spiazzi, 2nd ed. (Turin: Marietti, 1954).
[77] *Super Ioan* 5, lec. 6 (Marietti no. 812).
[78] *Super Ioan* 14, lec. 6 (Marietti no. 1941).
[79] *Super Ioan* 14, lec. 6 (Marietti no. 1942).

Like the Baptist, Mary Magdalene shares in this burning charity: she is named in John 20 as the first to see the open tomb, and so receive the revelation of Christ's resurrection, because she was "more fervent and more devoted to Christ than the other women."[80] As soon as the Sabbath was over, before daylight, Mary Magdalene came to the tomb, "incited by the exceeding ardor of her love: 'its lamps are lamps of fire,' namely, of charity" (gloss 7).[81]

The notion of the impetus or stimulus of love is especially seen where Thomas links Song of Songs 8:6 with 2 Corinthians 5:14, as he does in some of the texts above, and in other places, including his *Commentary on Second Corinthians* itself. Paul says that "the charity of Christ urges us" (gloss 8) because:

To urge is the same as to stimulate. As if he said: the love of God, as a stimulus, stimulates us to do what charity commands, namely, to procure the salvation of our neighbor. This is the effect of charity: "Those who are led," i.e., stirred, "by the Spirit of God are sons of God" (Rom 8:14); Song 8:6: "Its lamps, as lamps of fire," etc. [82]

For Thomas, the burning ardor of charity urges one on especially to work for the salvation of souls. And this kind of spiritual fire, Thomas says in a *Summa* article on devotion, is the effect of meditation or contemplation arousing love; he quotes Psalm 38[39]—"In my meditation a fire shall flame forth"—a text he also uses where he describes the invisible mission of the Holy Spirit in the infused gift of charity.[83]

The final piece of this picture, then, is that this burning love, born of contemplation and bearing fruit for the salvation of souls,

---

[80] *Super Ioan* 20, lec. 1 (Marietti no. 2472).

[81] *Super Ioan* 20, lec. 1 (Marietti no. 2473).

[82] *Super II Cor.* 5, lec. 3 (Marietti no. 181). Also see, e.g., *Super Psalmos* 26[27], no. 3; speaking there of the perfection of desire, Thomas says that "love solicits, as if it were a goad [*stimulus*] and a fire: Cant. 8: *its lamps are lamps of fire*, and 2 Cor 5: *the charity of God urges us.*"

[83] *ST* II-II, q. 82, a. 3; I, q. 43, a. 5, ad 2. See also *ST* II-II, q. 180, a. 1: "Gregory makes the contemplative life consist in the 'love of God' inasmuch as loving God we are aflame to gaze on his beauty. And since everyone delights when he obtains what he loves, it follows that the contemplative life terminates in delight, which is seated in the affective power, the result being that love also becomes more intense."

comes from the work of the Holy Spirit, who not only inebriates the lovers of God but also sets them on fire. Charity itself is a participation in the Holy Spirit, who is always at work in the children of God, leading and prompting them by the *instinctus* of grace to enkindle charity into act and to carry out love's commands. [84] Thomas refers to the Spirit's inflammatory agency in connection with these Song texts multiple times, such as in his commentaries on the Psalms and on John (glosses 9, 10, and 11). The Holy Spirit ignites;[85] it warms and nourishes the heat of love;[86] it stimulates and elevates the heart with fervor and warmth and burns up sins.[87] Thomas uses a rich variety of fiery words.

CONCLUSION

Does Thomas's exegesis of the Song import an element of spiritual *eros* into his understanding of charity as friendship with God? I argue *yes*—but in a distinctively Dominican mode. Thomas does not develop a spousal mysticism like St. Bernard. The wedding of Christ and his members takes place more on the Cross than in a mystical embrace. Yet the bride in Thomas's Song is intoxicated and rushed onward by the fire of a love fed by the Holy Spirit, which nothing can extinguish. With an ardor born of contemplation, she ecstatically longs to see the face of God—not alone, but in the company of all who will be the friends of God through her eager cooperation with charity's urging. It cannot be said that Thomas, in comparison with many of his peers, presents a theology of charity that is notably "hot and sticky" (or, affective and experiential). But it glows deeply with passionate love nonetheless, a fervent desire for union with God and the salvation of souls, for to be Christ's friend—made into his other self—is to share in his charity, and so in the burning intention of his will. Thomas may not have spoken of the Song as he lay dying, but his biographers tell us that he did ardently and openly profess

---

[84] *ST* II-II, q. 24, a. 2, aa. 5 and 7; *Super Rom* 5, lec. 1 (Marietti no. 392); *Super Rom* 8, lec. 3 (Marietti no. 635).

[85] *Super Psalmos* 18[19], no. 4.

[86] *Super Psalmos* 44[45], no. 5.

[87] *Super Ioan* 4, lec. 2 (Marietti no. 577).

his faith and love to Christ in the Eucharist, receiving him "with devotion and tears."[88] As Thomas wrote of Paul, that other lover of Christ: "For this is the way of lovers, that they cannot hide their love in silence but assert and reveal it to their close friends and to their beloved," because they "cannot confine the flames within their heart."[89]

[88] William of Tocco, *Ystoria* 58.
[89] *Super Rom* 8, lec. 7 (Marietti no. 728).

1 *Super Isa 25.*

[In] convivium solemne caelestis curiae... proponit tria: Primo vinum ad ebrietatem. Cant. 5: "comedite amici, et bibite et inebriamini"; secundo mel ad satietatem (Ps 16). Tertio lac ad perfectionem corporis et animae. Cant. 5: "oculi tui sicut columbae."

2 *Super Isa 28.*

Inebriantur sancti... incentivo amoris. Cant. 5: "comedite amici, et inebriamini."

3 *In sent.* prol.

Partus ipsius Christi sunt fideles Ecclesiae, quos suo labore quasi mater parturivit... Fructus autem istius partus sunt sancti qui sunt in gloria: de quo fructu Cant. 5:1: "veniat dilectus meus in hortum suum et comedat fructum pomorum suorum." Istos inebriat abundantissima sui fruitione; de qua fruitione et ebrietate Psalm. 35:9: "inebriabuntur ab ubertate domus tuae."

FIGURE I
SONG OF SONGS 5:1

Veniat dilectus meus in hortum suum, et comedat fructum pomorum suorum. Veni in hortum meum, soror mea, sponsa; messui myrrham meam cum aromatibus meis; comedi favum cum melle meo; bibi vinum meum cum lacte meo; comedite, amici, et bibite, et inebriamini, carissimi.

6 *Super Psalmos 35, no. 4.*

Et quod plus est, inebriantur, inquantum supra omnem mensuram meriti desideria implentur: ebrietas enim excessus quidam est: Isa. 64: "quod oculus non vidit," etc. Cant. 5: "inebriamini carissimi." Et qui sunt ebrii, non in se sunt, sed extra se.

7 *Super II Cor 5, lec. 3.*

Haec sobrietas non opponitur ebrietati, quae est de vino, quae ad bella trahit in terra, sed opponitur ebrietati quae est a spiritu sancto, quae rapit hominem ad divina, de qua dicitur Cant. 5:1: "bibite, amici, et inebriamini, charissimi." Nam illa scilicet sobrietas est propter utilitatem proximi, sed haec ebrietas est propter amorem Dei.

4 *Super Ioan 2, lec.* **1.**

Vinum laetificat cor . . . et quantum ad hoc dicitur vinum sapientia . . .Vinum similiter inebriat, Cant. 5:1, "bibite, amici, et inebriamini, carissimi," et secundum hoc caritas dicitur vinum, Cant. 5:1, "bibi vinum meum cum lacte meo." Et dicitur caritas etiam vinum ratione fervoris. . . . Christus aquam timoris convertit in vinum caritatis, quando "dedit spiritum adoptionis filiorum, in quo clamamus, abba pater," Rom. 8:15, et quando "caritas Dei diffusa est in cordibus nostris," Rom. 5:5.

5 *Super Psalmos 22, no. 2.*

Hic calix est donum divini amoris qui inebriat: quia ebrius non est in se, nec secundum se loquitur, sed secundum impetum vini; sic ille qui est plenus divino amore, loquitur secundum Deum: est enim in extasim factus. Cant. 5: "comedite amici, et inebriamini."

8 *Homo quidam fecit cenam magnam 2.*

Tertio preparauit nobis Christus refectionem pertinentem ad affectum, unde in cantico: "comedite amici mei," scilicet hic per gratiam, "et inebriamini carissimi," scilicet in futuro per gloriam. Istam refectionem facit nobis Christus in quantum habet plenitudinem divinitatis. Ps.: "gratiam et gloriam dabit dominus."

9 *Super Matt* [rep. Leodegarii Bissuntini] **26, lec. 3.**

Et quod dicit "accipite," ad spiritualem receptionem debet referri, quia non debet accipi nisi in fide et caritate; Io. 6:55: "qui manducat carnem meam, et bibit sanguinem meum, in me manet, et ego in eo." Item inducit ad comestionem, "comedite," non solum spiritualiter, sed etiam sacramentaliter; Cant. 5:1: "comedite, amici, et bibite."

10 *Summa theologiae* **III, q. 79, a. 1, ad 2.**

Et ideo per hoc sacramentum, quantum est ex sui virtute, non solum habitus gratiae et virtutis confertur, sed etiam excitatur in actum, secundum illud 2 Cor. 5:14, "caritas Christi urget nos." Et inde est quod ex virtute huius sacramenti anima spiritualiter reficitur, per hoc quod anima delectatur, et quodammodo inebriatur dulcedine bonitatis divinae, secundum illud Cant. 5, "comedite, amici, et bibite; et inebriamini, carissimi."

1 *Super Rom* 8, lec. 7.

Alio modo sic: dictum est, quod magna beneficia Deus sanctis suis confert, ex quorum consideratione adeo charitas Christi in cordibus nostris fervet, quod nihil eam extinguere potest. Cant. ult. "aquae multae non potuerunt extinguere charitatem."

2 *Super Rom* 8, lec. 7.

Tangit magnitudinem virtutis, cum dicit "neque fortitudo," id est, neque quaecumque creatura fortis, potest me separare a Christo, puta fortis ignis, aut fortis aqua: quia, ut Cant. 8:6 dicitur, "fortis est ut mors dilectio."

3 *Summa Theol* II-II, q. 24, a. 10.

Sed contra est quod caritas in Scriptura igni comparatur, secundum illud Cant. 8, "lampades eius, scilicet caritatis, lampades ignis atque flammarum." Sed ignis, quandiu manet, semper ascendit.

4 *De decem praeceptis*, prol.

Manifestum est enim quod quando gravia pro eo quem diligimus, sustinemus, amor ipse non destruitur, immo crescit. Cant. 8:7: "aquae multae (idest tribulationes multae) non potuerunt extinguere caritatem." Et ideo sancti viri qui adversitates pro Deo sustinent, magis in eius dilectione firmantur; sicut artifex illud artificium magis diligit in quo plus laboravit.

FIGURE II
SONG OF SONGS 8:6–7

quia fortis est ut mors dilectio, dura sicut infernus æmulatio: lampades ejus lampades ignis atque flammarum.

5 *Super Ioan* 5, lec. 6.

Primo quidem, quia ignis inter omnia corpora est magis activus: sic et ardor caritatis, intantum quod nihil eius impetum ferre potest, secundum illud 2 Cor. 5:14: "caritas Christi urget nos." Secundo, quia sicut ignis per hoc quod est maxime sensitivus, facit multum aestuare, ita et caritas aestum causat quousque homo consequatur intentum; Cant. ult. 6: "lampades eius lampades ignis atque flammarum." Tertio sicut ignis est sursum ductivus, ita et caritas, intantum quod coniungit nos Deo; 1 John 4:16: "qui manet in caritate, in Deo manet, et Deus in eo."

Aquæ multæ non potuerunt extinguere caritatem, nec flumina obruent illam.

6 *Super Ioan* 14, lec. 6.

Quando ergo voluntas hominis intensa est ad Deum, qui est finis eius, movet omnes vires ad faciendum ea quae ad ipsum ducunt. Intenditur autem in Deum per caritatem; et ideo caritas est quae nos servare mandata facit 2 Cor 5:14: "caritas Christi urget nos;" Cant. 8, "lampades eius, lampades ignis." Et per obedientiam homo efficitur idoneus ad videndum Deum.

7 *Super Ioan* 20, lec. 1.

Statim transacto sabbato ante lucem primae sabbati venit ad monumentum: nam nimius ardor amoris eam sollicitabat; Cant. 8:6: "lampades eius lampades ignis," etc.

8 *Super II Cor* 5, lec. 3.

"Caritas Christi urget nos" ad hoc. Et dicit urget, quia urgere idem est quod stimulare; quasi dicat: charitas Christi, quasi stimulus, stimulat nos ad faciendum ea, quae charitas imperat, ut scilicet procuremus salutem proximorum. Hic est effectus charitatis. Rom. 8:14: "qui spiritu Dei aguntur," id est agitantur, etc. Cant. 8:6: "lampades eius, ut lampades ignis."

9 *Super Psalmos* 18, no. 4.

Spiritus sanctus calefacit: Cant. 8: "lampades ejus lampades ignis." Sed numquid multi non recipiunt calorem ejus?

10 *Super Psalmos* 44, no. 5.

Tertio, quia oleum est diffusivum, sic spiritus sanctus est communicativus: 2 Cor. ult. "communicatio sancti spiritus sit semper cum omnibus vobis"; Rom. 5: "caritas Dei diffusa est in cordibus vestris per spiritum sanctum." Item oleum est fomentum ignis et caloris, et spiritus sanctus fovet et nutrit amoris calorem in nobis: Cant. ult.: "lampades ejus lampades ignis."

11 *Super Ioan* 4, lec. 2.

Et dicendum, quod per aquam intelligitur gratia spiritus sancti: quae quidem quandoque dicitur ignis, quandoque aqua, ut ostendatur quod nec hoc, nec illud dicitur secundum substantiae proprietatem, sed secundum similitudinem actionis. Nam ignis dicitur, quia elevat cor per fervorem et calorem, Rom 12:11: "spiritu ferventes," etc., et quia consumit peccata; Cant. 8: "lampades eius, lampades ignis atque flammarum."

Scripture as a Guidepost for How Not to Read Scripture: Aquinas on the Apologetic Function of Scripture

Jörgen Vijgen
Tilburg University, Netherlands

Introduction

Reading St. Thomas's biblical commentaries, one often encounters St. Thomas forcefully engaging with a large and varied number of heresies. Since this procedure might strike the contemporary reader of his biblical commentaries as being at odds with the aims of a historical-critical method, it is worthwhile to ask why St. Thomas takes such an interest in engaging with these heresies and ultimately in refuting them. Even more important for our purposes is the question regarding the method St. Thomas employs in order to achieve such a refutation.

In his systematic writings on the nature and goal of sacred doctrine, the "destruction of errors" is a recurrent theme and constitutes, together with the "manifestation of the truth," an integral part of St. Thomas's sapiential theology.[1] Commenting on Peter Lombard's

---

[1] These expressions are taken from *Summa contra gentiles* [*SCG*] I, ch. 9 (trans. Anton C. Pegis [Notre Dame, IN: University of Notre Dame Press, 1975]; unless otherwise noted, all translations of *SCG* are from this edition). In what follows,

prologue to the *Sentences*, St. Thomas notes that someone who is zealous for the house of God, the Church, possesses such an intense love that he is not weighted down by the opposition, but rather his zeal rather kindles him to react against the "infidels" who attack the Church. He identifies these infidels with the "carnal and animal men" of Lombard's—and Augustine's—text,[2] meaning with those who prefer to follow the disorderly desires of the flesh (Rom 13:14) and, in doing so, reject divine providence and the immortality of the soul. As a result, they are of the opinion that their sins will be left unpunished. These are "animal men" in so far as they think they can judge divine things using merely "corporeal" reasons. Lombard's stated intention to wall the faith with "the bucklers of the tower of David or rather to show that it is walled" (inspired by Song of Songs 4:4—"Thy neck is as the tower of David, which is built with bulwarks: a thousand bucklers hang upon it, all the armor of valiant men") is of singular importance here. For St. Thomas, it means that, in order to transmit the truth as it comes from Christ (David) and is being handed on through the faith of the Church (the neck), the exclusion of errors becomes an integral part of the transmission of the faith. Such an exclusion of errors happens, he writes, by way of the "reasons and authorities of the saints" (*rationes et auctoritates sanctorum*).[3] While both Lombard and St. Thomas have the argu-

---

I make use of the Latin texts as provided by the Leonine [LE] and Marietti editions (particularly the Scripture commentaries; with Marietti numbers in parentheses), unless otherwise noted. For the *Summa theologiae* [*ST*], I use the English translation by the Dominican Fathers of the English Province edition (New York: Benziger Brothers, 1947). For the *Scriptum*, I use the translation of the Aquinas Institute (in Wyoming) published by Emmaus Academic Press.

[2] Peter Lombard is paraphrasing a passage from Augustine's prologue to *De Trinitate* 3 (CCSL 50, 127): ". . . pro studio quo fidem nostrum adversus errorem carnalium et animalium hominum munire inardesco necesse est me pati . . ."

[3] *In I sent., prol. divisio textus*: "*Zelus* secundum Dionysium est amor intensus, unde non patitur aliquid contrarium amato. *Domus Dei*, idest Ecclesia. *Quo inardescentes*, scilicet dum non patimur Ecclesiam ab infidelibus impugnari. *Carnalium*, quantum ad illos qui inueniunt sibi errores, ut carnis curam faciant in desideriis, sicut qui negant prouidentiam diuinam de rebus humanis et anime perpetuitatem, ut impune possint peccare. *Animalium*, quantum ad errantes, ex eo quod non elevantur supra sensibilia, set secundum rationes corporales uolunt de divinis iudicare. *Davidicae turris*: hic sumitur Cant. IV '*Sicut turris David*' etc.—per David significatur Christus: turris ejus est fides vel Ecclesia, clypei sunt rationes et auctoritates sanctorum. *Vel potius munitam ostendere*, quia ipse non invenit rationes, sed potius ab aliis inuentas compilavit. Et in hoc tangit

ments of the Church Fathers in mind in this text, St. Thomas finds additional support for this approach in Aristotle's demonstration by refutation of the principle of noncontradiction in his *Metaphysics* 4, chapters 4–5.[4]

Even more important for our purposes is a frequently cited passage from Aristotle's *Sophistical Refutations* in which Aristotle writes that two things pertain to the work of a wise man: not to lie about things he knows and to be able to refute the one who does lie.[5] St. Thomas uses this passage from Aristotle both to corroborate 2 Timothy 3:16 ("All Scripture is inspired by God and profitable for teaching, for reproof, for correction, and for training in righteousness") and when commenting on Titus 1:9 concerning the bishop's task to "hold firm to the sure word as taught, so that he may be able to give instruction in sound doctrine and also to confute those who contradict it."[6] In other words, not only should a sapiential reading and preaching of the Word of God include the destruction of errors, but Scripture contains already in itself the motive, content, and argumentation to refute those who contradict it.

It should not be surprising therefore that St. Thomas's biblical commentaries also contain numerous instances in which he notes that a certain biblical passage is explicitly written to refute an error or observes that the Apostle Paul uses a certain concept or phrase to exclude an error.[7] Moreover, for St. Thomas, both the Letter to the

---

unam utilitatem, scilicet exclusionem erroris" (*Les débuts de l'enseignement de Thomas d'Aquin et sa conception de la sacra doctrina*, ed. A. Oliva [Paris: J. Vrin, 2006], 334[ln. 52]–35[ln. 65]).

[4] See *Super Boethium de Trinitate*, q. 2, a. 2, ad 4 ("Articuli autem fidei in hac scientia non sunt quasi conclusiones, set quasi principia, que etiam defenduntur ab impugnantibus sicut Philosophus in IV Metaphisice disputat contra negantes principia . . ." [LE, 50:96]), and a. 3: ". . . tertio ad resistendum his que contra fidem dicuntur, siue ostendendo ea esse falsa, siue ostendendo ea non esse necessaria" (LE, 50:99).

[5] Aristotle, *De sophisticis elenchis* 1.165a24–27: "Est autem, ut sit ad unum dicere, in unoquoque opus scientis non mentiri quidem eum de quibus novit, mentientem autem manifestare posse" (*Aristoteles Latinus* edition [https://hiw.kuleuven.be/dwmc/al/editions/index.html#section-0], vol. VI 1–3, p. 6). See also *SCG* I, ch. 9: "Ex praemissis igitur evidenter apparet sapientis intentionem circa duplicem veritatem divinorum debere versari, et circa errores contrarios destruendos . . ."

[6] *Super II Tim* 3, lec. 3 (no. 127); *Super Tit* 1, lec. 3 (no. 24); see also *Principium biblicum* II (*partitione Sacrae Scripturae*).

[7] See, e.g.: *Super Col* 1, lec. 4 (no. 32: "Hoc autem excludit apostolus. . ."); *Super II Cor* 3, lec. 1 (no. 32: "Et hoc est contra Pelagianos dicentes . . ."); *Super Phil* 2,

Hebrews and the first four propositions of the prologue to John's Gospel are in their entirety written with the refutation of errors in mind.[8]

In order to formulate an answer to the questions raised above, we will first analyze St. Thomas's view on the importance and nature of heresy in general. Second, we will discuss the different types of argumentation used to refute heresies in his biblical commentaries, showing as well how and to what extent these different types are interwoven with each other.[9] In doing so, we hope to shed more light on St. Thomas's apologetic method in reading Scripture and the role of Scripture itself in this regard.

THE IMPORTANCE AND NATURE OF HERESY

The fight against heresies had been an integral part of St. Dominic's vision as early as his travels with Bishop Diego of Osma in southern France from 1203 onward.[10] Bishop Fulco of Toulouse's episcopal charter approving the young preaching movement in 1215 described its tasks as follows: "to eradicate depraved heresy, expel vices, teach the rule of faith and imbue sound morals."[11] The German historian Peter Segl recently described the fight against heresies as the rai-

---

lec. 2 (no. 62: "Et per hoc etiam excluditur error Photini . . ."); *Super Hebr* 1, lec. 1 (no. 23: "In hoc ergo removet errorem Manichaei . . .").

[8] See *Super Hebr* 1, lec. 1 (no. 6: "Scripsit autem epostolam istam contra errores . . .").

[9] St. Thomas uses the Latin *haeresis* and its cognates in his own discourse (excluding explicit and implicit citations) 136 times in his biblical commentaries. He explicitly mentions twenty-two heretics or heretical movements. With seventy-five mentions, Manichaeism holds by far the first place in terms of explicit mentions, followed by Arianism (fifty-four), and Nestorius and Pelagius holding a joint third place with twenty-five each. Sabellius is fourth on the list with twenty-two mentions, followed by Photinus (seventeen), Valentinus (fourteen), and Apollinaris and Elvidius are mentioned twelve times each. Others such as Eutyches, Macedonius, Novatianus, and Priscillianism have less than five mentions each.

[10] See Guy Bedouelle, *Saint Dominic: The Grace of the Word* (San Francisco: Ignatius Press, 1987).

[11] *Monumenta diplomatica S. Dominici*, ed. V.-J. Koudelka and R.J. Loenertz, Monumenta Ordinis Fratrum Praedicatorum historica 25 (Rome: Istituto storico domenicano di S. Sabina, 1966), 57: ". . . ad extirpandam hereticam pravitatem et vitia expellenda et fidei regulam educendam et homines sanis moribus imbuendos."

son d'être of the community of preachers founded by St. Dominic.[12] According to one of St. Dominic's earliest disciples, Moneta of Cremona, whose *Adversus Catharos et Valdenses* St. Thomas used when writing his *Summa contra gentiles*, the mission to confute heresy with the sword of the Word of God, to strengthen the faith, and to defend the Church is the principal reason why St. Dominic founded the order and defines Moneta's own vocation as a member of that order.[13]

As a son of St. Dominic, St. Thomas fully adhered to this vision. He was profoundly perceptive of the influence of ancient and contemporary errors and heresies on the faith and life of the Church of his day.[14] Consequently, we find him vigorously defending his order's

---

[12] See Peter Segl, "Deutsche Dominikaner im Kampf gegen Dämonen, Ketzer und Hexen," in *Die deutschen Dominikaner und Dominikanerinnen im Mittelalter*, ed. Sabine von Heusinger, Elias H. Füllenbach, and Walter Senner (Berlin: De Gruyter, 2016), 499–530, at 509.

[13] Moneta of Cremona, *Adversus Catharos et Valdenses*, praefatio: "Tempus ergo est ex parte Dei faciendi, idest intellectum dandi mihi, & aliis pro Fide eius certare volentibus; quia dissipaverunt legem eius Haeretici. Tempus etiam est propter eandem caussam faciendi huiusmodi Opusculum ex divinis testimoniis mihi sua gratia inspiratis, suffragante orationum instantia, & copia meritorum B. Dominici Patris mei, cuius totum fuit desiderium, & conatus per se suosque filios spirituales spretis saeculi nugis demoliri opere & sermone Haereticorum dogma perversum, & beatam credulitatem Fidelium adaugere. Ad quod felicius consumandum Sancti Spiritus consilio fretus primus primum Praedicatorum excogitavit Ordinem, & erexit. Cuius Ordinis devictus precibus, adiutus meritis, & documentis edoctus imbecillis Athleta ecce vibrare audeo gladium Verbi Dei in confutationem haeresum, ad robur Fidei, & Catholicae Ecclesiae firmamentum" (cited from the electronic edition at mlat.uzh.ch/MLS/xanfang.php?tabelle=Moneta_Cremonensis_cps4&corpus=4&lang=0&allow_download=). In a recent essay, Riccardo Parmeggiani has argued that, for Moneta of Cremona, Paul of Hungary, and Roland of Cremona, "Scripture and its interpretation was in fact the main issue of contention between the Preachers and the heretics, and the ground for controversy on which they faced each other" ("From the University to the Order: Study of the Bible and Preaching against Heresy in the First Generation of Dominicans at Bologna," in *Bibelstudium und Predigt im Dominikanerorden. Geschichte, Ideal, Praxis*, ed. Viliam Stefan Dóci and Thomas Prügl [Rome: Angelicum University Press, 2019], 21–38, at 27).

[14] This becomes apparent in a work such as *De articulis fidei et Ecclesiae sacramentis*, composed around the same time (1261–1265) as *SCG* II. In this work, he sets out, at the request of the archbishop of Palermo, to discuss briefly (*breviter*) the articles of faith and the sacraments, as well as corresponding errors which need to be avoided (LE, 42:245 [lns.1–13]). It is remarkable that, in such a "pastoral" work, Aquinas enumerates at length century-old errors, often quoting verbatim from Augustine's *De haeresibus*. He was also aware, probably due to the use of Moneta

right to teach as the right to engage in a spiritual combat against heresies—as the right to defend the Church against her enemies.[15] In fact, he finds support for the Dominican vision in the medieval glosses on Song of Songs 2:15 ("Catch us the little foxes that destroy the vines"). St. Thomas concurs with the identification of the "little foxes" with the "schismatics and heretics" and adds a gloss which aptly captures the essence of the Dominican vision: "It is not enough for us to spend our lives in setting an example and giving a good sermon to others, unless we correct those that are in error, and defend the weak against their snares."[16] Moreover, and alluding to 2 Corinthians 10:4 ("the weapons of our warfare are not carnal, but powerful through God"), we find him frequently complaining about the "carnal men" who "reckon as folly what is of the spirit of God" and identifying them as heretics, as those who "strive to glorify themselves in the name of Christ."[17] To be fair, St. Thomas is equally severe concerning those whose state necessarily entails the salvation of the souls, for "one bad bishop, for sure, means ruin in many," and of those, St. Thomas writes, "the Lord complains in Ezekiel 13:5

---

of Cremona's *Adversus Catharos et Valdenses*, of some of the heresies of his time, as is evident from the remark in *De articulis fidei* about the error of "quorundam modernorum hereticorum," who thought that, in the resurrection, souls would be united with celestial bodies and not with their own bodies (LE, 40:249, 290–97), or from the explicit reference in the same work to the Poor of Lyons, a heretical group closely related to the Waldensians (LE, 40:255 [ln. 288]–56 [ln. 287]). For more, see the introduction by René-Antoine Gauthier to *Saint Thomas d'Aquin: Somme contre les gentils* (Paris: Cerf, 1993), 136–40, and John Inglis, "Emanation in Historical Context: Aquinas and the Dominican Response to the Cathars," *Dionysius* 17 (1999): 95–128.

15 *Contra impugnantes*, ch. 2 (LE, 41A:58 [lns. 228–42]), with reference to 2 Cor 10:4.

16 *Contra impugnantes*, ch. 15: "Item. Cant. II, 15: 'capite nobis vulpes parvulas,' Glosa 'schismaticos et haereticos'; quia, ut in alia glosa ibidem dicitur, 'non sufficit nobis vitam nostram aliis in exemplum proponere, et bonam praedicationem facere, nisi et errantes corrigamus, et infirmos ab insidiis aliorum defendamus'" (LE, 41A:147 [lns. 83–90]). The first gloss is an interlineary gloss stemming from Bede the Venerable's commentary; the second gloss is a marginal gloss. See *Glossa ordinaria, Pars 22: in canticum canticorum*, ed. Mary Dove, CCCM 170 (Turnhout, BE: Brepols, 1997), 185–87. For a comprehensive analysis of St. Thomas's reception of Song of Songs, see Serge-Thomas Bonino, O.P., *Saint Thomas d'Aquin: Lecteur du Cantique des cantiques* (Paris: Les Éditions du Cerf, 2019).

17 *Contra doctrinam retrahentium*, ch. 1 (LE, 41C:39 [lns. 43–57]) ; see also *Super II Cor* 11, lec. 3 (no. 405).

saying 'You have not placed yourselves upon the wall to defend the Lord's house,' namely against the heretics and all who are evil."[18]

It is therefore not surprising that, as a result of his many responses to the ancient and contemporary errors and heresies, one of the recurring themes in St. Thomas's iconography is precisely his triumph over pagan thinkers and Christian heretics.[19] These depictions should not, at least from Thomas's own perspective, be seen as triumphalist expressions of his own achievements but rather, and most fundamentally, should rest upon his confidence in God's metaphysical and epistemological providence regarding man's search for the truth. Hence, he says: "As the good is in relation to things, so is the true in relation to knowledge. Now in things it is impossible to find one that is wholly devoid of good. Wherefore it is also impossible for any knowledge to be wholly false, without some mixture of truth. Hence Bede says that 'no teaching is so false that it never mingles truth with falsehood.'"[20]

In this respect, it is worthwhile to mention his response to the question of whether one should interact with a heretic. On the basis of such scriptural passages as 1 Corinthians 15:33 ("Bad company ruins good morals") and 2 John 10 ("If any one comes to you and does

---

[18] *Sermo XXI Beatus vir*: "Unus episcopus malus occasio est ruine in multis. . . . set conqueritur Dominus de malis in Ezechiele dicens: *'Non ascendistis ex'* diverso nec *'opposuitis vos* in *'murum pro domo Domini,'* id est contra hereticos et malos quoscumque" (LE, 44.1:335 [lns. 293–300]).

[19] See, e.g., Andrea Bonaiuti's fresco (ca. 1365) in the *Cappella degli Spagnoli* of the S. Maria Novella in Florence, Filippino Lippi's fresco (ca. 1493) in the *Capella Caraffa* in S. Maria sopra Minerva in Rome, and Benozzo Gozzoli's *Triumph of St. Thomas Aquinas* (ca. 1471; Louvre, Paris). See Gregor Martin Lechner, "Iconographia Thomasiana," in *Thomas von Aquin: Interpretation und Rezeption*, ed. Willehad Paul Eckert (Mainz: Matthias Grünewald, 1974), 933–74.

[20] *ST* II-II, q. 172, a. 6, corp. Bede the Venerable (see his *In Lucae evangelium expositio* in CCSL 120:312 [lns. 664–65]) is himself quoting Augustine's *Quaestiones evangeliorum* (CCSL 44B:98 [lns. 24–25]), where Augustine reflects on the identity of the ten lepers in Luke 17:12. See also St. Thomas's frequent use of Ambrosiaster's phrase "Omne Verum, a quocumque dicatur, a Spiritu Sancto est"; see Serge-Thomas Bonino, O.P., "'Toute vérité, quel que soit celui qui la dit, vient de l'Esprit saint': Autour d'une citation de l'Ambrosiaster dans le corpus thomasien," *Revue thomiste* 106 (2006): 101–47. Note, however, that, in his prologue to Lombard's *Sentences*, Bede's phrase is used as a sed contra to which Thomas responds: "The true things they say, although these things are true in themselves, yet they are false with respect to their use, because they use them falsely" (Oliva, *Les débuts*, 338 [lns. 110–12]).

not bring this doctrine, do not receive him into the house or give him any greeting") and their interpretation by the glosses, St. Thomas repeats the traditional reluctance to having interactions with heretics because these could endanger the faith of oneself or of others directly, or even indirectly, by giving the impression of approving a heretical position. He ends his response, however, with an important qualifying remark: "This, however, should be understood as follows: unless we are talking with one of them in view of their salvation."[21] In other words, the traditional arguments against having interactions with heretics should be put aside when their salvation is at stake. Moreover, as long as one is living in this world, there remains a "place for repentance," as the Letter to the Hebrews (12:17) says. To hold a different position, St. Thomas warns, would in itself constitute a heresy, specifically the heresy of Novatianus, who is said to defend the position that no one could rise to penance after baptism.[22]

Given that faith entails an adherence of the mind to the truths revealed by God on account of the veracity of God,[23] what follows is that, by picking and choosing of the faith according to one's own personal criteria and obstinately rejecting some truths revealed by God, the heretic rejects both these particular truths and the very reason why he ought to believe all the articles of faith. In doing so, the heretic elevates his own judgment over that of the authority of God and prefers to glorify himself, rather than submitting himself

---

21 *Quodlibet* 10, q. 7, a. 1 [15] (LE, 25, 145, 25–53): "Hoc tamen intelligendum est, nisi cum aliquo loqueremur de eius salute." For a similar argument regarding those who are excommunicated see *In IV sent.*, d. 18, q. 2, a. 4, qc. 1, corp.: "Sed quia Ecclesia excommunicationem ad medelam, et non ad interitum, inducit; excipiuntur ab hac generalitate quaedam in quibus communicare licet; scilicet in his quae pertinent ad salutem: quia de talibus homo licite cum excommunicato loqui potest; et etiam alia verba interserere, ut facilius salutis verba ex familiaritate recipiantur" (ed. M. F. Moos [Paris: Lethielleux, 1947], 962).

22 See *Quodlibet* 10, q. 7, a. 2 [16] (LE, 25:146 [lns. 12–24]); see also *Super Heb* 6, lec. 1 (no. 291). This seems to go against Heb 12:17. Thomas argues, however, that Esau's penance was not genuine because he repented "not from a love of justice, but from the fear of punishment or temporal harm" (*Super Heb* 12, lec. 3 [no. 694]).

23 Lawrence Feingold has defined faith as follows: "the freely chosen, firm, stable, joyful, and self-abandoning adherence of the mind, moved by divine grace, to the truths revealed by God about Himself and His plan of salvation, not on account of their own intrinsic evidence, but based on the veracity of God, who cannot err or deceive" (*Faith Comes from What Is Heard: An Introduction to Fundamental Theology* [Steubenville, OH: Emmaus Academic, 2016], 41).

to God. The heretic's assent to *some* truths of the faith is based solely on his own judgment and will and is therefore a corruption of
the faith.[24] While the heretic might intend to assent to God as the
primary truth and ultimate end, he fails in his choice of the means
toward that end because he does not assent to what truly belongs to
God's teaching, but rather "to what his own mind suggests," to his
own "false opinion."[25]

St. Thomas places a heavy emphasis on such a privatization of the
faith over and against what he calls the "common faith that is called
Catholic"[26] because "the mystical body is first brought together by
the unity of the true faith."[27] It belongs, moreover, to the authority
of the universal Church, and in particular to the pope, in whom
this authority principally dwells, to define what belongs to the true
faith[28] and, in doing so, to preserve the unity of the faith, and hence
of the Church.[29] The heretic, however, "prefers his own feelings to
the entire Church" and, in doing so, "spurns the judgment of the
Church."[30] Now, if faith is the foundation upon which the firmness
of the entire structure of the Church relies, as St. Thomas states in

---

[24] See: *ST* II-II, q. 5, a. 3, corp. ("aliomodo . . . quam per fidem"); *ST* II-II, q. 5, a.
3, ad 1 ("propria voluntate et iudicio"); *ST* II-II, q. 10, a. 1, ad 2; *ST* II-II, q. 10,
a. 6, corp. For a contemporary treatment see Feingold, *Faith Comes from What Is
Heard*, ch. 2.

[25] *ST* II-II, q. 11, a. 1, corp. and ad 2.

[26] *In IV sent.*, d. 13, q. 2, a. 1, corp. (Moos ed., 564): ". . . haeresis consistit in singu-
lari opinione praeter communem opinionem." "Haereticus secundum nos dicitur
qui a communi fide, quae Catholica dicitur, discedit." See also *Super Cor* 11,
lec. 14 (no. 627): ". . . de ratione haeresis est, quod aliquis privatam disciplinam
sequatur, quasi per electionem propriam: non autem disciplinam publicam, quae
divinitus traditur."

[27] *In IV sent.*, d. 13, q. 2, a. 1, corp. Whereas heresy is opposed to faith, schism is
opposed to charity. Because of the difference between faith and charity, heresy
and schism are two different vices. However, "just as the loss of charity is the
road to the loss of faith, according to 1 Tim. 1:6: 'From which things,' i.e. charity and the like, 'some going astray, are turned aside into vain babbling,' so too,
schism is the road to heresy" (*ST* II-II, q. 39, a. 1, ad 3).

[28] *ST* II-II, q. 11, a. 2, ad 3.

[29] *SCG* IV, ch. 76. On numerous occasions, Ulrich Horst has clarified the relation
between Scripture, Tradition, and the papal magisterium in St. Thomas and the
Thomist tradition. See for example his *Dominicans and the Pope: Papal Teaching
Authority in the Medieval and Early Modern Thomist Tradition* (South Bend, IN:
University of Notre Dame Press, 2006).

[30] *Super I Cor* 11, lec. 14 (no. 627): "Talis autem pertinacia procedit ex radice super-
biae, qua aliquis praefert sensum suum toti Ecclesiae."

his commentary on Colossians 1:23,[31] the gravity of the sin of heresy becomes intelligible: because heresy subverts "the foundation of all goods," it is more harmful than any other sin.[32]

In this respect, his answer to the objection that the sin of heresy is not counted among the capital vices is telling. St. Thomas responds:

> As the Philosopher says in *Ethics* 7, bestiality is counted outside the number of other human wickednesses, because it goes beyond the human manner. In the same way, the saints count heresy outside the number of sins that are found among the faithful, as more serious than they. And this is why it is not reckoned among the capital vices.[33]

St. Thomas is referring here to a passage in *Nicomachean Ethics* 7.1.1145a15–22 wherein Aristotle mentions in passing the existence of a "superhuman virtue" (*hyper hēmas aretēn*), a heroic (*hērōikēn*) and divine (*theian*) kind of virtue," as opposed to brutishness (*thēriotēs*). Aristotle seems to say later in *Nicomachean Ethics*, at 7.6.1150a1–8, that brutishness is not in the strict sense a vice at all, because it involves the total absence of reason, not merely its corruption. In other words, the extremes of defect and excess, constitutive for a vice, are entirely absent from brutishness. Pleasures are permissible if they are enjoyed in accordance with right reason (*orthos logos*), whereas a brutish person enjoys pleasures which are simply against nature, as for instance in the case of cannibalism.[34] Hence, those states which are called brutish (or "beastly" in another translation) are referred to as such only on account of a metaphor. When we apply this to heresy, one could say that, in the strict sense, it cannot be applied to the faithful unless by extension, through a *façon de parler*, because it not merely harms a particular good, but subverts the foundation of all goods, and hence is more destructive, in so far as it destroys the act of faith altogether.

St. Thomas illustrates the gravity of the sin of heresy with the help of another metaphor taken from the animal kingdom. In the

---

[31] *Super Col* 1, lec. 5 (no. 57).
[32] *In IV sent.*, d. 13, q. 2, a. 1, corp.
[33] *In IV sent.*, d. 13, q. 2, a. 2, ad 1 (Moos ed., 567).
[34] *Nicomachean Ethics* 7.6.1148b15–1149a24.

prologue to his *Sentences*, Lombard had already emphasized the apologetic nature of the work by stating that it contains not only "the examples and the doctrine of [our] elders [*maiorum*]," but also an attempt to bring to light "the fraudulence of the viper's doctrine" (*vipereae doctrinae fraudulentiam*) "through a sincere profession of faith in the Lord."[35] St. Thomas briefly and enigmatically comments as follows: "Vipers, heretics: for heretics in giving birth to others in their heresy give birth like vipers (*uipera*)."[36] He is referring to the mistaken but widespread idea, going back to Pliny the Elders's *Natural History*, that vipers bear their young "at the rate of one a day, to the number of about twenty; the consequence is that the remaining ones get so tired of the delay that they burst open their mother's sides, so committing matricide."[37] In light of what has been said above regarding the relation of the heretic to the Church, it is very plausible that, by this brief remark, St. Thomas considers heretics and their privatization of the faith as committing murder against the Church who gave birth to their authentic faith.

St. Thomas, together with Jerome and Hilary, holds that the novelty of a heretical position is grounded in an interpretative error regarding the Scriptures, in expounding the sense of the Scriptures in a sense other than, as Jerome says, "that of the Holy Spirit by Whom they were written."[38] Whereas the heretic, in doing so, "distorts the meaning of Holy Scriptures,"[39] the faithful believer approaches Holy Scriptures in accordance with the interpretative rules set out by the Holy Spirit and formulated by the universal Church.

The importance of this claim becomes even more apparent if one realizes that, for St. Thomas, the "ultimate effect of Scripture"[40] is "to order us towards God and to lead us towards Him"[41] (that is to

---

[35] Peter Lombard, *Sententiae, prol.*, ed. Collegii S. Bonaventurae ad Claras Aquas (Rome: Grottaferrata, 1971), 3.

[36] *In* I *sent., prol. divisio textus*: ". . . quantum ad rationes: *uiperee*, idest heretice: heretici enim pariendo alios in sua heresy pereunt sicut uipera" (Oliva, *Les débuts*, 339 [lns. 128–29]).

[37] Pliny the Elder, *Natural History* 10.82, trans. Harris Rackham (Cambridge, MA: Harvard University Press, 1967), 400.

[38] *ST* II-II, q. 11, a. 2, obj. 2, quoting from Jerome's *Commentary on Galatians* (*PL* 26:417A).

[39] *ST* II-II, q. 11, a. 2, ad 2.

[40] *Super II Tim* 3, lec. 3 (no. 128).

[41] *Super Heb* 6, lec. 4 (no. 314).

say, to be "a man of God").[42] Hence, the maturity or perfection to which Hebrews 6:1 invites us (*feramur ad perfectionem*) consists in the perfection of loving God and one's neighbor. The invitation of Hebrews 6:1 therefore becomes an invitation to follow "the impulse of the Holy Spirit because 'Whoever are led by the Spirit of God, they are the sons of God' (Rom. 8:14)."[43] For St. Thomas, however, the fourfold effect of Scripture he enumerates on the basis of 2 Timothy 3:16—teaching the truth, reproving falsehood, rescuing from evil, and inducing good—is an integral part leading toward the ultimate effect of Scripture. It is for this reason, I would argue, that he assigns an important, albeit *per accidens*, role to heresies in the life of the Church. Together with St. Paul in 1 Corinthians 11:19 ("For there must be factions [*haireseis*] among you in order that those who are genuine among you may be recognized") and St. Augustine, he shares the conviction that, from the perspective of God's power and providence, "the malice of heretics" is ordained by God "to the good of the faithful."[44] A heresy offers believers and the Church as a whole an occasion for a more careful analysis, a clearer understanding and a more effective preaching of the truth, and a more firm adherence to the truth, all of which occur when a heresy provokes the faithful to long for a better understanding of Scripture.

While obstinacy and pride or covetousness[45] are crucial, formal

---

[42] *Super II Tim* 3, lec. 3 (no. 128).

[43] *Super II Tim* 3, lec. 3 (no.128).

[44] *Super I Cor* 11, lec. 14 (no. 628), drawing on Augustine's *De civitate Dei* 16.2; see also *ST* II-II, q. 11, a. 3, ad 2, drawing on Augustine's *De Genesi contra Manichaeos* 1.1.

[45] Ultimately the cause of heresy lies in "pride or covetousness" (*oritur ex superbia vel cupiditate*). Why does he equate pride with covetousness? Here we have to distinguish between the root (*radix*) and the beginning (*initium*) of sin. Pride is not the root of sin, but rather the beginning. If we were to say that pride was the root of sin, we would admit that evil could be the object of the corrupted action, and therefore that the will could desire evil as such. Pride as the beginning of sin admits to the presence of a free act, although defect, standing at the origin of every sin. As such, sin entails an act of pride (*aversio*) and, as act conditioned by the objects of vice (*conversio*), an act of covetousness. In other words, for St. Thomas, there exists in man a *pronitas* to turn toward the objects of vice, as well as a complete responsibility in every evil act. Pride is a beginning, but a beginning that, as free, cannot be explained by a *pronitas* in man towards evil, because this *pronitas* is produced by the object of the vice, whereas pride does not have, properly speaking, a foundation; see *In II sent.*, d. 42, q. 2, a. 1, ad 1: "peccatum non habet fundamentum ex parte illa qua auersio est" (ed. P. Mandonnet [Paris:

criteria for discerning a heretic, St. Thomas also gives two objective, material criteria for discerning the heretical nature of a theological position. First, in his *Contra errores Graecorum* St. Thomas reminds his readers that "the Son of God appeared precisely in order to destroy the works of the devil, as stated in 1 John 3:8."[46] The devil is "a liar and the father of lies" (John 8:44), to such an extent that, as St. Thomas remarks elsewhere, the Lord forbade the devil to profess even truths about his divinity in Mark 1:24 and Luke 4:34–35 so as not to give the slightest impression that there is any truth coming from the devil,[47] because he "speaks of his own" (John 8:44); that is to say, of himself, he has only lies and sins.[48] The devil's principal lie (1 John 2:22) consists in denying that Jesus is the Christ, and in doing so, destroying the salvific mission of Christ. The devil's attempt to destroy the work of Christ continues until this day, St. Thomas remarks, but whereas, in the beginning, the devil used tyrants to inflict bodily death on the Christians, he now works through heretics wanting to kill the faithful spiritually. In both cases, the persecution and doctrinal confusion has as its aim to subtract members from the Church. In the case of heresies, however, their principal aim is to "diminish the dignity of Christ."[49] In his commentary on Hebrews 10:29 ("How much more, do you think he deserves worse punishments, who has trodden underfoot the Son of God?"), he notes that scorning the faith that is announced to you deserves a more severe punishment because it constitutes an act of contempt and ingratitude toward the most precious gift God has given, the gift of his only begotten Son.[50] For St. Thomas, therefore, any attempt to diminish the unique dignity of Christ serves as a theological criterion to discern

---

Lethielleux, 1929], 1070.

[46] *Contra errores Graecorum*, pars altera, prol. (LE, 40A:87 [lns. 4–6]).

[47] *De malo*, q. 7, a. 9, ad 4.

[48] See *ST* II-II, q. 172, a. 6, ad 3: "Ad tertium dicendum quod propria Daemonum esse dicuntur illa quae habent a seipsis, scilicet mendacia et peccata. Quae autem pertinent ad propriam naturam, non habent a seipsis, sed a Deo. Per virtutem autem propriae naturae quandoque vera praenuntiant, ut dictum est. Utitur etiam eis Deus ad veritatis manifestationem per ipsos fiendam, dum divina mysteria eis per Angelos revelantur, ut dictum est."

[49] *Contra errores Graecorum*, pars altera, prol. (LE, 40A:87 [lns. 12–14]): "unde si quis diligenter inspiciat, haereticorum errores ad hoc principaliter videntur tendere ut Christi derogent dignitati."

[50] *Super Heb* 10, lec. 3 (nos. 526–28).

whether a theological position is heretical or not.[51]

The second objective, material criterion can be gathered from a passage from one of Thomas's sermons. In his sermon *Attendite a falsis prophetis*, St. Thomas asks a rhetorical question: "Arius was a liar—was he not?—as well as the ones like him, who wanted to 'correct' the doctrine of Christ."[52] This resembles something he writes in his *Scriptum*: "Every opinion that does not have its start in Christ's teaching, which is the foundation, is considered to be new, no matter how ancient it is in time."[53] St. Thomas seems to point to the idea that, even more fundamental than diminishing the unique dignity of Christ, the willingness to come up with a "better" understanding of Christ serves as the ulterior motive of all heretics and something which unifies them all. But such a willingness can never be the result of inspiration by the Holy Spirit; it can come only from either the devil or the own spirit of such false prophets who follow merely human reasoning.[54]

---

[51] In fact, in the remainder of the passage from *Contra errores Graecorum*, he lists no less than twelve positions which, on the basis of this criterion, diminish the unique dignity of Christ, and hence are heretical. For instance, Arius "diminished the dignity of Christ by destroying that He was the Son of God consubstantial with the Father and by asserting Him to be a creature. Macedonius, by asserting that the Holy Spirit is a creature, who took from the Son the honor of spirating a divine person. Mani diminished the dignity of Christ when he claimed that visible things were created by an evil God, thereby denying that all things were created through the Son." *Contra errores Graecorum*, pars altera, prol. (LE, 40A:87 [lns. 15–25]).

[52] Sermon 14 (LE, 40.1:217, [lns. 127–29]).

[53] *In IV sent.*, d. 13, q. 2, a. 1, ad 8 (Moos ed., 566). Here one should take into account the distinction between that which belongs to the faith directly, such as divinely taught truths about the Trinity, the Incarnation, etc., and that which belongs to the faith indirectly, the denial of which entails something against the faith, such as the denial of a historical truth of Scripture, for such a denial would entail that Scripture is false. In the former case, an obstinately held false opinion constitutes heresy. In the latter case, a dissident opinion may be held if the matter in question has not been settled as having consequences against the faith and if no obstinacy is being shown. Once the Church has made a decision that the dissident opinion contains a consequence against the faith and one still holds onto it, the error becomes heresy. See *ST* I, q. 32, a. 4, corp.; see also *Super I Cor* 11, lec. 4 (no. 627).

[54] St. Thomas also seems to imply that a heretic sins by excess or by deficiency. The theological virtues do not as such observe the mean because, for instance, in the case of the theological virtue of faith, one can never believe in God as much as one should, but rather one's faith increases the more one approaches God;

In concluding this section, we would like to draw attention to a passage where Thomas argues for the fittingness of a final, general judgment on the last day in addition to the judgment immediately after one's death. There he observes that a man's temporal life continues in multiple ways even after one's death, such that it is impossible to reach a perfect and final judgment in the present time. One of these ways has to do with the outcome of one's actions in the future. He writes: "Thirdly, as to the result of his actions: just as from the deceit of Arius and other false leaders unbelief continues to flourish down to the close of the world; and even until then faith will continue to derive its progress from the preaching of the apostles."[55] For Thomas, the progeny of ancient heretics will continue to exert its influence, which underscores again the importance of regarding the destruction of errors as an integral part of *sacra doctrina*. But equally so, the faith as preached by the apostles will continue to grow as well.

STRATEGIES FOR REFUTING HERESIES

In this section, we discuss a number of passages in order to gain an idea of the strategies he uses to refute heresies, limiting ourselves to the five most-mentioned heresies in his biblical commentaries.[56]

Manichaeism

The principal reason for the high number of references to Manichaeism is that St. Thomas, following Augustine's *De haeresibus* as

---

but in reference to us, "faith holds a middle course between contrary heresies." For instance, against the true faith of Christ being one Person and two natures, Nestorius sins by excess in holding that there are two persons and two natures in Christ, whereas Eutyches sins by deficiency in holding that there is one person with only one nature. See *ST* I-II, q. 64, a. 4, especially obj. 3 and ad 3.

[55] *ST* III, q. 59, a. 5, corp. I thank Andrew Hofer, O.P., for drawing my attention to this passage.

[56] See note 9 above for the exact numbers. For other heresies not treated in this contribution, see for example Gilles Emery, "Le photinisme et ses précurseurs chez saint Thomas: Cérinthe, les ébionites, Paul de Samosate et Photin," *Revue thomiste* 95 (1995): 371–98.

one of his principal sources in this respect, considers Manichaeism as a collection of multiple heresies. We often find St. Thomas attributing to one or two verses the power to refute multiple heresies by the same author or by multiple authors. Regarding the Manichaeans, Romans 1:2–3 ("Which he had promised before, through his prophets, in the holy Scriptures. Concerning his Son, who was made to him of the seed of David, according to the flesh") enables us to refute three of their heresies, because these verses show: first, that "the God of the Old Testament and the Father of our Lord Jesus Christ" are the same; second, that their condemnation of the Old Testament is incorrect, because St. Paul calls them "holy"; and third, that their claim that Christ merely had an imaginary body is erroneous.[57]

This latest claim, together with a negative view of the flesh in general, receives considerable attention in his commentary on Romans. Romans 7:18—"For I know that nothing good dwells within me, that is, in my flesh"—seems at first to favor the Manichaeans. However, the good to which St. Paul refers is not the good of nature, Thomas explains, but the good of grace "by which we are freed from sin."[58] Similarly, Romans 8:3, which is about God "sending his own Son in the likeness of sinful flesh," should not be read as favoring the "imaginary body" theory of the Manichaeans. On the contrary, Luke 24:39 says, "A spirit has not flesh and bones as you see that I have." "Likeness," therefore, operates as a qualifier of "sinful" and not of "flesh."[59] Nor does Romans 8:7—"Because the wisdom of the flesh is hostile to God. For it is not subject to the law of God, nor can it be"—support the Manichaeans, because here it is not the *nature* of the flesh that is at stake, but the prudential *use* of it.[60]

Another group of heresies focusing on Christ's humanity can be found in Aquinas's commentary on Matthew 1:1—"The book of the genealogy of Jesus Christ, the son of David, the son of Abraham." In fact, "the son of David, the son of Abraham" contains in itself already the rejection of all heresies regarding Christ's humanity. Even more interesting is the fact that St. Thomas sees a historical development regarding these heresies which starts from the Manichaean position and which subsequently was adjusted to meet criticism.

---

[57] *Super Rom* 1, lec. 2 (no. 41).
[58] *Super Rom* 7, lec. 3 (no. 573).
[59] *Super Rom* 8, lec. 1 (no. 608).
[60] *Super Rom* 8, lec. 2 (no. 623).

The first to err about his humanity was Manichaeus, who said that he took up, not a true body, but the appearance of a body. Contrary to this is what the Lord says: "handle, and see: for a spirit does not have flesh and bones, as you see me to have" (Luke 24:39). Second, after Manichaeus, Valentinus erred, who said that he took for himself a celestial body, and that he did not take it up from the Virgin but rather passed through her like water through a canal. But contrary to this it is said: "who was made to him of the seed of David, according to the flesh" (Rom 1:3). The third error was that of Apollinaris, who said that he took only a body and not a soul, but that he had the divinity in place of a soul. But contrary to this is what is frequently said: "now is my soul troubled" (John 12:27). But because of this saying, Apollinarus himself later changed his position and said that Christ had a vegetative and a sensitive soul, but nonetheless not a rational soul, but rather in its place the divinity. But in this case something unfitting would follow, namely that Christ would be no more a man than one of the brutes.[61]

Each of these heresies receives additional scriptural refutation. The Manichaean position is refuted by Luke 24:39. Valentinus's position is refuted by Romans 1:3—"who was made to him of the seed of David, according to the flesh." Apollinaris's position is rejected by John 12:27—"now is my soul troubled." At this point in the commentary, Thomas adds a purely philosophical reasoning, which applies to all these heresies and in which it is argued that sonship necessarily implies having the same specific nature, which in turn implies having a true and natural body, which implies the presence of a rational soul.[62]

Another interesting passage occurs in response to an objection raised against John 1:7—"He came as a witness, that he might bear witness to the light, so that through him all men might believe." For, if the Son is already the light to the Gentiles (Luke 2:32), sufficient

---

[61] *Super Matt* 1, lec. 1 (no. 21).

[62] See *Super Matt* 1, lec. 1 (no. 22). See also *Super Ioan* 1, lec. 7 (nos. 167–68), where he argues that Christ's marvel in Matt 8:10 implies the presence of an intellectual part in Christ's soul. Again he adds a purely rational argument (*per rationem*). Just as human flesh requires a human soul—that is, a rational soul—assumed flesh requires a rational soul as well. Otherwise, no assumption of human flesh took place and, hence, the proposition "God became man" is false.

in and of itself to make all things known, why is there need of a witness? Such an objection, he says, is raised by the Manichaeans and is meant to destroy the Old Testament. In what follows, he gives four reasons for why Christ wanted to have the testimony of the prophets, three from Origen and one from Chrysostom. When one compares the three reasons from Origen as they appear in St. Thomas's commentary on John with both St. Thomas's *Catena Aurea* on John and Origen's own commentary on John, it becomes clear that St. Thomas not only rearranges and paraphrases Origen's text but also expands on it significantly. The clearest example is the first reason he gives.

> The first is that God wanted to have certain witnesses, not because he needed their testimony, but to ennoble [*nobilitet*] those whom he appointed witnesses. Thus, we see in the order of the universe that God produces certain effects by means of intermediate causes, not because he himself is unable to produce them without these intermediaries, but he deigns to confer on them the dignity of causality because he wishes to ennoble these intermediate causes. Similarly, even though God could have enlightened all men by himself and led them to a knowledge of himself, yet to preserve due order in things and to ennoble certain men, he willed that divine knowledge reach men through certain other men. "'You are my witnesses,' says the Lord" (Isa 43:10).[63]

Only the first sentence of the English translation is a paraphrase from Origen.[64] St. Thomas corroborates the argument from tradition with a metaphysical and typically Thomist reasoning about the dignity of secondary causes, applies it to shed light on the process of revelation through the prophets, and concludes with a passage from Isaiah by way of confirmation of the whole argument.

Jesus's response to Mary in John 2:4 ("Woman, what does that have to do with me and you? My time has not yet come") also gave

---

[63] *Super Ioan* 1, lec. 4 (no. 119).

[64] Compare *Super Ioan* 1, lec. 4 (no. 119), with Aquinas's presentation of Origen's commentary on John 1:6–8 in his *Catena aurea* (*Ioan*) (ed. Martin Morard and *Centre national de la recherche scientifique [CNRS]*, 2019 [https://gloss-e.irht.cnrs.fr/sources/catena/04_Thomae_de_Aquino_Catena_aurea_in_Iohannem.pdf], matching p. 335 in the Marietti edition), and with Origen, *Commentary on John* 2.202–8 (*SChr*, 120:346–49).

rise to a group of three heresies. Some, like the Manichaeans and Valentinus, understood Jesus's words to mean, "I have received nothing from you," and concluded that Christ's body was either an imaginary one (Manichaeans) or a celestial one (Valentinus). Scripture refutes this in Galatians 4:4—"God sent his Son, made from a woman"—as well as in John's Gospel itself when John writes, "the mother of Jesus was there" (John 2:1).[65] A second heresy concerns Mary's virginity: Ebion said that Christ was conceived from a man's seed, and Elvidius denied Mary's virginity after Jesus's birth on the basis of the use of the word "woman," which implies the loss of virginity. Galatians 4:4, however, shows that "woman" can also refer to the female sex. There is, moreover, Genesis 3:12—"The woman whom you gave me as a companion, gave me fruit from the tree, and I ate it"—which, given that Eve was still a virgin in paradise, clearly shows that "woman" indeed can refer to a virgin.[66] Elsewhere he will explicitly call upon "our faith" as the authority for the belief in Mary's perpetual virginity.[67] The second part of John 2:4 ("My time has not yet come") is interpreted by the Priscillianists as implying that all things, including those of Christ, happen by fate and are predetermined. This position is clearly contrary to the fact that Christ is Lord of heaven and earth.

John 10:7–8 ("Truly, I say to you, I am the door of the sheep. All who came before me are thieves and robbers; but the sheep did not heed them") can also give rise to the heretical position of the Manichaeans that "the fathers of the Old Testament, who came before Christ, were evil and have been damned." St. Thomas refutes this position by arguing for the need to contextualize "all who came before me are thieves and robbers," and by making the necessary distinctions. First, the passage should be seen in relation to John 10:1 ("Truly, truly, I say to you, he who does not enter the sheepfold by the door but climbs in by another way, that man is a thief and a robber"), and hence as a qualification of those who do not enter the fold through Christ the door. The patriarchs and prophets, however, were sent by Christ as the forerunners of God's Word. Second, one needs to distinguish between those prophets sent by Christ and those who rely on their own authority, and hence are not sent by Christ. Finally, the fact that it says, "but the sheep did not heed them," shows that

---

[65] *Super Ioan* 2, lec. 1 (no. 349).
[66] *Super Ioan* 2, lec. 1 (no. 350).
[67] *Super Ioan* 2, lec. 2 (no. 370).

"those whom the sheep did heed were not thieves and robbers."[68]

John 12:30 ("Now shall the ruler of this world be cast out") presents an example of yet another distinction that is necessary for a correct understanding of a passage. In order to avoid the error of the Manichaeans calling the devil the creator and lord of all that is visible, a distinction has to be made between a natural right of dominion and a usurpation of that right. The latter is the case here because, when people reject Christ, they subject themselves to the devil, as 2 Corinthians 4:4 says: "The god of this world has blinded the minds of the unbelievers."[69]

These few examples already give us an indication of St. Thomas's argumentative strategy.[70] It is worthwhile, however, to consider briefly a few other major heresies.

Arianism

In the mind of Thomas, Arianism constitutes one of the worst heresies, possibly the worst. Interestingly, he finds support for this judgment in Scripture itself in John 5:18: "Consequently, the Jews tried all the harder to kill him, because he not only broke the Sabbath rest, but even called God his own Father, making himself equal to God,"

---

[68] *Super Ioan* 10, lec. 2 (no. 1384).

[69] *Super Ioan* 12, lec. 5 (no. 1669); see also *Super Ioan* 14, lec. 8 (no. 1975).

[70] Multiple other examples can be given. For instance, the miracle at the Cana wedding in John 2 illustrates that these created material substances are good in themselves (*Super Ioan* 2, lec. 1 [no. 358]). The same argument is used regarding the feeding of the people in John 6 (*Super Ioan* 6, lec. 1 [no. 860]). The reference to the temple as "my Father's house" in John 2 refutes the claim that the God of the New Testament was the Father of Christ but not the God of the Old Testament (*Super Ioan* 2, lec. 1 [no. 390]). The passages in Matt 14:26 and Luke 34:37 where Christ corrects his disciples for their fear of seeing a "spirit" or a "ghost" refutes the claim that flesh is a creature of the devil. Jesus's touching the leper and saying, "I will; be clean" (Matt 8:3) contains a refutation of three errors: Jesus indeed has a true body, contra the Manichaeans; he has a will, contra Apollinaris; and in curing the leper, he shows himself to be truly God, contra Photinus (*Super Matt* 8, lec. 1 [no. 686]). Jesus's saying in Matt 12:40 that "the Son of man [will] be three days and three nights in the heart of the earth" refutes the Manichaean claim that Jesus did not truly die (*Super Matt* 12, lec. 3 [no. 1051]). The opening lines of the Letter to the Hebrews affirm that God is the author of the Old Testament and the creator of temporal things (*Super Hebr* 1, lec. 1 [no. 23]).

showing that the "blindness of the Arians"[71] prevented them from understanding what even the Jews were able to understand.

In commenting on the first words of John's prologue, he asks how the Word can be coeternal, since he is begotten by the Father, a question directed against the Arians. First, he gives three reasons for why an originative principle is prior in duration. Next, he denies that this priority can be found in the generation of the Word, for that would introduce potency into a pure act. Next, he gives the example of the brightness of fire, which naturally and without succession issues from the fire. He concludes by invoking the Council of Ephesus as an argument from authority.[72]

Given that it is metaphysically impossible for a finite creature to receive an infinite goodness, the "his" in John 3:16 ("For God so loved the world that he gave his only begotten Son") cannot refer to an adopted, created son, but rather the immensity of God's love must refer to the Father's natural Son.[73]

Following Hilary, he sees John 6:58 ("Just as the living Father has sent me, and I live because of the Father, so whoever eats me, he also will live because of me") as a rejection of Arius. The argument proceeds in a logical-deductive fashion. If (nam si) we live because of Christ, because we have something of his nature (and the truth of this claim is based on John 6:55—"Whoever eats my flesh and drinks my blood has eternal life"), and if the nature of the Father is simple and indivisible, then Christ too lives because of the Father, because he has in himself the nature of the Father. Therefore (ergo), Christ has the entire nature of the Father.[74]

Christ's words to Philip in John 14:9 ("He who has seen me has seen the Father") constitutes another refutation of Arius on philosophical grounds: "For it is impossible to see the uncreated substance by seeing some created substance, just as by knowing a substance of one genus, one cannot know a substance of another genus."[75]

St. Thomas thinks John 8:54—"Jesus answered, 'If I glorify myself, my glory is nothing; it is my Father who glorifies me, of whom you say that he is your God'"—is used by the Arians to claim that the

---

[71] *Super Ioan* 5, lec. 2 (no. 742).
[72] *Super Ioan* 1, lec. 1 (no. 41).
[73] *Super Ioan* 3, lec. 1 (no. 477).
[74] *Super Ioan* 6, lec. 7 (no. 978).
[75] *Super Ioan* 14, lec. 3 (no. 1888).

Father is greater than the Son because "one who glorifies is greater than the one glorified by him." Thomas contextualizes this verse canonically by quoting John 17:1: "Father, the hour has come: glorify thy Son that thy Son may glorify thee."[76] Similarly, John 14:20—"In that day you will know that I am in my Father, and you in me, and I in you"—cannot be taken as an argument for likening the relation between the Son and the Father to that between the disciples and Christ if one properly contextualizes the statement "I am in my Father" canonically by reading it alongside "I and the Father are one" in John 10:30 and "the Word became flesh" in John 1:1.[77] Also, "the Father is greater than I" (John 14:28) should be read in light of the immediately preceding words, "I go to the Father," as well as in light of the fact that, given that the Son is from eternity with the Father, only his human nature can be said to go the Father, which is attested by Hebrews 2:9—"We see Jesus, who was made a little lower than the angels."[78]

We find an interesting example of a combination of speculative reasoning and a canonical reading, inspired by Hilary, when Thomas comments on John 17:3: "And this is eternal life, that they know you the only true God, and Jesus Christ whom you have sent." The major premise is drawn from Hilary: if something exercises true activities of a species, it must belong to that species. The minor we find in John 5:19—"Whatever he [the Father] does, that the Son does likewise." Therefore, the Son, who performs true works of divinity, must also possess the true nature of God. And this refutes Arius's claim that Father is the only true God.[79]

Sabellianism

Sabellianism is often treated together with Arianism because, following St. Augustine, St. Thomas sees them as two extremes addressed in John 10:30 ("I and the Father are one"): "One" establishes that the Father and Son are not different in nature, whereas "I and the Father" establishes that the Father and the Son are not the same

---

[76] *Super Ioan* 8, lec. 8 (no. 1278).
[77] *Super Ioan* 14, lec. 5 (no. 1930).
[78] *Super Ioan* 14, lec. 8 (no. 1970).
[79] *Super Ioan* 17, lec. 1 (no. 2187).

person.[80] Similarly, John 5:26 ("Indeed, just as the Father possesses life in himself, so he has given it to the Son to have life in himself") shows that, "if the Father gave life to the Son, it is obvious that the Father, who gave it, is other than the Son, who received it."[81] Also, it is impossible to make sense of John 14:10 ("The words that I say to you I do not speak of myself") if the Father and Son are the same.[82] Further refutations can be found in Matthew 11:25—"I confess to you, O Father, Lord of heaven and earth."

Most important for our purposes are Thomas's comments on Romans 1:3: "Concerning his Son, who was made to him of the seed of David, according to the flesh." This passage offers an occasion for a lengthy discussion on the nature of this sonship, as well as on the Incarnation. The passage refutes Photinus, Arius, and Sabellius, because all three in some way defend a temporal origin of the Son. Regarding the last, he argues that, if Sabellius's position were correct—if the Father himself became incarnate and took the name of Son, "such that the person would be the same and the names alone different"—we would not expect to find a sending of the Son by the Father, as we do in John 6:38 ("I have come down from heaven"). Such a logical inference finds confirmation in the fact that St. Paul says "his Son," in which "his" refers to God's "very own and natural" sonship. Finally, he draws on the Tradition by way of two phrases much in use already in Lombard's *Sentences*: Hilary's statement that "this true and personal Son is a Son by origin and not by adoption, in truth and not in name only, by birth and not by creation,"[83] and Augustine's comment on John 10:30 ("I and the Father are one") that "the fact that he says 'one' frees you from Arius; that he says 'we are' frees you from Sabellius."[84] Regarding the temporal origin, he infers from "was made to him of the seed of David, according to the flesh," that it is impossible for the Son to be made *for* the Father if the Son was the same person as the Father, as Sabellius held.[85]

---

[80] *Super Ioan* 10, lec. 5 (no. 1451).

[81] *Super Ioan* 5, lec. 5 (no. 783).

[82] *Super Ioan* 14, lec. 3 (no. 1895).

[83] Hilary, *De Trinitate* 3.11 (*PL*, 10:82A–B); Peter Lombard, *Sent.* III, d. 8, c. 2.

[84] Augustine, *In Iohannis evangelium tractatus* 36.9 (*CCSL*, 36:330) and *De Trinitate* 5.9.10. See Lombard, *Sent.* I, d. 31, c. 4.

[85] *Super Rom* 1, lec. 2 (nos. 33–34). For other refutations of Sabellianism, see for instance John 5:19 (*Super Ioan* [no.749]), John 5:26 (*Super Ioan* [no. 583]), and John 14:10 (*Super Ioan* [no. 1895]).

Nestorius and Eutyches

Regarding the Incarnation itself, something noteworthy occurs when discussing Nestorius. Commenting on the opening verses of Romans, St. Thomas presents Nestorius's position as the claim that the union of the Word with human nature consisted merely in an indwelling. But because it is obviously true that the dweller and that in which someone dwells are substantially distinct (*alia est substantia inhabitantis et inhabitati*), Thomas argues, Nestorius was led to the position that the person of the Son of God was distinct from the person of the son of man. Thomas refutes this position by combining Philemon 2:7 ("He emptied himself") with John 14:23, where it is said of the Father and the Spirit that "we will come to him and make our home with him." The implication of Nestorius's position, there-fore, leads to the "absurd" conclusion that the Father and the Spirit empty themselves as well. Finally, Thomas returns to Romans 1:2 by suggesting that, if the union were a mere indwelling, then St. Paul, in saying that "his Son, who was made to him of the seed of David, according to the flesh," would have employed a wholly inadequate way of speaking.[86]

The expression "was made" in Romans 1:3, however, seems to play into the hands of Eutyches,[87] who held that, as result of a change, after the Incarnation there is only one nature. Given that God cannot change, as Malachi 3:6 says ("I, the Lord, do not change"), the new union in question must be the result of a change in the creature, and more specifically a relational change similar to a person who remains in one place but comes to be on the right of an object when that object was moved from his right to his left. Equally troublesome is "according to the flesh," because it seems to give credence to the posi-tion of Apollinaris and Arius that the Incarnation did not involve the assumption of a soul. St. Thomas finds support for his view that flesh stands for the entire man in the Vulgate version of Isaiah 40:5 ("all

---

[86] *Super Rom* 1, lec. 2 (no. 35). See also *Super Rom* 9, lec. 1 (no. 747), on Rom 9:5. When one reads Rom 9:5 as "He [Christ] is from the patriarchs according to the flesh who is God over all things," the verse rejects Nestorius's claim that the Son of man was other than the Son of God.

[87] The monophysite Eutyches (ca. 380–456) should not be confused with Euty-chius, patriarch of Constantinople (512–582), who was held to believe that the resurrected bodies would be like air or wind.

flesh shall see it together for the mouth of the Lord has spoken").[88]

In his comments on Matthew 1:18—"When his mother Mary was espoused to Joseph"—he defends Mary as Mother of God against Nestorius by arguing that "his" refers to God. In doing so, he reads Revelation 12:1 ("a woman clothed with the sun") as an indication that Mary was "entirely filled with the divinity." Furthermore, he draws on Cyril of Alexandria's example for further clarification. Cyril explains that, in the generation of men, the mother provides the substance for the formation of the body while God provides the rational soul, yet the woman is called the mother of the whole man because "that which is taken from her is united to the rational soul." "Similarly," St. Thomas continues, following Cyril, "since the humanity of Christ was taken from the Blessed Virgin, the Blessed Virgin is called the mother not only of a man, but also of God, on account of the union with the divinity, although the divinity is not taken from her, just as the rational soul is not taken from the mother in others."[89]

Pelagianism

The clearest refutation of Pelagianism comes from Christ himself in the Lord's Prayer. In asking God to forgive us, it is shown that no one can live without sin, as Pelagius thought.[90] Similarly, in asking that his will be done, we acknowledge the need for divine help, contra Pelagius. The penultimate petition also refutes Pelagius in two respects, because it shows that, (1) contrary to Pelagius, no one can persevere without the help of God and that (2) God can indeed change the will, for otherwise God would not ask us to pray that we

---

[88] *Super Rom* 1, lec. 2 (nos. 37–38). See also *Super Ioan* 1, lec. 7 (no. 166): a mixture of natures, as Eutyches held, must be rejected on the basis of simple logical reasoning. If the Word was God and if God is immutable, as it is said in Mal 3:6 ("I am the Lord, and I do not change"), a conversion (*convertatur*) of one nature into another is impossible.

[89] *Super Matt* 1, lec. 4 (no. 108). Here the example is attributed to Ignatius Martyr. See, however, Thomas's presentation of Cyril's commentary on Matt 1:18 in the *Catena aurea* (1:18, no. 9; Morard and CNRS; Marietti edition, p. 23) and its source in Cyril, *Epistola ad Monachos Aegypti* (*Venerunt quidem*).

[90] The same petition also shows that it is possible to do penance even if one has sinned after baptism, contrary to Novatian, for otherwise Christ would be asking us to pray in vain for forgiveness (*Super Matt* 6, lec. 3 [no. 596]).

do not consent to the temptation.[91] In fact, John 15:5—"Apart from me you can do nothing"—is equally directed against Pelagius.[92] This includes the beginning of a good work, as is said in 2 Corinthians 3:5 ("Not that we are sufficient of ourselves to claim anything as coming from us; our sufficiency is from God")[93] and Phil. 1:6 ("He who began a good work in you will bring it to completion").[94]

Thomas treats Pelagianism extensively when commenting on Philippians 2:13—"for God is at work in you, both to will and to work for his good pleasure"—a verse which refers to four constitutive errors of Pelagianism. First is the claim of salvation by one's own free will without God, against which it is said in John 14:10, "The Father who dwells in me does his works," and John 15:5, "Apart from me you can do nothing." Second is the denial of the existence of free will in favor of determinism, against which it is said, "God is at work *in you*"—that is to say that God moves the will from within the will. Third is the attribution of the will to us and the accomplishment to God, against which it is said in Romans 9:16 that justice depends not on the will of man, but on God's mercy. Fourth and finally, there is the claim that, while God accomplishes every good in us, he does so through our merits. In order to reject this claim, it is said, "according God's good pleasure."[95]

The expression "by nature" in Romans 2:14 ("For when Gentiles who have not the law do by nature what the law requires, these, although they have not the law, are a law to themselves") seems to favor Pelagianism. St. Thomas offers two possibilities: "by nature" can refer to Gentiles who are already converted and are beginning to obey the law with the help of God's grace; or the expression can refer to the light of natural reason but not exclude the need of grace to move the affections, "any more than the knowledge of sin through the Law (Rom 3:20) exempts from the need of grace to move the affections."[96]

---

[91] *Super Matt* 6, lec. 3 [no. 598].

[92] *Super Ioan* 15, lec. 1 [no. 1993].

[93] *Super II Cor* 3, lec. 1 [nos. 86–87]. St. Thomas finds support for this in Aristotle's *Liber de bona fortuna*, a collection of two passages from the *Eudemian Ethics* and *Magna moralia*.

[94] *Super Phil* 1, lec. 1 [no. 12].

[95] *Super Phil* 2, lec. 3 [no. 77]. This reading can be found *ad sensum* in Augustine's *De dono perseverantiae* 13.33.

[96] *Super Rom* 2, lec. 3 (no. 216).

Conclusion

St. Thomas is a passionate interpreter and defender of Scripture, and from time to time, we can catch a glimpse of this fact shining through the Scholastic divisions, distinctions, and oppositions in his biblical commentaries. At one point, he writes: "With these two sets of distinctions in mind, it is easy to solve a difficulty which arises here."[97] Elsewhere we find him using expressions such as "we can clearly see that this is false" or "hence, in no way can it be said that."[98] Even more vehement are expressions such as "how great then is the blindness of the Arians"[99] and "this shows their folly"[100] and the claim that certain heretics teach "the basest things in private, . . . things which a man would blush to teach and preach openly."[101] Equally vehement are the use of verbs such as "to blaspheme," "to contrive" (*fingere*), and "to be out of one's mind" (*delirare*). But the stakes could not be higher, for the salvation of souls depends on a correct understanding of Christ's divinity and humanity.

Any apologetic approach in this regard should be based on Scripture, and more particularly, it should start with God as the Author of Scripture, for it is God, St. Thomas writes, following Luke 24:45 ("Then he opened their minds to understand the Scripture"), and not our frail human minds, who "opens up the words of the Scriptures" and is the "revealer of mysteries" (Dan 2:47).[102]

Given what Scripture teaches about God as the Author of Truth, of any truth and of his veracity, any argumentation can in principle be used, whether it is from Scripture itself, from Tradition, or based

---

[97] *Super Ioan* 1, lec. 5 (no. 129).

[98] *Super Ioan* 1, lec. 7 (no. 166).

[99] *Super Ioan* 5, lec. 2 (no. 742).

[100] *Super Ioan* 7, lec. 3 (no. 1055).

[101] *Super Ioan* 16, lec. 3 (no. 2101): "The statement, 'you cannot bear them now' [John 16:12], has been used by certain heretics as a cover for their errors. They tell their adherents the basest things in private, things they would not dare to say openly, as though these were the things the disciples were not then able to bear, and as though the Holy Spirit taught them these things which a man would blush to teach and preach openly" (trans. Fabian Larcher).

[102] See *Super Threnos*, prol.: "Deus enim aperit Scripturarum verba: unde dicitur Luc. ult.: aperuit illis sensum ut intelligerent Scripturas. Revelat occulta mysteria. Dan. 2: vere Deus noster Deus deorum, et dominus regum, revelans mysteria" (Parma ed., 14:668). The authenticity of this commentary on Lamentations is disputed.

on metaphysical truths or logical inferences. This is why we seldom find St. Thomas relying on just one scriptural passage to refute a heresy, and also why he is indeed able to find such refutations of the same heresies throughout different chapters or books of the Bible. For the same reason, we seldom find him relying on Scripture alone, but rather deepening and developing arguments on the basis of Tradition[103] and reason. These latter arguments do not seem, we would argue, to go beyond Scripture in the sense of introducing something foreign into Scripture,[104] but are rather introduced to bring out the inner coherence of Scripture, to reinforce the argumentation provided by Scripture itself, to show the fittingness of a theological exegesis which tries to retrieve the full doctrinal and moral content of the text, and so on.

For this reason, St. Thomas explicitly recommends the study of Scripture as a protection against heretics,[105] for in giving Scripture as his revealed word, God has also given everything necessary to defend the faith.[106]

---

[103] Regarding the argumentative force of Tradition, one should take into account *ST* II-II, q. 1, a. 7, ad 4, where it is argued that, because Christ came in "the fullness of time" (Gal 4:4), those who were nearest to Christ chronologically possessed a fuller knowledge of the mysteries of faith.

[104] For instance, Scripture can be a premise for inferring a truth implicit in Scripture.

[105] *Super Tit* 1, lec. 3, no. 24: "Ut custodian (doctrinam sanam) contra haereticos . . . per studium sacrae Scripturae."

[106] See Aquinas, *Traités: Les raisons de la foi; Les articles de la foi et Les sacraments de l'Eglise*, trans. Gilles Emery with introduction and annotation (Paris: Cerf, 1999), 202.

Aquinas's Pauline Understanding of Perfection as Defining of the Christian Moral Life: The Case of Sexual Practice

Paul Gondreau
Providence College

As the Apostle says. This phrase, or the near equivalent, is well familiar to the reader of Thomas Aquinas. Its appearance—coming well over several hundred times in his *opera*—signals the fact that a deep Pauline undercurrent runs throughout Aquinas's writings. It indicates the formative role that Paul's thought played in Aquinas's theology, to the extent that it would be impossible to overstate how thoroughly Pauline, and thus biblical, Aquinas's theology is.

If this holds true anywhere, it is in Aquinas's doctrine of law, or more specifically, of the New Law of the Christian Gospel—and, by extension, of the role that law (in this case, the New Law) plays in his overarching vision of the moral life. It concerns, to be more precise, Aquinas's understanding of perfection as defining of the New Law, or of New Testament (Evangelical) morality. And in this element of his teaching, St. Thomas draws heavily (quite heavily) from "the Apostle."

This essay shall aim to bear this out, doing so in two moves: first, by offering, after a cursory look at the role of law in Thomas's overarching vision of the moral life, an overview of Aquinas's Pauline view that perfection defines New Testament (New Law) morality; and second, by considering how this moral perfection plays out in sexual practice.

Aquinas on Perfection as Defining
New Testament Morality

Recall that Thomas's vision of the moral life is predicated on the teleological ordering of the human being to beatitude, our supreme end, which will consist in our attaining to the *visio Dei*.[1] The means to our attaining this end, he goes on to make clear in the prologues to the treatise on habits (*habitus*) and the treatise on law in the *Summa theologiae*, are the intrinsic principle of virtue and the extrinsic principles of law and grace.[2] As for law, its fundamental purpose, on Aquinas's account, is to instruct us of our good, the good that orders us to our end of happiness: "the extrinsic principle moving to good is God, who both instructs us by means of his law, and assists us by his grace," writes Aquinas in the same prologue to the treatise on law.[3] While the natural law instructs of our natural good, the good proportionate to reason, the divine law instructs us of our proper supernatural good, since our ultimate end is of course a supernatural one, an end that exceeds our nature. As Thomas puts it:

> It is by law that man is directed on how to perform his proper acts in view of his last end. . . . And since man is ordained to the end of eternal happiness, which exceeds the proportion of man's natural faculty, it was necessary that . . . man should be directed to his end by a law given [or revealed] by God.[4]

---

[1] See *Summa theologiae* [*ST*] I-II, q. 1, prol. ("The end is the rule of whatever is ordained to the end. And . . . the last end of human life is said to be happiness"; translations of *ST* are taken from the Dominican Fathers of the English Province edition), and q. 3, a. 8 ("Final and perfect happiness can consist in nothing else than the vision of the Divine Essence").

[2] *ST* I-II, q. 49, prol. ("The intrinsic principle [of human acts] is power and habit; but as we have already treated of powers [in I, q. 77], it remains for us to consider . . . virtues and vices and other like habits, which are the principles of human acts"), and q. 90, prol.

[3] *ST* I-II, q. 90, prol.

[4] *ST* I-II, q. 91, a. 4. As regards the natural law, see q. 94, a. 4: "To the natural law belongs those things to which man is inclined naturally; and among these it is proper to man to be inclined to act according to reason." See also q. 91, a. 4, ad 1: "By the natural law the eternal law is participated proportionately to the capacity of human nature. But to his supernatural end man needs to be directed in a yet higher way. Hence the additional [divine] law given by God."

The divine law, then, plays a crucial function in the moral life, for which reason it plays a prominent role in Aquinas's moral system. Without the divine law, we could never attain to eternal happiness, our supreme end.

Notably, the divine law was issued or revealed in two installments: the Old Mosaic Law, the law of the Old Covenant; and the New Law of Christ, the Evangelical Law, the law of the Christian Gospel. How these two laws relate to each other has ever vexed Christian thinkers, with the notorious second-century heretic Marcion representing one extreme position. The Marcion option (the easy-way-out option) stands always before us, beckoning us to pit the two laws against each other, to drive a wedge between the two testaments, whether that wedge be hard and firm or soft and muted. Many take the Marcion bait, especially in the modern age, which is wont to equate distinction with separation.

"There Is But One God of the New and of the Old Testament"

But neither Paul nor Aquinas take the Marcion bait. Aquinas can put his anti-Marcion position no more clearly and succinctly than when he writes: "there is but one God of the New and of the Old Testament."[5] And it is the Apostle himself who provides him with the key to unlocking the link uniting the two laws, the two testaments. The crucial passage comes in Galatians 3:23–25:

> Now before faith came, we were confined under the law, kept under restraint until faith should be revealed. So that the law [the Old Law] was our custodian until Christ came, that we might be justified by faith. But now that faith has come, we are no longer under a custodian.

The key term here is "custodian"—in Greek *paidagōgos*, or *pedagogus* in the Latin Vulgate, which the Revised Standard Version (cited here) translates as "custodian," but which other translations (like the New American Bible) render as "disciplinarian." To say this passage from Galatians has a seismic impact on Thomas's under-

---

5   *ST* I-II, q. 107, a. 1.

standing of Gospel morality and of how it relates to Old Testament morality would not be overstating the matter. Let us quote the key passage from the *Summa*:

> Now things may be distinguished . . . as between perfect and imperfect in the same species, for example, a boy and a man, and in this way the divine law is divided into Old and New. Hence the Apostle compares the state of man under the Old Law to that of a child "under a pedagogue," but the state under the New Law to that of a full-grown man, who is "no longer under a pedagogue."[6]

Likening this role of "pedagogue" or "disciplinarian" to that of a father issuing commands or "house rules" to his children in echo of Deuteronomy 8:5 ("as a man disciplines his son, so the Lord God disciplines you"), Aquinas continues:

> As the father of a family issues different commands to the children and to the adults, so also does the one King, God, in his one kingdom give one law [or moral instruction] to men while they were yet imperfect, and another more perfect law [moral instruction] when, by the preceding law, they had been led to a greater capacity for divine things.[7]

Contrary, then, to a Marcion-styled reading of how the two biblical testaments relate, Aquinas the Pauline theologian takes the view that the moral teaching of the two testaments is fitted to two organically unified stages of moral development: the first to a more child- or adolescent-like stage, and the second to a proper adult-like stage. The "one God" of the New and Old Testaments is like the same father who disciplines his young and adult children differently. It is not God who is different, but man and where he finds himself in his respective stage of moral development, to which the two laws are fitted.

Put simply, salvation history involves a process of moral and spiritual reform. This permits us to look upon the moral teaching of the

---

[6] *ST* I-II, q. 91, a. 5, corp. Aquinas goes on in the *corpus* here to delineate the various ways by which we should understand this "perfection and imperfection."

[7] *ST* I-II, q. 91, a. 5, ad 1; for a fuller treatment of this, see q. 107, a. 1, ad 2.

Old Testament as something suited, say, to those in what we might call "reform school," and thus to appreciate why there is a developing morality even within the Old Testament. The moral teaching of the New Testament is instead suited to those already "reformed," principally by the grace of Christ, in which, on Aquinas's account, the New Law of the Gospel consists principally: "The New Law *is chiefly* the grace itself of the Holy Spirit."[8] Just as we hold children to one standard of conduct and adults to another higher standard, so also Old Testament morality permits things like polygamy and divorce, whereas New Testament morality does not. (Examples of sexual morality are chosen intentionally; more on this shortly below.)

The Person of Christ as the New Source of the Moral Life

Note the crucial turn Aquinas makes in his exegesis of the Pauline distinction between "under a pedagogue" and "no longer under a pedagogue," moving from imperfection to perfection. On Thomas's reading of Galatians, then, perfection is the defining trait of New Testament morality ("no longer under a pedagogue").

And what makes this perfection possible? Nothing other than the Person of Christ and the grace of the Holy Spirit he gives. Whereas Jewish moral teaching, to which Saul the Pharisee at first adhered, places the emphasis on adherence to God's Torah, and Greek moral teaching holds up human reason, or natural wisdom, as the principal source of moral action, Gospel morality, now championed by Paul the Apostle, instead identifies the Person of Christ as the new and principal source of moral action. That the Person of Christ was found guilty by and accursed under Jewish law and had the most gruesome and tortuous of Roman executions imposed upon him explains why, in 1 Corinthians 1:23, Paul understands how "scandalous" (to Jews) and "foolish" (to Greeks) it is at first sight to propose such a man as the new center of gravity in the moral life.

Paul would have us understand that the baptized believer lives not according to an abstract moral theory or set of ideas, nor to a set of moral imperatives as stipulated by the Torah. Rather, the baptized

---

8 *ST* I-II, q. 106, a. 1 (emphasis added); see also a. 2. Here we see again how, in Thomas's moral system, law and grace converge in the New Divine Law.

believer first and foremost lives in a relationship with the Person of Jesus Christ, God's incarnate Son, a relationship that the grace of the Holy Spirit makes possible. The moral life is first and last relational.

On Paul's account, the implications of this Christocentric and Pneumacentric relational way of conceiving the moral life are put in the following terms: we must "live to" the Person of Christ (Rom 14:8), "belong to" him (Gal 5:24), and even "put on" this Person, the Lord Jesus Christ, while "mak[ing] no provisions for the flesh, to gratify its desires" (Rom 13:14). Our relationship with the Person of Christ implies a transformation of our moral comportment in a way that suits the moral maturity of a "reformed" person (reformed by grace) who acts "no longer as under a pedagogue."

Biblical Natural Law

We should point out that this Christocentric and Pneumacentric way of conceiving the moral life does not rule out human reason as a veritable source of moral action (as the Greek philosophical tradition so honors), as Aquinas well knows. On the contrary, reason plays an integral role in "putting on" Christ.

It does this principally through the natural law. The Apostle makes this clear, as Aquinas attests, at the outset of the Letter to the Romans, where he affirms that the Gentiles, by virtue of "the law . . . written on their hearts," were able to observe "by nature what the law [of Moses] requires" (Rom 2:14–15).[9] The harmony between the duty to follow nature and the duty to follow Christ is evidenced in Paul's affirmation later in Romans that obedience to the moral law known through conscience is not opposed to the effort of "putting on the Lord Jesus Christ" (13:14). According to the moral theologian Servais Pinckaers, the Person of Christ and the natural law mark "the two major poles of the moral teaching of St. Paul."[10]

The natural law is so omnipresent—not simply in the Pauline corpus, but in the entire biblical witness—that we can speak of a ver-

---

[9] See Aquinas, *Super Rom* 2, lec. 3: "'By nature' can be taken to mean by the natural law showing them [the Gentiles] what should be done." (Trans. F. R. Larcher [Lander, WY: Aquinas Institute for the Study of Sacred Doctrine, 2012], 75).

[10] Servais Pinckaers, *Morality: The Catholic View*, trans. Michael Sherwin (South Bend, IN: St. Augustine's Press, 2001), 16.

itable biblical natural law. The French biblical scholar Ceslas Spicq observes how the role of natural law in St. Paul's moral teaching is consistent with the New Testament as a whole: "The entire New Testament," Spicq tells us, "makes use of and presupposes as incontrovertible (the natural law's) first given; namely, that good is distinct from evil, and that we should do good and avoid evil."[11] For a Gospel passage portraying Jesus, he points to Mark 3:4 ("And he said to them, 'Is it lawful on the Sabbath to do good or to do harm, to save life or to kill?'"). One could also point to Matthew 12:35 ("'The good man out of his good treasure brings forth good, and the evil man out of his evil treasure brings forth evil'"), or to Jesus's appeal to reason and common sense in moral matters, as in Luke 12:57 ("'And why do you not judge for yourselves what is right?'"). For references in St. Paul, Spicq cites Romans 2:9–10 ("There will be tribulation and distress for every human being who does evil . . . but glory and honor and peace for every one who does good") and 16:19 ("I would have you wise as to what is good and guileless as to what is evil") and Galatians 6:10 ("let us do good to all men"). Spicq concludes: "In a sense, nothing is more human than New Testament morality. It denounces the same vices and prescribes the same virtues as the Jewish, Greek, and Roman moral codes."[12]

The biblical scholar Amos N. Wilder extends this further: "We have every right to recognize the equivalent of natural law in the [entire] Bible."[13] Among the many passages he points to for evidence,

---

[11] Ceslas Spicq, *Théologie morale du Nouveau Testament*, 2 vols. (Paris: J. Gabalda, 1965), 1:394–406 (Appendix 2: "La loi naturelle dans Le Nouveau Testament"), at 401 (translation mine). See also Spicq's much later *Connaissance et Morale dans la Bible* (Paris: Editions du Cerf, 1985), 50–67 ("La connaissance de la volonté de Dieu par la Loi naturelle, la Tôrâh et la loi positive"), at 56, where he observes (noting an important caveat): "As with any 'human' morality, the New Testament reaffirms the first principle of the natural law: do good and avoid evil, though the revulsion of evil and the attachment to good will be made possible only by charity" (translation mine).

[12] Spicq, *Théologie morale du Nouveau Testament*, 1:404 (translation mine). For agreement, see C. H. Dodd, "Natural Law in the New Testament," in *New Testament Studies* (Manchester, UK: Manchester University Press, 1953), 129–42, at 139.

[13] Amos N. Wilder, "Equivalents of Natural Law in the Teaching of Jesus," *Journal of Religion* 26, no. 2 (1945): 125–35, at 129. See also: Matthew Levering, "God and Natural Law: Reflections on Genesis 22," *Modern Theology* 24, no. 2 (2008): 151–77; Levering, "Knowing What is 'Natural': Thomas Aquinas and Luke Tim-

Genesis 1–2 figures prominently. To put it in the words of the scholar Jean-Baptiste Edart, the Genesis creation account "presents a clear vision of the man-woman structure in the act of creation . . . and this divine will or divine law is inscribed in nature."[14]

Taking this argument further, Matthew Levering, in his work *Biblical Natural Law*, points out that what we find not only in Genesis, but in the entire biblical revelation, is a theocentric and teleological account of creation and providence, of God's ordering wisdom. And to say "providential governance or teleological ordering to predetermined ends," particularly in reference to the human being, is to say natural law. We see this when God fashions the human being in view of what Levering terms "goods constitutive of true human flourishing":

> The early chapters of Genesis, within a profoundly theocentric context, reveal human beings to be intrinsically teleological, ordered to certain goods constitutive of a flourishing proper to human beings. This aspect of Genesis 1–2 can be overlooked when one views God's commands as extrinsic rather than intrinsic to the human person. Yet in appealing, with regard to marriage, to 'the beginning' (Matt. 19:4, 8), Jesus himself emphasizes the teleological dimension of Genesis 1–2. In Genesis 1–2 God's commands and actions do not set up extrinsic norms, but rather indicate, in a theocentric fashion, the intrinsic norms that express the goods constitutive of true human flourishing.[15]

---

othy Johnson on Romans 1–2," *Logos* 12, no. 1 (2009): 117–42; Anver M. Emon, Matthew Levering, and David Novak, *Natural Law: A Jewish, Christian, and Islamic Trialogue* (Oxford: Oxford University Press, 2014); Dodd, "Natural Law in the New Testament," 135–36; and Cajetan Cuddy, "Thomas Aquinas on the Bible and Morality: The Sacred Scriptures, the Natural Law, and the Hermeneutic of Continuity," in *Towards a Biblical Thomism: Thomas Aquinas and the Renewal of Biblical Theology*, ed. Piotr Roszak and Jörgen Vijgen (Pamplona, ES: Eunsa Press, 2018), 173–97.

14 Innocent Himbaza, Adrien Schenker, and Jean-Baptiste Edart, *The Bible on the Question of Homosexuality*, trans. Benedict Guevin (Washington, DC: Catholic University of America Press, 2012), 98. For agreement, see Jacques Dupont, *Mariage et divorce dans l'Évangile* (Bruges, BE: Desclée de Brouwer, 1959), 34: "[Divorce] ignores a fundamental law of nature, expressive of the will of the Creator" (translation mine).

15 Matthew Levering, *Biblical Natural Law: A Theocentric and Teleological Approach*

Levering's mentioning of Jesus is noteworthy. To reinforce his point, by appealing to Genesis 1–2 in his moral teaching on marriage (see Mark 10:4–12), Jesus makes an unmistakable, albeit implicit, appeal to the law of nature, to the law that precedes the Torah and that holds authority over the Torah, the law that originates with and remains imbedded in human nature itself.[16] Additionally, Jesus constantly points to God's providential ordering of nature in his use of metaphors and examples: trees, fruits, mustard seeds, foxes, sparrows, ravens, thorns, thistles, weather patterns, lilies, grass, grains of wheat, and so on.[17]

When considering the role of natural law in Aquinas's moral system, then, we are not speaking merely of what he inherits from the Greek philosophical tradition, but of a thoroughly biblical element in his moral teaching as well.

MORAL PERFECTION IN THE CASE OF SEXUAL PRACTICE

We turn now to sexual practice in the interests of giving practical consideration, in this area at least, to moral perfection as defining New Testament morality. After all, "universal moral discourse is less useful [in moral considerations]," Thomas reminds us in the prologue to his treatise on the virtues and vices, "since actions occur in the singular."[18] The choice of sexual practice is not a marginal or random one. Placing the moral meaning of sex in the top three notions that Paul is most "eager" to expound upon, the New Testament scholar N. T. Wright adds: "Sexual holiness is mandatory, not optional, for followers of Jesus. . . . Sexual holiness isn't just a 'rule,' an arbitrary commandment. It is part of what it means to turn from idols and serve the true and living God. It is part of being a genuine, image-bearing human being

---

(Oxford: Oxford University Press, 2008), 60.

[16] For support, besides Wilder's "Equivalents of Natural Law," see Dodd, "Natural Law in the New Testament," 135–36, and A.-M. Dubarle, *Le péché original dans l'Écriture* (Paris: Édition du Cerf, 1958), 107.

[17] See Wilder, "Equivalents of Natural Law," 133–34. For agreement, see Spicq, *Théologie morale*, 1:394.

[18] *ST* II-II, q. 1, prol.

. . . [and is] to be built into the Christian DNA from the start."[19]

The same is true for Aquinas the biblical theologian, whose whole moral vision is structured around a view of the human person in whom "the biological dimension [inclusive of our sexuality and more generally of our affectivity] is vitally integrated in a spiritual nature," to quote Servais Pinckaers.[20] To this end, the virtue of chastity, understood in quite Pauline (and Aristotelian) terms, inasmuch as our sexuality is integrated through reason into "the service of true love" (Pinckaers), figures prominently, as we shall see below.[21]

A Hetero-Normative View of Human Sexuality

Two Pauline texts emerge as especially foundational in his teaching on sexual morality: 1 Corinthians 7:1–16 and Ephesians 5:21–33. In both we find Paul deferring to preestablished authorities as a ground for his own position: in the first, the authority of Jesus "the Lord"; and, in the second, that of Genesis 2. In the 1 Corinthians passage, the Apostle writes: "To the married I give charge, not I but the Lord [Jesus], that the wife should not separate from her husband . . . and that the husband should not divorce his wife" (1 Cor 7:10–11). In the Ephesians passage, Paul directly cites Genesis 2:24 in his effort to underscore the unitive love of husband and wife: "Husbands should love their wives as their own bodies . . . 'For this reason a man shall leave his father and mother and be joined to his wife, and the two shall become one flesh'" (Eph 5:28–31). (Paul directly references Gen 1–2 in his appeal to "the Lord" in the 1 Corinthians passage as well, given that Jesus had invoked it in his prohibition of remarriage after divorce.) Paul makes his own these two foundational sources, Jesus the Lord and the Genesis creation account, from which he forges what one biblical scholar affirms is a veritable vision of the meaning and purpose of human sexuality.[22]

Paul's appeal to the Genesis creation account in particular—both

---

[19] N. T. Wright, *Paul: A Biography* (New York: HarperCollins, 2018), 217–18.

[20] Servais Pinckaers, *The Sources of Christian Ethics*, trans. Mary Thomas Noble (Washington, DC: Catholic University of America Press, 1995), 441; see also 446. See also my own essay, "The Passions and the Moral Life: Appreciating the Originality of Aquinas," *The Thomist* 71 (2007): 419–50.

[21] Pinckaers, *Sources*, 439.

[22] Himbaza, Schenker, and Edart, *The Bible on Homosexuality*, 124.

directly and via his invoking Jesus "the Lord"—shows that, for him, there can be no doubt that male–female complementarity, or sexual dimorphism, marks a fundamental structure of human nature. Genesis 1–2 sets forth the male–female anthropology, expressive of God's creative design, as normative for human sexual comportment. Put more directly, the two creation accounts of Genesis (in conjunction with natural law) present human sexuality as a gift from God to provide us with a means both for propagating the human race (Gen 1:28) and for attaining oneness in the deepest bonds of human love or companionship (Gen 2:18–25)—that is, for the joint purposes of procreation and unitive love, to use the language of today.

God thus endowed us with a sexed nature for the express purpose of marriage (the union of man and woman), since only marriage unites the joint goods of procreation and unitive love. Sex, in the biblical perspective, is inherently nuptial in meaning. Hence, in his commentary on the Ephesians passage, Aquinas puts forth the view that, by appealing to Genesis, Paul underscores how "the devotion of conjugal love" (the unitive love shared by the spouses) is "so strong in each that they both leave their parents behind," specifically in order to enjoy a "carnal union" that by its very nature is ordered to "the act of generation."[23]

Because this unitive-procreative meaning bears on any who share this sexed design, Paul sees imbedded in the Genesis creation account a universal standard of conduct that is "applicable to all people at all times," to quote Edart.[24] Significantly for the purposes of highlighting the perfection that is defining of New Testament morality, this universal standard includes the indissoluble nature of the marriage bond, the Mosaic compromise of which Gospel morality no longer tolerates, as seen in the teachings of "the Lord" cited by Paul: "For your hardness of heart Moses allowed you to divorce your wives, but from the beginning it was not so" (Matt 19:8); "What therefore God has joined together, let not man put asunder'" (Mark 10:9). As the German biblical scholar Rudolf Schnackenburg puts it: "The fact of indissolubility alone was enough to elevate the early Christian ethics

---

[23] Aquinas, *Super Eph* 5, lec. 10 (trans. Matthew Lamb [Lander, WY: Aquinas Institute for the Study of Sacred Doctrine, 2012], 325–26).

[24] "The reference to the creation story is the foundation of the universal character of Paul's judgment [on sexual immorality]. According to him, it is applicable to all people at all times" (Himbaza, Schenker, and Edart, *The Bible on Homosexuality*, 124).

of marriage far above the level of those of Judaism and paganism."[25]

To say that marriage is indissoluble means we cannot pretend something that is truly one is in fact two. To acknowledge the permissibility of divorce is to acknowledge the fracturing of a merely apparent—not real—union. Indeed, it is deeply telling how nuptial vows today, even in the purely civil arena, promise permanence ("until death do us part") and do not admit of "back-out" clauses (along the lines of, say, and to put it in terms of contemporary idiom, "I promise to be true to you, until things don't work out," or "until things get difficult," or "until my feelings change," and the list goes on).

Further, since the Mosaic permission for divorce was tantamount to the Jewish male right to divorce, to affirm the indissolubility of marriage is to affirm the fundamental equality of husband and wife in the marriage covenant. Generally speaking, only Jewish men had the right to divorce. Basing itself on Deuteronomy 24:1–2, the Talmud, for instance, states that only the husband can initiate a divorce, and that this can be for any reason, including the spoiling of his dinner, or for practically no reason—an ancient form of "no-fault" divorce.[26] Jewish law thus relegated women to secondary status, to the status of property of their husbands. In rescinding this male right, New Testament morality makes clear that women are not to be so regarded or treated. Not at the disposal of their husbands' mere whim or wish, wives enjoy the security of full rights and responsibilities that come with any true partnership.

For Aquinas, this means marriage sits at the very summit of human friendship, in that marital love holds the rank not only of *aequalis amicitia*, "friendship of equality," but of *maxima amicitia*, "highest friendship."[27] Only a biblically minded theologian, noting that God's

---

[25] Rudolf Schnackenburg, *The Moral Teaching of the New Testament*, trans. J. Holland-Smith and W. J. O'Hara (New York: Herder and Herder, 1965), 250.

[26] In the Mishnah, the School of Hillel states that a man may divorce his wife "even due to a minor issue, e.g., because she burned or over-salted his dish, as it is stated: 'Because he has found some unseemly matter in her' [Deut 24:1]," while Rabbi Akiva adds, "He may divorce her even if he found another woman who is better looking than her and wishes to marry her, as it is stated in that verse: 'And if it comes to pass, if she finds no favor in his eyes' [Deut 24:1]" (b. Git. 90a; sefaria.org/Gittin.90a?lang=bi).

[27] *Summa contra Gentiles* [*SCG*] III, ch. 123. In this passage, Aquinas makes clear that marriage implies *aequalis amicitia* and *maxima amicitia* because it constitutes an "indivisible union of souls" (*indivisibili coniunctione animorum*), or a "domes-

first response to Adam's social nature and need for friendship is to create not another man, but a woman, could call marriage *maxima amicitia*. Nothing satisfies the human need for friendship more than the love of man and woman in marriage.

Based on the 1 Corinthians and Ephesians passages cited above, then, we can say that, at the core of the Pauline vision of human sexuality, at the heart of the effort at "putting on" Christ in the arena of sexual practice, is the principle that marriage acts as the normative good of our sexuality. Paul's hetero-normative vision of human sexuality could be summed up simply as a morality of conjugal love—though understood in properly relational terms ("belonging to Christ"). For the Apostle, what renders a sexual act good and holy is the measure by which it respects the unitive and procreative orderings of the marital act. Any sexual act falling short of this will fail to attain what God intends for human sexual practice. Paul's remarks on sexually immoral behavior make this quite clear.

"A Great Mystery"

Before we get to those remarks, though, we should point out that the Ephesians passage also advances an entirely new understanding of marriage. In it, Paul terms marriage a "great mystery" (*mystērion mégas* in Greek; *sacramentum magnum* in the Vulgate), in that it signifies the nuptial union of Christ and the Church (Eph 5:32). Marriage, in other words, marks a sacrament.[28] (By Jerome's day, the Greek Fathers had long since been using the term *mystēria* to designate those Christian rites that the Latin tradition was referring to as *sacramenta*, "sacraments.") Here, then, we find ourselves at the summit of Gospel perfection relative to the moral meaning and direction of human sexuality: our sexuality is not merely ordered to marriage; it is ordered to a partaking in our redemption, since all the sacraments give us a share in Christ's redemption. As Aquinas,

---

tic society of loving personal communion" (*domesticae conversationis consortium*), which enjoys the "sweet bond" (*suavem societatem*) of sexual procreative union. In other words, marriage attains to the level of *maxima amicitia* because it unites the two essential dimensions of human sexuality, procreative and unitive.

[28] For more on the meaning of marriage as a sacrament, see my essay "The Redemption and Divinization of Human Sexuality through the Sacrament of Marriage: A Thomistic Approach," *Nova et Vetera* (English) 10, no. 2 (2012): 383–413.

wishing to stress how the sacraments are, at bottom, dynamic actions of the Person of Christ on the Cross, puts it: "Christ's Passion is, so to speak, applied to man through the sacraments. . . . The merit and power of Christ's Passion operates in the sacraments."[29]

"*Shun* Porneia"

As for Paul's view on immoral sexual practice, he uses a catchword that encompasses all types. That word is *porneia*, as when he exhorts us to "shun *porneia*" in 1 Corinthians 6:18. Difficult to translate, *porneia* is best rendered, generally, as sexual immorality or unchaste action, or more precisely, as any sexual act, whether of an extramarital or unnatural sort, that dishonors marriage in its procreative-unitive nature. (Jerome's Vulgate offers *fornicatio* as the Latin rendering of *porneia*, meaning fornication in its broad, not narrow, sense.) With this term *porneia*, Paul approximates closely Jesus's condemnation of "adultery of the heart" (Matt 5:27–28), in that he targets the urgency of exercising internal self-mastery over our sexual urges: Aquinas reads Paul's exhortation here as "avoiding entirely all unclean thoughts and all occasions whatsoever [of sexual immorality]."[30]

So, when Paul says to the Christian community in Corinth that "the body is not meant for *porneia*" (1 Cor 6:13), what he means is the body is meant for no other form of sexual intimacy than that between husband and wife, in an embrace of procreative-unitive love. To "shun *porneia*" means to shun those sexual practices that seek pleasure as the ultimate aim, to shun those sexual acts that oppose or divide in any way the procreative and unitive orderings of the marital embrace. Paul enumerates several specific examples of this, including adultery (inclusive of remarried divorced persons), fornication (*koitais*), lust (*orēxis*), orgies (*kōmois*), prostitution (*pornē*), incest, and, most famously—and most controversially from a contemporary standpoint—homosexual practice.

---

[29] *ST* III, q. 61, a. 1, ad 3, and q. 64, a. 3. Also, in q. 62, a. 5, he writes: "The sacraments of the Church derive their power from Christ's Passion." See Jean-Pierre Torrell, *Aquinas's Summa: Background, Structure, and Reception*, trans. Benedict M. Guevin (Washington, DC: Catholic University of America Press, 2004), 59.
[30] Aquinas, *Super I Cor* 6, lec. 3 (trans. F. R. Larcher [Lander, WY: Aquinas Institute for the Study of Sacred Doctrine, 2012], 115).

Chastity Safeguards the Meaning and Purpose
of Human Sexuality

On this issue of avoiding sexual immorality, Aquinas adverts to the Greek language of virtue. Specifically, he appends the term "chastity" to this biblical teaching on shunning *fornicatio (porneia)* as part and parcel of a life of moral perfection in sexual practice. Only through the virtue of chastity, the self-mastery and balanced regulation of bodily desire and pleasure of a sexual sort, can one attain to moral perfection in the sexual arena of human life. "It belongs to chastity," Aquinas writes in the *Summa*, "that a man make moderate use of his bodily members [sexual organs] in accordance with the judgment of his reason and the choice of his will."[31] And this requires that one gain self-mastery over his interior thoughts and desires, the source of outward action.

To be sure, Aquinas holds that chastity is not foreign to the moral scope of Old Testament morality, as the Decalogue's proscription of adultery and lust (commandments 6 and 9) prompt us to the practice of chastity, he says, just as the other eight commandments inculcate other respective virtues.[32] The difference, though, centers on the New Law's placing the spotlight on our internal acts, the source of moral action, whereas the Mosaic Law tends to focus on external action: "The New Law surpasses the Old Law, since the New Law directs our internal acts. . . . Hence the saying that 'the Old Law restrains the hand, but the New Law controls the mind,'" writes Aquinas, citing Peter Lombard.[33]

Focus on the external act or on legal obligation, which is defining of the Old Law, is insufficient for good moral living. The com-

---

[31] *ST* II-II, q. 151, a. 1, ad 1.

[32] See *ST* I-II, q. 100, a. 11, obj. 3 and ad 3; see also q. 108, a. 3, ad 3, where Aquinas explains: "The moral precepts [of the Old Law] necessarily retained their force under the New Law, because they are of themselves essential to virtue."

[33] *ST* I-II, q. 91, a. 5: "The New Law surpasses the Old Law, since the New Law directs our internal acts. . . . Hence the saying [by Peter Lombard, *Sentences* III, d. 40] that 'the Old Law restrains the hand, but the New Law controls the mind.'" Later, in q. 107, a. 2, Aquinas adds: "In His doctrine Christ fulfilled the precepts of the (Old) Law . . . by explaining the true sense of the Law. This is clear in the case of murder and adultery, the prohibition of which the Scribes and Pharisees thought referred only to the exterior act: wherefore Our Lord fulfilled the Law by showing that the prohibition extends also to the interior acts of sins." See also q. 108, a. 3.

plete shaping of one's moral character requires more. Only by loving the good as befitting the mature adult who does the good for its own sake (in this instance, loving the virtue of chastity for its own sake, which the grace of the Holy Spirit makes possible) will one attain moral perfection in sexual practice.[34] The person animated by grace strives via the virtue of chastity for mature, interior self-mastery, specifically as regards one's sexual thoughts and desires: "because it requires greater virtue to conquer sexual desire entirely on account of the vehemence of sexual pleasure," Aquinas writes in his commentary on 1 Corinthians, "it is necessary that this desire be . . . subjected to reason."[35] Chastity is the virtue, then, that serves and safeguards the meaning and direction of human sexuality.

Homosexuality

Paul's censure of homosexual practice and its place in New Testament (Evangelical) morality merit closer consideration, since modern scholarship has witnessed myriad attempts either to dismiss outright or to soften the otherwise moral juggernaut presented by the passages in which Paul condemns homoerotic activity. Usually these efforts are put forward on the following two grounds: first, that the so-called homosexual "orientation," and by extension loving, stable homosexual relationships, were unknown in the ancient world, with the result that what Paul condemns was more pederasty or abusive/violent sex (such as between master and slave) or prostitution than committed homosexual relationships as we understand them today;[36] second, that the meaning of the Pauline passages (as well as those

---

[34] "The imperfect, who as yet do not possess the habit [*habitus*] of virtue, are directed to perform virtuous acts . . . through the threat of punishment, or the promise of extrinsic rewards, such as honor, riches, and the like. Hence the Old Law, which was given to men who were imperfect, is called the 'law of fear,' since it induces men to observe its commandments by threatening them with penalties. . . . On the other hand, those who possess the habit of virtue are inclined to do virtuous deeds through the love of virtue" (*ST* I-II, q. 107, a. 1, ad 2).

[35] Aquinas, *Super I Cor* 7, lec. 1 (Larcher trans., 121).

[36] For arguments in favor of this position, see: Robin Scroggs, *The New Testament and Homosexuality* (Philadelphia: Fortress, 1983), 84; Gerald Coleman, "The Vatican Statement on Homosexuality," *Theological Studies* 48 (1987): 727–34, at 728–89; and Adriano Oliva, *Amours: l'Église, les divorcés remariés, les couples homosexuels* (Paris: Cerf, 2015).

in the Old Testament, which are foundational for Paul) remain obscure and, in any case, ever-evolving in light of cultural and historical change and modern scientific findings, if not eclipsed by these changes and findings.[37] One well-known author, John Boswell, sums up the upshot of these efforts when he declares that the Bible takes "no demonstrable position" on sexual intimacy between members of the same sex within the context of a stable, affirming relationship.[38] These conclusions find recycled airplay in those who appeal to them as authoritatively definitive, and it is not uncommon even to find high-ranking Churchmen calling today for a reexamination of the biblical teaching on homosexuality.[39]

Suffice it to say that any honest "reexamination" will recognize that it is inconceivable that the moral perfection that defines New Testament (Evangelical) morality would embrace homoerotic practice of any sort, whether "affirming and committed" or not. Aquinas, for one, would be aghast at the modern move to grant biblical blessing to homosexual unions. Particularly if we keep in mind that New Testament morality takes the moral rigor of the Mosaic Law on sexual practices—itself without parallel in the ancient world—and intensifies and elevates it. That Jesus, who himself heralded this elevation in moral rigor, pronounced no word on homosexuality is of little consequence, given that Israel, to which Jesus was sent exclusively (see Matt 15:24), had, according to the first-century Jewish

---

[37] For an example of a proponent of this position, see Daniel A. Helminiak, "Preface to First Edition," in *What the Bible Really Says about Homosexuality* (Tajique, NM: Alamo Square Press, 2000). This position was also put forward by a homosexually active Episcopal priest at a panel discussion on same-sex marriage that I participated in at Rhode Island College in Providence, RI, in March of 2009.

[38] John Boswell, *Christianity, Social Tolerance, and Homosexuality: Gay People in Western Europe from the Beginning of the Christian Era to the Fourteenth Century* (Chicago: University of Chicago Press, 1980), 92. For Scroggs, the Old Testament expresses "indifference" to homosexual acts (*The New Testament and Homosexuality*, 70). For an outlining of these various arguments dismissing the Pauline condemnation of homosexual practice, see Himbaza, Schenker, and Edart, *The Bible on Homosexuality*, 81–83.

[39] For instance, see Gary Gutting's op-ed "Unraveling the Church Ban on Sex," *The New York Times*, March 12, 2015 (opinionator.blogs.nytimes.com/2015/03/12/unraveling-the-church-ban-on-gay-sex/?_r=2). For an example of the call to reexamine the biblical teaching on homosexuality by certain leading Churchmen, see the comments of Bishop Franz-Josef Overbeck of Essen, Germany, in the February 2019 issue of the German theological monthly *Herder Korrespondenz*.

historian Josephus, been "set apart from the unnatural sexual practices" that were otherwise prevalent among the pagan Gentiles.[40] In short, homosexuality was a non-issue for the Jewish audience of Jesus's day, as it enjoyed "no social visibility," to quote the scholar Edart.[41] Further, if Jesus opposed divorce on the grounds that, as he says, "from the beginning of creation, 'God made them male and female'" (Mark 10:6), it would have been exceedingly incongruous, to say the least, if he should have moved in a more lax direction on homoerotic relationships and not also have opposed them on the same grounds: namely, that they violate the male–female complementary structure of human sexuality.

In point of fact, the position of the Old Testament on the inherently immoral nature of homosexual conduct (see the Sodom and Gibeah stories of Gen 19:1–29 and Judg 19:11–25, and Lev 18:22 and 20:13) easily suffices for the standard of the New Law, as Paul's teaching unmistakably shows. In Romans 1:26–27, Paul employs the prepositional phrase "against nature" *(para physin)* to denounce homosexual activity ("men committing shameless acts with men" and "women exchang[ing] natural relations for ones against nature"). From the pen of Paul, the phrase *para physin* is particularly potent, carrying with it the full weight that the (natural law) male–female anthropology of the Genesis creation account would accord it. As the biblical scholar Edart tells us, the phrase *para physin* relays Paul's view "that sexual differentiation is willed by the Creator, and that it is a fundamental structure of the human being, a characteristic that is negated in the homosexual act."[42]

---

[40] Josephus's remark comes in *Contra Apionem*, quoted in Joseph Fitzmyer, *Romans*, Anchor Bible 33 [New York: Doubleday, 1993], 286. The *Epistle of Aristeas*, another Jewish account from the second century BC, also testifies that, with regard to unnatural sexual practices, the ancient Jews "remained aloof from these vices" (*Lettre d'Aristée à Philocrate*, no. 152, trans. A. Pelletier, Sources chrétiennes 89 [Paris: Editions du Cerf, 1962], 175; cited in Himbaza, Schenker, and Edart, *The Bible on Homosexuality*, 85).

[41] "Jesus' silence on this matter [of homosexual acts] can only be interpreted as reflecting agreement with the tradition of Israel on this point. Besides, it is highly probable that he never directly came across this question in the Jewish milieu, since, given the existing prohibition, this behavior had no social visibility" (Himbaza, Schenker, and Edart, *The Bible on Homosexuality*, 114).

[42] Himbaza, Schenker, and Edart, *The Bible on Homosexuality*, 92; see also 97–98: "The context of Rom. 1:19–23 invites us to see in this nature [to which Paul appeals in vv. 26–27] the order willed by God and seen in his creation. From

In his commentary on Romans, Aquinas, contrary to the happy determination of today's scholars who seek to evade the plain sense of these Pauline passages, adheres closely to Paul's strong and unbending language. Aquinas observes that as a sin "against nature" (*contra naturam*, as the Vulgate renders the Greek *para physin*), homosexual behavior debases us in a particularly dehumanizing way:

> If sins of the flesh are shameful, since through them man is lowered to what is bestial in him, much more so are sins against nature [*contra naturam*], through which man sinks beneath the level of the bestial. . . . [For] something is said to be against man's nature by reason of his general class, which is animal. Now it is obvious that according to the intent of nature, sexual union in animals is ordained to the act of generation; hence, every form of union from which generation cannot follow is against the nature of animal as animal. . . . The same is true of every act of intercourse from which generation cannot follow.[43]

Elsewhere in the *Summa*, Aquinas's term of choice for homoerotic acts is *deformitatis*, "deformed," since these acts fail to observe what is "suitable [*convenit*] for the human species," in that they involve sexual practices "not with the proper sex [*non debitum sexum*], as male with male or female with female, as the Apostle says in Romans 1:26–27."[44]

Paul offers another unequivocal condemnation of homosexual activity in 1 Corinthians 6:9: "Do not be deceived; neither the sexually immoral [*pornoi*], nor idolaters, nor adulterers, nor homosexuals [*malakoi oute arsenokoitai*] . . . will inherit the kingdom of God." While the RSV here collapses the two terms *malakoi* and *arsenokoitai*

---

this perspective, 'against nature' can legitimately be understood with reference to Genesis 1. . . . They [homosexual relations] are called 'against nature' because they are contrary to the plan of the Creator since they 'unite' two people of the same sex."

[43] *Super Rom* 1, lec. 8 (Larcher trans., 52). See *SCG* III, ch. 122, for the same teaching. In *ST* II-II, q. 154, a. 11, Aquinas expressly lists masturbation ("procuring ejaculation without sexual union for the sake of sexual pleasure"), bestiality ("copulating with a thing not of the same species"), and homosexual acts as examples of sins *contra naturam*.

[44] *ST* II-II, q. 154, a. 11.

into the one "homosexuals," this is for convenience's sake. Paul employs these two terms to describe the nature of the male homosexual act in somewhat graphic language. Difficult to translate, *malakos* means "soft" or "effeminate one," though here it is best rendered as "the man who desires to be penetrated." *Arsenokoitēs*, a term that Paul seems to be the first to have employed in all of Greek literature, literally means "male bedder" or "male seeder," one who beds/seeds a male. In other words, by these terms, "Paul has simply laid out the active and passive roles in a homosexual act," to quote Edart (with *arsenokoitēs* obviously corresponding to the active role and *malakos* to the passive role).[45]

There is further biblical depth to Paul's use of *arsenokoitēs*. It centers on the fact that, as "one who is knowledgeable in the Torah, Paul could not ignore the weight of [the condemnation of homosexual activity in] Leviticus 18 and 20," to quote the biblical scholar Adrien Schenker.[46] Significantly, in the Septuagint's Greek renderings of Leviticus 18:22 and 20:13, the key terms used to describe the homosexual act are *arsenos* ("male") and *koitēn* ("bed" or "sleep"), as in 20:13: "Whoever sleeps with a man [*arsenos*] as one sleeps [*koitēn*] with a woman, it is an abomination." Sticking closely to this language of the Septuagint, Paul pens the neologism *arsenokoitēs* as a way of continuing in the line of Leviticus on the gravely immoral nature of homosexual relations.[47] (The two rabbinic Talmuds do much the same thing when, in drawing upon the Hebrew text of Lev 18:22 and 20:13, they use the Hebrew phrase "to sleep with a male," *miškab zâkûr*, to signify homosexual conduct.)[48] Paul's use of *arsenokoitēs*, in other words, draws a direct allusion to Leviticus 18:22 and 20:13, and in so doing, gives a Christian echo of the Torah's censure of homosexual relations as an "abomination" (*tô'ēbâ* in Hebrew, which can be rendered either as "abomination" or as "repugnant filth").

Perhaps modern sensibilities would have preferred Paul to have distanced himself and his vision of the Christian moral life in a Marcion-like manner from the harsh tone of Leviticus, as well as from the entire Old Testament precedent. But he does not. He opts for the

---

[45] Himbaza, Schenker, and Edart, *The Bible on Homosexuality*, 78.
[46] Himbaza, Schenker, and Edart, *The Bible on Homosexuality*, 71.
[47] See Himbaza, Schenker, and Edart, *The Bible on Homosexuality*, 77.
[48] For support of the rabbinic usage, Edart cites a number of Talmud passages: b. Sanh. 54a; b. Šab. 17b; b. Sukkah 29a; y. Ber. 9:50, 13c (Himbaza, Schenker, and Edart, *The Bible on Homosexuality*, 77).

opposite approach, and no amount of gerrymandering exegesis can alter this fact. His language is severe (at least to contemporary ears) and uncompromising ("against nature," "shameless acts," "will not inherit the kingdom of God"), with no confusion of referent, such as pederasty or male prostitution, and with no exceptions, such as for homosexual orientation.

Ever the theologian obedient to the biblical witness (not to mention proponent of the natural law), Aquinas follows suit. Like Paul's, his language is stern and unbending, and he makes clear that Christian moral perfection strictly precludes homoerotic practice in any form. It is pure revisionist wishful thinking to suppose that homosexual unions can somehow satisfy the standard of Gospel morality.

As a final word on this topic, we must bear in mind that it is the conduct itself that Paul (and Aquinas after him) condemn, not the persons themselves as persons. Jesus of course provides the model for this distinction between persons and moral behavior when he says to the woman caught in adultery, "neither do I condemn you," while at the same time instructing this woman to "sin no more," thereby making clear his stance on the conduct itself of adultery (see John 8:11). We must do the same when treating the Pauline (and Thomist) position on homosexuality: "It is only homosexual acts and the desires at their origin that are condemned," Edart observes, "[since] only acts and desires to which one fully consents can be qualified as good or evil."[49]

Nor should we think Paul is singling out homosexual conduct for excessively disproportionate censure. To repeat, Paul comes down severely on all forms of *porneia*, of which homoerotic conduct is simply one (albeit attention-catching) type. As already seen, Paul's statement that "the body is not meant for *porneia*" (1 Cor 6:13) means the body is meant for no other form of sexual intimacy than that between husband and wife, in an embrace of procreative-unitive love.

The same is true for Aquinas. It is noteworthy that, in the afore-cited passage from his commentary on Romans, where he condemns homosexual conduct as especially dehumanizing on account of its making us "sink beneath the level of the bestial, of the nature of animal as animal," he adds: "The same is true of every act of intercourse from which generation cannot follow." This would include artificial contraception, to choose an example that is wide-

---

[49] Himbaza, Schenker, and Edart, *The Bible on Homosexuality*, 106.

spread among today's *Humanae Vitae* generation, not to mention all forms of autosexual practices (masturbation, pornographic viewing, sexting, etc.).

Virginity (Celibacy): The Eschatological Virtue

If we see the New Law's higher standard for sexual conduct vis-à-vis the Old Law in Paul's affirmation of the indissolubility and sacramental meaning of marriage or in the targeting of internal acts consonant with imbibing the virtue of chastity and the shunning of all forms of sexual immorality (*porneia*; *fornicatio*), we see it also and especially in that virtue that is unique to Gospel morality: virginity, the perpetual sacrifice of sexual pleasure, the state of which is called celibacy, of course. (See Paul's recommendation that all "remain single as I do" in 1 Cor 7:7–8 and Jesus's teaching on "eunuchs for the sake of the kingdom of heaven" in Matt 19:12.)

Ordering us not simply to an "earthly" good, as does the Mosaic Law, but to our ultimate, supernatural end (eternal life), the New Evangelical Law of Christ transforms human sexuality by extending its meaning and purpose beyond the carnal or earthly nature of the marital relationship to the very supernatural, glorified end of human life. As Aquinas puts it: "The New Law which derives its pre-eminence from the spiritual grace instilled into our hearts . . . is described as containing spiritual and eternal promises, which are objects of the virtues, chiefly of charity [but also of chastity and virginity]."[50]

By renouncing the earthly good of sexual pleasure, virginity/celibacy gives witness to Paul's declaration that "this world [including our bodies] in its present form is passing away" (1 Cor 7:31) and anticipates the glorified state of our bodies at the final resurrection,

---

[50] *ST* I-II, q. 107, a. 1. To be sure, chastity and virginity would in this case be infused virtues (i.e., caused by grace), since the objects of these virtues, insofar as they contain spiritual and eternal promises, formally relate to God, and "effects must needs be proportionate to their causes and principles" (I-II, q. 63, a. 3). Earlier, in I-II, q. 91, a. 5, Thomas explains: "to this (sensible and earthly good) man was directly ordained by the Old Law. Thus, at the very outset of the law, the people were invited to the earthly kingdom of the Canaanites (Ex 3:8–17). . . . But to this (our spiritual and heavenly good) man is ordained by the New Law. Thus, at the very beginning of his preaching, Christ invited men to the kingdom of heaven, saying (Mt 4:17): 'Repent, for the kingdom of heaven is at hand.'"

where men and women "neither marry nor are given in marriage" (Matt 22:30). Even if retaining its sexed design, the human body on the Last Day will yet be raised "celestial," "imperishable," "spiritual," "immortal," and with "power" and "glory," to use Paul's vocabulary in 1 Corinthians 15:40–44. Because it gives witness to the glorified state that awaits the final resurrection, virginity is sometimes called the eschatological virtue, and celibacy the eschatological state.[51]

For Aquinas, the spiritualized resurrected body means that "the soul will, to a certain extent, communicate to the body what properly belongs to itself as a spirit."[52] That is, at the final resurrection, the glory of the beatified soul will redound or overflow unto the resurrected body, so that the body will receive what Aquinas terms an "incorruptible being" (*esse incorruptibile*).[53] Part and parcel of the body's *esse incorruptibile*, Aquinas further explains, is "subtlety" (*subtilitas*), whereby the body, entirely subject to the spirit and sharing fully in the soul's spiritual enjoyment of God, will not engage in the bodily activities of eating, drinking, and sexual union, as these "serve the corruptible life."[54]

Lest one consider virginity or celibacy an affront to God's command "to be fruitful and multiply" (Gen 1:28), Aquinas links virginity (and by extension the celibate state) to this command by suggesting that the divine command implies not only physical or bodily fecundity, but spiritual fecundity as well. By devoting themselves "to

---

[51] See: Spicq, *Théologie morale*, 2:562; Pinckaers, *Sources*, 131; John Paul II, *Man and Woman He Created Them*, trans. and ed. Michael Waldstein (Boston: Pauline Books, 2006), 395 and 419 (General Audiences of December 16, 1981, and especially March 24, 1982).

[52] *ST* I, q. 97, a. 3; see also q. 98, a. 2, ad 1. As for the glorified, spiritualized, resurrected body retaining its sexed design, St. Thomas Aquinas writes: "[Humans] shall rise again of different sex. And though there be difference of sex, there will be no shame in seeing one another, since there will be no lust to invite them to shameful deeds which are the cause of shame" (*ST* Suppl., q. 81, a. 3).

[53] See *ST* III, q. 54, a. 2, ad 2, and *SCG* IV, ch. 86. See also *ST* II-II, q. 18, a. 2, ad 4. For more on all this, see Philippe-Marie Margelidon, O.P., *Les fins dernières, De la résurrection du Christ à la résurrection des morts*, 2nd ed. (Paris: Éditions Lethielleux, 2016). For more on what this *esse incorruptibile* spells in terms of the healing of our bodies, particularly in the case of those with disabilities, see my essay, "Disability, the Healing of Infirmity, and the Theological Virtue of Hope: A Thomistic Approach," *Journal of Moral Theology* 6, special issue 2 (2017): 70–111.

[54] *SCG* IV, ch. 86; see also ch. 83 and *ST* Suppl., q. 83, aa. 1–6.

the contemplation of divine things for the beauty and welfare of the entire human race," Thomas writes, those who practice virginity fulfill the *spiritual* thrust of God's command to be fruitful and multiply, as in accord with the spiritual and eternal goods to which the New Law orders us.[55]

CONCLUSION

For Thomas Aquinas the biblical theologian, the Pauline view of perfection as defining of New Testament (Evangelical) morality provides the key to understanding the essential role that the divine law (constituted of both Old and New) plays in the moral life. Law in general, on Aquinas's account, provides instruction of our proper good or end, and thus of proper moral action. What the divine law, culminating in the New Law, instructs us is that our ultimate end falls nothing short of eternal life with God, a supernatural end, and that perfection is the code of conduct that targets this end. For Paul, and Aquinas after him, perfection sets the standard of the Christian moral life—an elevated standard, indeed! Moral perfection is made possible by the gift of divine grace, in which the New Law in fact consists.

"The Apostle" was most eager to inform Christian believers as to what this perfection means in terms of sexual practice. And so, too, was the Pauline Aquinas. It means to shun sexual immorality of all types *(porneia; fornicatio)*, which follows upon exercising interior self-mastery over one's sexual thoughts and desires and loving the good for its own sake, in this instance, loving the virtue of chastity for its own sake. It means observing the principle that marriage acts as the normative good of our sexuality, that the body is meant for no other form of sexual intimacy than that between husband and wife, in an embrace of procreative-unitive love. It means to shun those sexual practices that seek pleasure as the ultimate aim and which oppose or divide in any way the procreative and unitive orderings of the marital embrace, such as adultery, remarriage after divorce, fornication, and homosexual conduct. New Law (Evangelical) morality, biblical morality, demands nothing less.

---

[55] *ST* II-II, q. 152, a. 2, ad 1. See Pinckaers, *Sources*, 458–59.

SIN AND GRACE IN THE CHURCH
ACCORDING TO PAUL AND AQUINAS

MATTHEW LEVERING
Mundelein Seminary

INTRODUCTION

Few theologians have thought about sin as much—or as insight-fully—as did St. Thomas Aquinas. Immersed in their sins, habitual sinners sometimes have difficulty perceiving the harm that they are causing to themselves and others. Saints such as Aquinas, by contrast, see it clearly. Of course, Aquinas never reflected on sin or vice to the neglect of study of grace and the life of charity. Contemporary Thomists rightly make much of the fact that Aquinas's *secunda pars* of the *Summa theologiae* begins with reflection upon beatitude and proceeds to explore life in Christ in terms of the outpouring of the Holy Spirit, who bestows upon Christians the infused virtues (theological and moral), the gifts of the Spirit, and the beatitudes, as well as the gratuitous graces.[1]

The present moment in the Church's history, however, suggests that we need to attend more carefully to Aquinas's realism about the corrupting and harmful place of sin and vice in the life of the

---

[1] See for example Servais Pinckaers, O.P., *The Sources of Christian Ethics*, trans. Mary Thomas Noble, O.P. (Washington, DC: Catholic University of America Press, 1995).

Church of Christ, the inaugurated kingdom of God.[2] In the *Summa theologiae*, Aquinas treats a vast profusion of sins and vices that afflict not only non-Christians but also, very painfully, the members of the Church. Many of these sins are mortal: they cut people off from the body of Christ because of their gravity. In the *secunda secundae*, Aquinas discusses over one hundred vices in extensive detail. He also treats Adam and Eve's original sin at some length. In the *prima secundae*, furthermore, he explores vice and sin in general, in preparation for treating the particular vices.

All this attention to sin does not detract from Aquinas's affirmation that, as the Psalmist says, "the Lord is good; his mercy endures for ever, and his faithfulness to all generations" (Ps 100:5) and the Lord "has revealed his vindication in the sight of the nations" (Ps 98:2). Aquinas is deeply attuned to the salvific gifts of law and grace, by which God overcomes sin.[3] God is continually pouring out "varieties of gifts" upon his Church, so that "to each is given the manifestation of the Spirit for the common good. To one is given through the Spirit the utterance of wisdom, . . . to another faith by the same Spirit, to another gifts of healing by the one Spirit, to another the working of miracles, to another prophecy, to another the ability to distinguish between spirits" (1 Cor 12:8–10). Yet, given the power and plenitude of the Spirit's gifts to the members of the Church— gifts that we recognize as present among us—why are there such grave sinners and horrific sins among God's people?

J. J. McCullough has recently published an online article in which he argues that "a Church whose most powerful appeal rests on transcendent claims now looks very much of this world."[4] He

---

[2] For some recent efforts to do this, see: Steven J. Jensen, *Sin: A Thomistic Psychology* (Washington, DC: Catholic University of America Press, 2018); Jensen, *Good and Evil Actions: A Journey through Saint Thomas Aquinas* (Washington, DC: Catholic University of America Press, 2010). See also my *The Betrayal of Charity: The Sins that Sabotage Divine Love* (Waco, TX: Baylor University Press, 2011). For Aquinas on the "kingdom of God," see his exposition of four meanings of the "kingdom" in his *Commentary on the Gospel of St. Matthew [Super Matt]*, trans. Paul M. Kimball (Camillus, NY: Dolorosa, 2012), 88; and see also *In IV sent.*, d. 49, q. 1, a. 2, qc. 5, in *Commentary on the Sentences Book IV*, 4 vols., trans. Beth Mortensen, ed. Jeremy Holmes and Peter Kwasniewski (Green Bay, WI: Aquinas Institute, 2018).

[3] See Thomas Aquinas, *Summa theologiae [ST]* I-II, q. 90, prol., trans. Fathers of the English Dominican Province (Westminster, MD: Christian Classics, 1981).

[4] See J. J. McCullough, "The Catholic Church Scandal Hits American Conserva-

points out: "If, as Catholics maintain, the Church's hierarchy derives its legitimacy from a transmission of spiritual authority passed down from the Apostles, then even isolated instances of malfeasance within that hierarchy can shake people's faith in this claim."[5] McCullough is rightly outraged about the terrible and sacrilegious sins that have been committed or covered up by many prelates. But his essay is off the mark in a crucial respect. He seems to think that the Catholic Church bases its claims for the truth of its transcendent spiritual authority upon the holiness of the episcopacy. In fact, this has never been even close to the case. Augustine tells his flock, "You already knew, didn't you, that bad people must be borne with in the Church of God and that schisms are to be avoided? And you surely knew before now that we have to hold out and persevere in these nets which hold both good and bad fish until we reach the final shore."[6]

In investigating Aquinas's teachings on sin and grace, I will proceed in three steps. First, I examine Aquinas's theology of the Old and New Laws.[7] Aquinas makes clear that, even though the New Law is the powerful outpouring of the Holy Spirit into our hearts, human freedom nonetheless means that the "state of the New Law"—the actual spiritual condition of Christians—will vary greatly in holiness at different periods in history, including very dark periods where falsehood and sin are prevalent. Likewise, the "state of the Old Law" varied greatly over time with respect to the spiritual condition of the people. Second, I explore Paul's commendation of the extraordinary spiritual blessings received by the Corinthian Christians. I ask how these spiritual blessings can cohere with Paul's frank exposure of the terrible sinfulness of many members of the Corinthian church. Third, I examine Aquinas's commentary on the passages in which Paul describes the sins of the members of the Corinthian church— their quarreling, jealousy, worldly wisdom, tacit approval of sexual

---

tives Hard," *National Review*, September 8, 2018, nationalreview.com/2018/09/catholic-abuse-scandal-challenge-for-american-conservatives/.

5   McCullough, "Catholic Church Scandal."

6   Augustine, "Exposition of Psalm 138 [139]," in *Essential Expositions of the Psalms by Saint Augustine*, selected and introduced by Michael Cameron, trans. Maria Boulding, O.S.B., with notes, ed. Boniface Ramsey (Hyde Park, NY: New City, 2015), 180–205, at 205.

7   For further discussion of some of these issues, see also my "Thomas Aquinas on Law and Love," *Angelicum* 94 (2017): 413–41, as well as my "Aquinas's Reception of Paul: Reading the Testaments Together," *Letter & Spirit* 11 (2016): 83–101.

immorality (incest), lawsuits against each other, and procurement of prostitutes.

I suggest that Aquinas's main contribution consists in highlighting Paul's distinction between the members of the Corinthian community who are living in accord with the Spirit and the members who, despite everything, are living in accord with the flesh. This distinction allows us to understand how a Church filled with spiritual gifts can also contain leaders who (in McCullough's words) "debase their positions through heretical beliefs or evil actions."[8] As Hans Urs von Balthasar reminds us, "The condition of fallen nature cannot simply be equated with 'the Gentiles,' nor can nature on its way toward restoration be equated with Judaism, nor can nature restored be equated with Christianity: each condition participates in all the others."[9] Christians, living under the "state of the New Law," may actually lack the New Law (the interior grace of the Holy Spirit); while the people of Israel and the Gentiles may in fact live in accordance with the New Law. The point is that the failures of professed Christians do not mean that the Holy Spirit has not been poured out at Pentecost; instead such failures mean that these Christians, separating themselves interiorly from Christ's body, tragically have chosen to live according to the flesh rather than according to the Spirit.

AQUINAS ON THE OLD (MOSAIC) LAW AND THE NEW LAW

Because sin obscures the light of natural law, God revealed the basic contents of the natural law to Israel at Mount Sinai, in the Decalogue. In addition, God gave Israel other laws to govern its moral, ceremonial, and judicial life. These laws served God's pedagogical preparation of his messianic people.

In Jesus Christ, then, we find the culmination of all law given to

---

[8] McCullough, "Catholic Church Scandal."

[9] Hans Urs von Balthasar, *Theo-Drama: Theological Dramatic Theory*, vol. 2, *The Dramatis Personae: Man in God*, trans. Graham Harrison (San Francisco: Ignatius Press, 1990), 13. He adds that "at most one could say that each of the three theological exponents of mankind predominantly represents one of these conditions" (ibid.).

humans: the New Law. Aquinas explains the New Law by reference to biblical prophecies such as Jeremiah 31:33, where God proclaims: "This is the covenant which I will make with the house of Israel after those days, says the Lord: I will put my law within them, and I will write it upon their hearts; and I will be their God, and they shall be my people." Similarly, God tells Israel through the prophet Ezekiel: "A new heart I will give you, and a new spirit I will put within you; and I will take out of your flesh the heart of stone and give you a heart of flesh. And I will put my spirit within you, and cause you to walk in my statutes and be careful to observe my ordinances" (Ezek 36:26–27). These promises are better than the written Law given through Moses because God makes clear that he will interiorize the Law and give his people the will to obey it through his indwelling Spirit.

The New Law is not only an interior law, of course. In a secondary way, the New Law reflects the fact that the people of God "needed to be instructed" about the grace of the Holy Spirit and the use of that grace, and so the New Law contains instructions—both oral and written—about what the people of God should believe and do.[10] Without in any way discounting the writings of the New Testament and the teachings of the Church, Aquinas nonetheless affirms that "the New Law is in the first place a law that is inscribed on our hearts."[11]

Aquinas notes that the Mosaic Law served not only to teach Israel holiness but also to show Israel its own inability to obey God's law adequately without the aid of divine grace. The Mosaic Law undermined human pride by showing that even a person who knows the divine law is unable to act upon his or her knowledge in an adequate manner without God's help. Many Israelites therefore prayed for God's grace and had faith in the future savior to come. In Aquinas's view, the priests and prophets often had an explicit faith in this messianic savior, whereas the regular people, through participation in the symbolic rites (such as the Passover lamb), often had an implicit faith.[12] Either implicit or explicit faith fully opened up the grace of the Holy Spirit to the Israelites, and so in this way, the "New Law" was present prior to Christ's coming.[13]

---

[10] *ST* I-II, q. 106, a. 1.

[11] *ST* I-II, q. 106, a. 1.

[12] See *ST* I-II, q. 102, a. 4, ad 4.

[13] See *ST* I-II, q. 106, a. 1, ad 3.

As Aquinas points out, the greatness of the Mosaic Law is found in its "chief intention," which is "to establish man in friendship with God" by making human beings like God in goodness.[14] He cites such precepts as: Leviticus 19:2, "You shall be holy; for I the Lord your God am holy"; Leviticus 19:18, "You shall love your neighbor as yourself"; and Deuteronomy 6:4, "You shall love the Lord your God with all your heart, and with all your soul, and with all your might." Such precepts are greatly helpful because, although "human reason could not go astray in the abstract, as to the universal principles of the natural law," human reason nonetheless, "through being habituated to sin, . . . became obscured in the point of things to be done in detail."[15]

Without doubt, the people of Israel, both individually and collectively, often habitually disobeyed the Mosaic Law. Due to such sins, a civil war soon split the people of Israel into two kingdoms, and the northern kingdom was sent into exile by the Assyrians in 722, never to be reinstated. The Babylonians sent the southern kingdom into exile in 587. The return of the Jews to Jerusalem later that century did not accomplish the promised restoration of the divine presence. The greatest heroes of Israel, such as David and Solomon, were in many ways notorious sinners; and Moses, preeminent above all other prophets and leaders of Israel, was punished by God for an act of pride.

Given the goodness of the Mosaic Law, and also given (as seen in Hebrews 11) the availability of grace to those who believed, how is it that even Israel's heroes committed grave sins? How is it that the prophet Isaiah could conclude with regard to God's people that "justice is far from us" and that "our transgressions are with us, and we know our iniquities: transgressing, and denying the Lord, and turning away from following our God, speaking oppression and revolt, conceiving and uttering from the heart lying words" (Isa 59:9, 12–13)? Like Isaiah, the Psalmist portrays God looking down upon his creatures and finding that, even in Israel, "they have all gone astray, they are all alike corrupt; there is none that does good, no, not one" (Ps 14:3). Despite the value of the Mosaic Law, the situation of the Israelites was often all too close to the situation of the uninstructed Gentiles in the days of Noah, when "God saw the earth, and

[14] *ST* I-II, q. 99, a. 2.
[15] *ST* I-II, q. 99, a. 2, ad 2.

behold, it was corrupt; for all flesh had corrupted their way upon the earth" (Gen 6:12).

Does Aquinas think that the New Law improved things much? He contends that, in its primary sense, as the grace of the Holy Spirit, the (interior) New Law of Christ is what has caused the salvation of all people who have ever been saved. This includes people from all times and places.[16] In a certain sense, therefore, the coming of Christ did not "change" things: by the grace of the Holy Spirit, implicit or explicit faith had united people to Christ even prior to Christ's coming.

Yet, Aquinas does think that the historical coming of Christ and the outpouring of the Spirit at Pentecost changed things. He argues that it was fitting that the grace of the Holy Spirit not be given abundantly "until sin, which is an obstacle to grace, had been cast out of man through the accomplishment of his redemption by Christ."[17] In Aquinas's view, this temporal delay in the abundant outpouring of the Spirit is the meaning of John 7:39, where the Evangelist observes that "as yet the Spirit had not been given, because Jesus was not yet glorified." In Isaiah 44:3, God promises that "I will pour my Spirit upon your descendants." This promise was fulfilled on the day of Pentecost.

Aquinas argues that it is fitting that God did not institute the fullness of the New Law (which he calls the "state of the New Law") from the outset, even though some people shared in the New Law through grace from the outset. Under the Mosaic Law, God's people learned how deeply sinful they were and how much they needed God's grace. This experience was necessary for the people of God. Without this experience, the people of God—both then and now—would not fully have known how much Christ was needed and would not have been able to turn as fervently to Christ. The people of God would also not have been able to grow over time toward Christ, through a succession of stages as befits a truly historical people. Aquinas takes this to be the central meaning of Galatians 3:24, where Paul states that "the law was our custodian [or pedagogue] until Christ came,

---

[16] See *ST* I-II, q. 106, a. 4, ad 2: "The state of mankind does not vary according to diversity of place, but according to succession of time. Hence the New Law avails for all places, but not for all times: although at all times there have been some persons belonging to the New Testament."

[17] *ST* I-II, q. 106, a. 3.

that we might be justified by faith." He also points to Paul's teaching about how the Mosaic Law revealed the extent of sin: "Law came in, to increase the trespass" (Rom 5:20).[18]

The abundant outpouring of the Spirit at Pentecost certainly improved the condition of the world, therefore. Nonetheless, Aquinas is well aware that certain epochs of Christian history are more devout—more filled with grace and more united to Christ—than other epochs. Again, whereas the "New Law" is present in all historical time periods (as the interior grace of the Spirit), the "state of the New Law" begins only after Christ's coming. In itself, this "state" is as perfect as earthly life can be. This is so because we simply cannot be united to God more perfectly than we are by the incarnate Lord who is now interceding for us at the right hand of the Father and who sends his Spirit upon us.[19] But, as noted above, the "state of the New Law"—the time of the Church—is nonetheless subject to much spiritual variation, just as was the "state of the Old Law." Aquinas explains that "the state of the New Law is subject to change with regard to various places, times, and persons, according as the grace of the Holy Spirit dwells in man more or less perfectly."[20] The spiritual ups and downs that we see in the history of the people of Israel are therefore present also in the history of the Church.

This explains why Aquinas, believing that Jesus has inaugurated his eschatological kingdom by pouring out his Spirit, did not lose his faith because of the monstrous sins of so many Christians of his day, including that of his own parents, who tried to tempt him to abandon his Dominican vocation by sending a prostitute to his room. Consider for instance Aquinas's discussion of the sin of simony. Simony means the intentional buying or selling of something spiritual. It takes its name from the attempted sin of Simon Magus in Acts 8:20. In treating simony, Aquinas cites the writings of Popes Gregory VII, Innocent IV, Paschal II, and Urban II against this sin. As this list of medieval popes shows, Aquinas knew all too well that the clergy and the bishops, despite being called to a state of life devoted to total service to Christ's flock, had been fleecing Christ's flock for monetary gain and had been accumulating power in the Church by means of vile bribery. Aquinas deems that such priests and bishops

---

[18] These two passages are cited in *ST* I-II, q. 106, a. 3.

[19] Cited in *ST* I-II, q. 106, a. 4.

[20] *ST* I-II, q. 106, a. 4.

lack the grace of their office, even though their ordination is valid. Although men who have bought their ecclesiastical position are validly ordained, they lack the right to exercise their office. Aquinas says all this despite knowing that in some (even many) dioceses, the bishop and the entire upper clergy secured their positions by simony. Imagine entire dioceses, archdioceses, and even the bishop of Rome himself being set in place by simoniacal means (or worse), and therefore lacking the grace to shepherd and govern God's flock. Aquinas is aware that such situations are likely to have occurred. In such a condition, when the Church is being led by "fierce wolves" (Acts 20:29), the spiritual situation of both the clergy and laity will be dire, easily rivaling Israel's worst days.

Aquinas affirms that "all external acts that are incompatible with righteousness, peace, and spiritual joy, are in opposition to the kingdom of God."[21] But Aquinas also emphasizes that the New Law is sufficient in every way. In terms of external acts, the New Law ensures that we receive grace by means of the sacraments, which unite us to Christ and enable us to receive the saving power of his Cross and resurrection. Aquinas adds that "the sermon, which Our Lord delivered on the mountain, contains the whole process of forming the life of a Christian."[22] Again, however, if the New Law is so perfectly suited for our needs, why is the Church often in such bad shape? To respond further to this question, let me turn to the letters of Paul, and specifically to the Corinthian correspondence (especially 1 Corinthians).

Paul's Letters to the Corinthians

Extraordinary Spiritual Gifts

Greeting "those sanctified in Christ Jesus, called to be saints" (1 Cor 1:2), Paul describes the spiritual gifts that the Corinthians have received in Christ. He tells the Corinthians, "I give thanks to God always for you because of the grace of God which was given you in Christ Jesus, that in every way you were enriched in him with all

---

[21] *ST* I-II, q. 108, a. 1, ad 1.
[22] *ST* I-II, q. 108, a. 3.

speech and all knowledge . . . so that you are not lacking in any spiritual gift" (1 Cor 1:4–5, 7). The Corinthians enjoy the "fellowship" of God's "Son, Jesus Christ our Lord" (1 Cor 1:9). They are "God's temple," in whom "God's Spirit dwells" (1 Cor 3:16). Paul informs the Corinthians that, in fact: "All things are yours, whether Paul or Apollos or Cephas or the world or life or death or the present or the future, all are yours; and you are Christ's; and Christ is God's" (1 Cor 3:21–23). Furthermore, in the Lord's Supper, the Corinthians partake in Christ and become "one body" in Christ (1 Cor 10:16–17). According to Paul, the very bodies of the Corinthians are "members of Christ" (1 Cor 6:15), united to his glorified body. In faith and baptism, the Corinthians have been "washed," "sanctified," and "justified" in Christ and by his Spirit (1 Cor 6:11).

In Christ, therefore, the Corinthians have received the following marks of the inaugurated kingdom: justification, sanctification, the grace of God, all knowledge, every spiritual gift, fellowship with the Son of God, the indwelling Holy Spirit, all earthly things, the status of being God's Temple, participation in Christ's body and blood, membership in Christ's glorified body, and the status of being "one body" in Christ.

Egregious Sins

Yet, the sins of many members of the Corinthian church take up the bulk of 1 Corinthians. Paul mentions that he has heard that "there is quarreling" (1 Cor 1:11) among the Corinthian Christians. The quarreling is rooted in factionalism: some say that they follow Paul, whereas others follow Cephas or Apollos or Christ.

Paul also informs the Corinthians that "there is jealousy and strife among you" (1 Cor 3:3). He warns that all who exhibit such jealousy are "behaving like ordinary men" and are "of the flesh" (1 Cor 3:3). So long as they are "puffed up in favor of one [apostle] against another" (1 Cor 4:6), they have failed to realize that the apostles are merely stewards of Christ.

Paul adds that some of the Corinthian Christians have deceived themselves by imagining themselves to be "wise in this age" (1 Cor 3:18). He cautions against such worldly wisdom, which is unable to perceive the power of the "foolishness of God" that is manifested by Christ's Cross (1 Cor 1:25). Worldly wisdom prevents people from understanding what makes for true status in the inaugurated kingdom of God: self-sacrificial charity. In terms of worldly status, the apostles cannot but appear to be "fools" and "a spectacle to the world," mere itinerant fanatics (1 Cor 4:9–10).

Furthermore, some of the Corinthian Christians are engaging in sexual immorality. Even worse, the whole Corinthian church appears to be supporting this immorality rather than condemning it. Paul puts them to shame: "And you are arrogant! Ought you not rather to mourn?" (1 Cor 5:2). Among other things, Paul fears that members of the Corinthian community have been soliciting prostitutes. Reminding the Corinthian Christians that their bodies are Christ's members, Paul asks rhetorically: "Shall I therefore take the members of Christ and make them members of a prostitute?" (1 Cor 6:15).

Not surprisingly, given the above sins, the Corinthian Christians are also suing each other in Roman (pagan) courts of law. Deploring this practice as unworthy of followers of Christ, Paul urges repentance and renewed appreciation of Christ's gifts. He concludes: "You are not your own; you were bought with a price. So glorify God in your body" (1 Cor 6:19–20).

The combination of internal wrangling and the community's seeming approval of sexual immorality leads Paul to issue a strong warning about the kingdom of God: grave and unrepentant sinners, no matter whether they claim to be following Christ, will not inherit the kingdom of God. Paul tells the Corinthians "not to associate with any one who bears the name of brother if he is guilty of immorality or greed, or is an idolater, reviler, drunkard, or robber" (1 Cor 5:11). Someone who "bears the name" of a Christian but who does such things without repentance, has in fact rejected the gifts of God. Paul observes: "Do not be deceived; neither the immoral, nor idolaters, nor adulterers, nor homosexuals, nor thieves, nor the greedy, nor drunkards, nor revilers, nor robbers will inherit the kingdom of God" (1 Cor 6:9–10).

At the same time, Paul exhorts the Corinthian Christians to remember the gifts they have received. After listing the actions that cut off a person from inheriting the kingdom of God, Paul reminds his audience: "And such were some of you. But you were washed, you were sanctified, you were justified in the name of the Lord Jesus Christ and in the Spirit of our God" (1 Cor 6:11). Paul urges the Corinthian Christians to remember that he is their "father in Christ Jesus through the gospel" and he asks them to "be imitators of me"

(1 Cor 4:15–16) in living the Gospel.

Paul goes on to compare the Christian to an athlete. We have to run the race of life by living in accordance with Christ's extraordinary gifts. If we slacken and depart from these gifts, we separate ourselves from Christ. The fault is not in the gifts themselves, which are powerful, but rather the problem is our choice to turn away. As Paul points out, athletes exercise "self-control in all things" merely in order that they might win "a perishable wreath" (1 Cor 9:25). Christians, then, must exercise self-control in order to win the "imperishable" prize (1 Cor 9:25) of everlasting glory. Paul's point is that, if Christians relax and seek to live according to the flesh, then like an out-of-shape athlete, they will be "disqualified" rather than attaining to the goal of Christian life (1 Cor 9:27).

Repentance and Forgiveness

Paul is stern toward unrepentant sinfulness, but to the repentant Christian he offers a renewed embrace. At the outset of his second letter, he states that, "if any one has caused pain, he has caused it not to me, but in some measure . . . to you all" (2 Cor 2:5). The sin of one Christian wounds the entire Church. Nonetheless, mercy is the proper response of the Christian community to a repentant believer. Paul urges the Corinthian believers to "forgive and comfort him [the repentant believer], or he may be overwhelmed by excessive sorrow" (2 Cor 2:7). He adds an even stronger, more personal exhortation: "I beg you to reaffirm your love for him" (2 Cor 2:8). Paul rejoices in the divine mercy. He proclaims that "in Christ God was reconciling the world to himself, not counting their trespasses against them, and entrusting to us the message of reconciliation" (2 Cor 5:19).

At the same time, he implores the Corinthians: "We beg you on behalf of Christ, be reconciled to God" (2 Cor 5:20). After all, despite the outpouring of divine forgiveness in Christ, it remains possible "to accept the grace of God in vain" (2 Cor 6:1). Even after accepting the gifts of God, Christians can choose to live according to the world rather than according to the Spirit. Paul therefore exhorts the Corinthians to seek holiness diligently, so as to respond appropriately to the gifts of God: "Since we have these promises, beloved, let us cleanse ourselves from every defilement of body and spirit, and make holiness perfect in the fear of God" (2 Cor 7:1).

AQUINAS ON GOD'S GIFTS AND CHRISTIAN SINFULNESS IN 1 CORINTHIANS

The letters of Paul to the Corinthians show that the Corinthian Christians have received extraordinary gifts from God but remain plagued by quarreling, jealousy, worldly wisdom, sexual immorality, lawsuits against each other, and procurement of prostitutes. How does Aquinas understand this situation, in which a people who should be holy are in many instances failing to be so, despite the amazing outpouring of the Spirit? Recall that Paul prefaces his sharp critique of the Corinthian Christians' jealousy and factionalism by telling them: "I . . . could not address you as spiritual men, but as men of the flesh, as infants in Christ" (1 Cor 3:1). Yet, Paul affirms that the Corinthian Christians "are not lacking in any spiritual gift" (1 Cor 1:7). How do these two statements fit together?

Commenting upon Paul's statement that the Corinthians "are not lacking in any spiritual gift," Aquinas suggests that Paul means that "various persons among them enjoyed all the Charismatic graces."[23] The members of the church have diverse gifts. They are united by charity, and in this way share in each other's gifts. Aquinas has in view 1 Corinthians 12, where (as noted above) Paul affirms that "there are varieties of gifts": "To each is given the manifestation of the Spirit for the common good. To one is given through the Spirit the utterance of wisdom, and to another the utterance of knowledge according to the same Spirit" (1 Cor 12:4, 7–8). Aquinas emphasizes that the Corinthian church truly possesses all the gifts Paul ascribes to it, but he makes clear that the gift-bearing community is constituted by the members who are united by charity.

Unfortunately, there are many professed Christians who lack charity. According to Aquinas, it is to this latter group that Paul addresses severe criticisms while urging repentance. They are still "men of the flesh" (1 Cor 3:1). Because they have turned away from God's gifts, their minds are "unspiritual," "of the flesh," and like "ordinary men" (1 Cor 2:14; 3:3). Commenting on their failure to

---

[23] Thomas Aquinas, *Super I Cor* 1, lec. 2 (Marietti no. 15), trans. F. R. Larcher, O.P., B. Mortensen, and D. Keating, in Aquinas, *Commentary on the Letters of Saint Paul to the Corinthians*, ed. J. Mortensen and E. Alarcón (Lander, WY: Aquinas Institute for the Study of Sacred Doctrine, 2012), p. 7 (*Super I Cor* = pp. 1–396). I quote only from Aquinas's commentary, not from the text of Peter of Tarentaise that has traditionally filled the gap in Aquinas's text.

grasp the things of the Spirit, Aquinas cites Romans 8:5, "For those who live according to the flesh set their minds on the things of the flesh, but those who live according to the Spirit set their minds on the things of the Spirit."[24]

Exploring the roots of the quarreling and jealousy among the Corinthian Christians, Aquinas points out that a jealous person wants another person's good and tries to take it, thereby producing strife. Jealousy and strife are characteristic marks of persons who live according to "the flesh" (1 Cor 3:3), for while spiritual goods can be shared, earthly goods are less easily shared. In this regard Aquinas comments that "material goods . . . cannot be possessed by many persons at the same time," whereas "spiritual goods, by which spiritual persons are attracted, can be possessed by several persons at the same time; consequently, one's good is not another's loss."[25]

No wonder, then, that Paul tells these members of the Corinthian church that he could not address them as "spiritual men." This is a heavy charge, given that Paul has just said that "the unspiritual man does not receive the gifts of the Spirit of God, for they are folly to him" (1 Cor 2:14). Aquinas comments that it is not surprising that Paul describes such persons as "ordinary men" (1 Cor 3:3), because, indeed, "the affections of human reason are moved by the things of the flesh, unless man's spirit is raised above man by the Spirit of God."[26] As fallen human beings, we need divine help to raise our minds above the material things that attract us. If the Corinthian Christians love power rather than God, then they will abuse God's gifts by forming factions.

Is it not appropriate, however, that Christians should "boast of men who are ministers of God," great and powerful leaders in the Church?[27] In reflecting upon this, Aquinas points out that God does not need human beings in order for God to be approached. The least powerful Christian can approach God directly in prayer, without needing a human minister's intervention. As Aquinas says, "Christ's faithful have access to God by faith."[28] In fact, therefore, leaders have no more access to God than does the poorest, simplest person in the

---

[24] *Super I Cor* 3, lec. 1 (Marietti no. 127; p. 49).
[25] *Super I Cor* 3, lec. 1 (Marietti no. 129; p. 49).
[26] *Super I Cor* 3, lec. 1 (Marietti no. 130; p. 49).
[27] *Super I Cor* 3, lec. 1 (Marietti no. 133; p. 50).
[28] *Super I Cor* 3, lec. 1 (Marietti no. 133; p. 50).

community. According to Aquinas, Paul sought to instill this very point. Paul tells the Corinthians: "I was with you in weakness and in much fear and trembling; and my speech and my message were not in plausible words of wisdom, but in demonstration of the Spirit and of power, that your faith might not rest in the wisdom of men but in the power of God" (1 Cor 2:3–5). Along these same lines, in discussing 1 Corinthians 3:6–7, Aquinas highlights the fact—taught by Paul— that "inasmuch as Paul planted and Apollo watered, they were but ministers of God, having nothing but what they received from God; and they worked only from without, God working within."[29]

Obviously, Paul is among the most important of the first Christians, and Paul was a uniquely privileged witness of the risen Christ. Yet, as Aquinas says, Paul emphasizes that he has "nothing but what [he] received from God"; and Paul warns that he is not "important and great" in any way that should lead anyone to glorify him.[30] God uses Paul as a minister, but God does the interior work. Aquinas observes, "God is independent and great by himself: for an action is not attributed to the instrument, which a minister is, but to the principal cause."[31] The point is this: the members of the Corinthian church who, in their factional jealousy, have their eyes fixed upon power and authority in the Church are not *interiorly* members of Christ, even though they are baptized Christians. Despite God's gifts to them, they continue to think and live in a worldly fashion.

Aquinas draws a close connection between quarreling, jealousy, and worldly wisdom. In 1 Corinthians 3:18–19, Paul states: "If any one among you thinks that he is wise in this age, let him become a fool that he may become wise. For the wisdom of this world is folly with God." What does Paul mean by "the wisdom of this world"? In answer, Aquinas explains that this kind of wisdom arrives only at knowledge of this world, by contrast to the true wisdom, which rises to God through reflection upon the things of this world. Those who are worldly-wise see the causal structure of this world, in which power and wealth are important. But they do not perceive God operative in and through created causes. Since they see only the empirical, they have no knowledge of the work of the Holy Spirit or of the power of the risen Christ. For this reason, their (worldly) wisdom is,

---

[29] *Super I Cor* 3, lec. 1 (Marietti no. 137; p. 51).
[30] *Super I Cor* 3, lec. 1 (Marietti no. 137; p. 51).
[31] *Super I Cor* 3, lec. 1 (Marietti no. 137; p. 51).

in God's eyes, mere "folly" (1 Cor 3:19).

In 1 Corinthians 3:19–20, Paul warns the worldly-wise by quoting Job 5:13 and Psalm 94:11: "For it is written, 'He catches the wise in their craftiness,' and again, 'The Lord knows that the thoughts of the wise are futile.'" Aquinas expounds the first passage (Job 5:13) by remarking that, when people make plans that go against God's plan, God ultimately "frustrates them and fulfills his own plan."[32] The wicked members of the Corinthian church, therefore, will not derail God's plan. Their thoughts are "futile" because, in their jealous factionalism, they suppose that the ministers of God matter most. In fact, it is *Christ* who matters most. True power is found in imitating and sharing in Christ's self-sacrificial love. Paul tells the Corinthian Christians that "all things are yours, whether Paul or Apollos or Cephas or the world or life or death or the present or the future" (1 Cor 3:21–22). But they will be able to understand this only if they have charity. To turn away from worldly wisdom, then, is to realize that no worldly power, if it is outside Christ and God, can ultimately count. Worldly Christians can never realize this, and therefore they become involved in all sorts of strife as they seek to increase their power.

In 1 Corinthians 5:1, Paul accuses a member of the Corinthian congregation of having sexual relations "with his father's wife." Aquinas approaches this situation in light of his view that the Corinthian church was divided between people who were living in accord with the flesh (or the world) and people who were living in accord with the Spirit. He first discusses incest as a grave sin. The "father's wife" is the son's mother or stepmother, forbidden as a sexual partner to the son by Leviticus 18:8, and even forbidden "among pagans," Paul says (1 Cor 5:1). On this basis, Aquinas attends to Paul's correction of the Corinthian church: "And you are arrogant! Ought you not rather to mourn? Let him who has done this be removed from among you" (1 Cor 5:2).

Aquinas identifies three points here. First, not only the man but also the whole Corinthian church—insofar as it tacitly allowed the man to go on with his incest while remaining in the church—must repent. The Corinthian Christians who went along with this situation are not "innocent as compared with the sinner."[33] Second, the

---

[32] *Super I Cor* 3, lec. 3 (Marietti no. 180; p. 67).
[33] *Super I Cor* 5, lec. 1 (Marietti no. 232; p. 88).

injustice of the Corinthian community is manifest inasmuch as it failed to "mourn" a grave crime committed by one of its own. Third, the Corinthian community bears guilt for failing to judge the man's actions and remove him from the community. Allowing grave sinners to continue about their business does not show compassion or mercy; rather, it shows simply that the community has neither a proper sense of justice nor a proper sense of mercy. Correcting a grave sinner is a merciful act in light of the harm done by the sinner as well as the prospect of divine punishment. It is also a merciful act with respect to others who might otherwise be tempted to sin in similar ways.

Aquinas thinks that the punishment Paul proposes for the sinner—that the man should be delivered "to Satan for the destruction of the flesh, that his spirit may be saved in the day of the Lord Jesus" (1 Cor 5:5)—may well be a formal excommunication of the kind practiced in Aquinas's day (as very occasionally in our own).[34] Whatever the case, it is clear that Paul expects his command to be obeyed by the Corinthian believers at their next assembly. Since this is so, Aquinas reasons that Paul must believe that the worldly members of the Corinthian community—the ones who would favor the sinner—are not in the majority.

The Corinthian Christians' lawsuits against each other further exhibit their worldliness. Aquinas lists four grounds for why their recourse to secular law courts is embarrassing, beginning with their failure to recognize the power of the Spirit, and ending with the opportunity they thereby give to pagan judges wishing to criticize and confound Christians. When discussing their lawsuits, Paul complains: "If then you have such cases, why do you lay them before those who are least esteemed by the Church? . . . Can it be that there is no man among you wise enough to decide between members of the brotherhood, but brother goes to law against brother, and that before unbelievers?" (1 Cor 6:4–6). Commenting on this passage, Aquinas supposes that Paul is suggesting that there are indeed wise men among the Corinthian Christians. The worldly members of the Corinthian church should therefore have appealed to these wiser Christian brethren rather than going to a pagan court. Instead

---

[34] Rather oddly, Aquinas also thinks that it could be evidence of the apostles' power over the demons. Given that the apostles could "cast out demons" (Matt 10:8), he supposes that the apostles had power to use the demons to purge the wicked of their wickedness.

of laying their lawsuits before people who are "least esteemed by the Church [Aquinas's Vulgate translation of 1 Cor 6:4 reads *contemptibiles, qui sunt in Ecclesia*]," they should have taken their cases to fellow Christians who merit esteem. Aided by the Vulgate's mistranslation, Aquinas holds that Paul here reiterates the distinction between Corinthian Christians who live according to the Spirit and Corinthian Christians who live according to the flesh.

Urging Corinthian believers to shun sex with prostitutes, Paul exhorts: "Do you not know that your body is a temple of the Holy Spirit within you, which you have from God?" (1 Cor 6:19). Commenting on this passage, Aquinas notes that "anyone in whom the Holy Spirit exists is called a temple of God."[35] It follows that Paul is speaking specifically to the Corinthian Christians who are in fact indwelt by the Spirit. After all, the Corinthian Christians who are fornicating with prostitutes have lost charity and have lost the indwelling Spirit. In short, Aquinas again appeals to the difference between the Corinthian Christians who have cooperated with God's gifts and those who have turned away from God's gifts.

CONCLUSION

Commenting on 2 Corinthians 6:1—where Paul says that "we entreat you not to accept the grace of God in vain"—Aquinas argues that the meaning is: "Let not the reception of grace be useless and vain for you, which it is when a person does not perceive the fruit of the grace he received."[36] This twofold fruit is the remission of sins (justification) and the elevation to a life of grace that leads to glory (sanctification). The implied premise of Paul's statement, of course, is that, when the Corinthians received the Gospel and were baptized, this did not mean that all of them were securely fastened on the path of salvation. On the contrary, they could still turn away from God's gifts. Aquinas remarks along these lines that "whoever does not use the grace he has received for avoiding sin and obtaining eternal life,

---

[35] *Super I Cor* 6, lec. 3 (Marietti no. 309; p. 116).

[36] Aquinas, *Super II Cor* 6, lec. 1 (Marietti no. 204; p. 490 [*Super II Cor* = pp. 401–631 in *Commentary on the Letters of Saint Paul to the Corinthians*, trans. Larcher]).

receives the grace of God in vain."[37] Were it not possible to misuse or neglect the powerful grace of the Holy Spirit in Christ's inaugurated kingdom, then Paul would not have urged his flock to hold "fast to the word of life" and to "work out your own salvation with fear and trembling" (Phil 2:12, 16).

As it stands, members of the community have fallen away from the grace of Christ. Thus, Paul tells some Corinthian Christians, "mend your ways" (2 Cor 13:11). Paul warns all the Corinthian believers: "Examine yourselves, to see whether you are holding to your faith. Test yourselves" (2 Cor 13:5). Those who fall away, however, cannot negate the goodness of those who cooperate with the gifts of God. In this vein, Paul praises the Corinthians as "a letter from Christ delivered by us, written not with ink but with the Spirit of the living God, not on tablets of stone but on the tablets of human hearts" (2 Cor 3:3). Rejoicing in the Corinthian Christians who cooperate with God's gifts, Paul gives "thanks to God always for you because of the grace of God which was given you in Christ Jesus, that in every way you were enriched in him with all speech and all knowledge—even as the testimony to Christ was confirmed among you—so that you are not lacking in any spiritual gift" (1 Cor 1:4–7).

How, then, would Paul have responded to McCullough's concerns that "a Church whose most powerful appeal rests on transcendent claims now looks very much of this world"? Paul would have certainly agreed that many members of the Corinthian community have a worldly understanding of what "power" is. Their lack of concern for sexual immorality in their church shows their worldly wisdom. But Paul would not have agreed that the Corinthian church as such, no matter how bad, was "of this world." Paul's awareness that there are professed Christians who are "swollen with conceit, lovers of pleasure rather than lovers of God, holding the form of religion but denying the power of it" (2 Tim 3:4–5) does not mean that he doubts the power of Christ and the Spirit "in the household of God, which is the Church of the living God, the pillar and bulwark of the truth" (2 Tim 3:15).

To put the matter in Aquinas's terminology, the difference between the state of the Old Law and the state of the New Law of Christ is not necessarily that, in every epoch of the state of the New Law (the inaugurated kingdom), there will be more holy people, per-

---

[37] *Super II Cor* 6, lec. 1 (Marietti no. 204; p. 490).

centage-wise, than there were in the state of the Old Law (or even among the Gentiles). No doubt, God's gifting is more apparent now that Christ has come and now that the Spirit has been poured out abundantly, in a manner that offers to the whole world freedom from idolatry and sin. But resistance to God's gifting is also, in certain ways, now more evident. Although such resistance was always present, sinful actions have, if anything, become more destructive. Jesus himself wondered whether, when he comes in glory, he will "find faith on earth" (Luke 18:8).

Jesus Christ envisioned the period after his death and resurrection (and prior to his coming in glory) as an apocalyptically heightened period. On the one hand, many people will not notice anything different about this period. Along these lines, Jesus remarks: "As it was in the days of Noah, so will it be in the days of the Son of man. They ate, they drank, they married, they were given in marriage, until the day when Noah entered the ark" (Luke 17:26–27). History will go on as normal in many ways: there will be "wars and rumors of wars," and "nation will rise against nation, and kingdom against kingdom, and there will be famines and earthquakes in various places" (Matt 24:6–7). All this is how life on earth has always been. During the time of the inaugurated kingdom—a time whose duration "no one knows" (Matt 24:36)—"many will fall away, and betray one another, and hate one another. And many false prophets will arise and lead many astray. And because wickedness is multiplied, most men's love will grow cold" (Matt 24:10–12). Anyone with a minimal knowledge of history knows that Jesus is not here describing something yet to come.

On the other hand, in this apocalyptic age, there will also be those who, under persecution and temptation, cleave to Jesus and to his self-sacrificial love. Jesus tells the Pharisees, "behold, the kingdom of God is in your midst" (Luke 17:21). The kingdom of God is present in those who, moved by the Spirit, humbly repent (Luke 18:14). The kingdom of God is present in those who "receive the kingdom of God like a child" (Luke 18:17)—namely, with childlike dependence upon the living God, by contrast to the worldly wisdom that seems more practical to those who live according to the flesh.

Urging believers not to "grow weary or fainthearted," the letter to the Hebrews points out that, in following Jesus to the Cross, they have "not yet resisted to the point of shedding [their] blood" (Heb 12:3–4). We must not give up due to our failures or be scandalized due to others' failures, since God in Christ is "rich in mercy" (Eph 2:4), and since, as Paul tells the Corinthians, "love bears all things, believes all things, hopes all things, endures all things" (1 Cor 13:7). The person who truly loves, Aquinas observes, "tolerates all the shortcomings of the neighbor" and does so "without disquiet."[38]

The Book of Revelation depicts the time after Christ's death and resurrection as a time of spiritual struggle, in which a particular church (or particular Christians) may "have the name of being alive" while in fact being spiritually "dead" (Rev 3:1). The risen Christ rejoices in the churches where believers "hold fast my name" even under persecution (Rev 2:13), and he will never abandon his Church. But the risen Christ is also aware that some Christians "have abandoned the love" for Christ that they "had at first" (Rev 2:4). The Book of Revelation depicts history as an ongoing struggle, even in the hearts of Christians, between pride (and its violence, lust, ambition, and greed) and self-sacrificial love.

In sum: Christ has conquered, but nonetheless, as members of the Church, we must still wait patiently for the final fall of the human "Babylon," the idolatrous city to which even many professed Christians—including we ourselves when we sin gravely—choose to belong, neglecting the wondrous love, mercy, and justice of Christ. The Book of Revelation provides the image of the blasphemous "beast" (an image of political and economic power) that "was allowed to make war on the saints and to conquer them": "And authority was given it over every tribe and people and tongue and nation, and all who dwell on earth will worship it, every one whose name has not been written before the foundation of the world in the book of life of the Lamb that was slain" (Rev 13:7–8). Aquinas and Paul (and Jesus Christ) recognize that many professed Christians will in fact worship this "beast."

Yet, as Aquinas says, every believer can fulfill the requirements of Gospel charity "by imploring the help of God; by striving to enter by the narrow door of perfect virtue; and by being wary lest we be led astray by evil influences."[39] Speaking of the Church founded upon Peter, Christ assures us that "the gates of Hades shall not prevail against it" (Matt 16:18). But, although the Catholic Church is

---

[38] *Super I Cor 13*, lec. 2 (p. 296). The Latin text reads "absque turbatione sustinet omnes defectus proximorum."

[39] *ST* I-II, q. 108, a. 3.

not Antichrist, it contains many members—including ourselves all too frequently—who are living according to the flesh rather than according to the Spirit. On behalf of ourselves and our fellow Catholics, let us therefore appeal ever more urgently to our Lord Jesus Christ, in whom "we have redemption through his blood, the forgiveness of our trespasses, according to the riches of his grace" (Eph 1:7). McCullough remarks: "If, as Catholics maintain, the Church's hierarchy derives its legitimacy from a transmission of spiritual authority passed down from the Apostles, then even isolated instances of malfeasance within that hierarchy can shake people's faith in this claim." Such instances of malfeasance, especially when the malfeasance is ongoing, understandably can shake people's faith profoundly. But, if we Catholics have read Paul—or Aquinas on Paul—then our faith will not be shaken so as to collapse. United in our own imperfect way to Christ's superabundant reparation of love, let us learn to "share abundantly in Christ's sufferings" in love (2 Cor 1:5), and even to "complete what is lacking in Christ's afflictions for the sake of his body, that is, the Church" (Col 1:24), "until we all attain to the unity of the faith and of the knowledge of the Son of God, to mature manhood, to the measure of the stature of the fulness of Christ" (Eph 4:13).[40]

---

[40] I thank Professor Michael Hahn for extraordinarily helpful comments on this essay.

Aquinas, Scripture, and the Divine Transcendence

Steven A. Long
Ave Maria University

This essay first briefly will consider the necessarily privileged instrumentality of metaphysics within Thomas's theology, and its importance for the understanding of Sacred Scripture. *Second*, it considers at length Thomas's commentary on Romans 9:13—which frames his further remarks—and Romans 9:14–23. I will not only advert to his direct remarks on the text, but consider aspects of his teaching regarding the divine simplicity, divine causality, and grace and his intellectualist account of freedom. *Third*, it engages a criticism offered by Fr. William Most (and many others) regarding the nature of the passages of Scripture, and offers brief response to this criticism. *Fourth*, this essay takes up the points where the accounts of Maritain and Marín-Sola regarding predestination and reprobation become inconsistent with the understanding of Aquinas. The point of this essay is simply that Aquinas offers a realistic reading of Sacred Scripture that, on the question of predestination and reprobation, arguably is the only account reconcilable with the conjoined evidence of nature and grace.

SACRA DOCTRINA AND METAPHYSICS

We begin with a very brief word about the necessary reliance of scriptural theology upon metaphysics, philosophic anthropology, and philosophy of nature. That brief word is supplied in the analysis of Aquinas in the *Summa theologiae* [*ST*] I, q. 1, a. 7, ad 1. The reasoning of the article, and of the reply to the first objection, must also be read in tandem with I, q. 45, a. 5. In q. 1, a. 7, Aquinas affirms that the subject of theology is God, and that other things are considered only insofar as they proceed from, or are ordered to, God. Yet, the first objection notes that we lack proper quidditative knowledge of God; we lack the vision of the divine essence. What, then, can "stand in" for this missing knowledge of the essence of the subject? His answer is that, just as in philosophy certain effects can stand in for the nature of the cause that produced them, so here the effects of nature and grace stand in for the lack of knowledge of the essence of God. In q. 45, a. 5, Thomas affirms that "among all effects the most universal is being itself: and hence it must be the proper effect of the first and most universal cause, and that is God."[1] Inasmuch as being is the proper effect of God, every other effect presupposes being, and all the effects of nature and grace stand in for the quidditative knowledge of God that is lacked, it is simply impossible that metaphysics should fail to assume a privileged instrumentality within *sacra doctrina*. The understanding of being, nature, substance, accidents, form, matter, and—most universally and as a condition for the principle of noncontradiction applying to being—the distinction of act and potency is of singularly great aid to the theologian. Revelation is bestowed in human language and logic, and ontologically presupposes the reality and intelligibility of the created natural order which is itself a divine effect. Thus the idea that scriptural interpretation must, or even intelligibly *may*, totally bracket philosophic considerations is necessarily erroneous, for any reading of Scripture requires certain essentially philosophic judgments. This does not imply that supernatural mysteries depend in themselves on finite nature, but rather that the participation of finite nature in the supernatural order does not subtract from finite nature which alike participates in the providential order.

---

[1] *Summa theologiae* [*ST*] I, q. 45, a. 5, corp.: "Inter omnes autem effectus, universalissimum est ipsum esse. Unde oportet quod sit proprius effectus primae et universalissimae causae, quae est Deus." Within quotes from Aquinas's works below, bold font indicates my own emphasis, so as to distinguish this from the convention of using italics for quotes of Scriptrue, Augustine, etc. within Thomas's works.

AQUINAS, SCRIPTURE, AND THE DIVINE TRANSCENDENCE

THE LETTER OF PAUL TO THE ROMANS, PREDESTINATION, AND REPROBATION

The scriptural passages that concern us are, first, Romans 9:13—Thomas's commentary about which frames his further consideration of predestination and reprobation—and then Romans 9:14–23. Romans 9:13 is the famous passage:

> **9:13** As it is written: *Jacob I have loved: but Esau I have hated.* [Marietti no. 762][2]

Romans 9:14–23 is as follows:

> **9:14** What shall we say then? Is there injustice with God? [no. 765] God forbid! [no. 768]

> **9:15** For he says to Moses: *I will have mercy on whom I will have mercy. And I will show mercy to whom I will show mercy.*

> **9:16** So then it is not of him who wills, nor of him who runs, but of God who shows mercy. [no. 775]

> **9:17** For the Scripture says to Pharaoh: *to this purpose have I raised you, that I may show my power in you and that my name may be declared throughout all the earth.* [no. 779]

> **9:18** Therefore he has mercy on whom he wills. And he hardens whom he wills. [no. 783]

> **9:19** You will say therefore to me: why does he still find fault? For who resists his will?

> **9:20** O man, who are you who replies against God? Shall the thing formed say to him who formed it: why have you made me thus? [no. 788]

---

2 *Super Rom* 9 (trans. Fr. Fabian R. Larcher, O.P. [Green Bay, WI: Aquinas Institute, 2018], 248). All paragraph numbers from Thomas's biblical commentaries will be the Marietti numbers.

9:21 Or has not the potter power over the clay, of the same lump, to make one vessel unto honor and another unto dishonour? [no. 791]

9:22 What if God, willing to show his wrath and to make his power known, endured with much patience vessels of wrath, fitted for destruction, [no. 793]

9:23 That he might show the riches of his glory on the vessels of mercy which he has prepared unto glory?

Manifestly, we cannot consider everything Thomas says in his commentary upon these lines of Sacred Scripture. I will direct attention to certain points that appear to me to be of conspicuous importance, beginning with Thomas's comments on 9:13 that frame the remainder of our consideration. Thomas unequivocally reads the love of God for Jacob, and the hatred of God for Esau, as pertaining to eternal predestination and reprobation. He comments that "one must say that God loved Jacob from all eternity"[3] and that "just as the love, about which we are speaking, pertains to God's eternal predestination, so the hatred about which we are speaking pertains to the rejection by which God rejects sinners."[4] He then articulates a decisive distinction between the order of election and love in God and man. He states:

> Election and love, however, are ordered differently in God than in man. For in men, election precedes love, for a man's will is inclined to love a thing on account of the good perceived in it, this good also being the reason why he prefers one thing to another and why he fixed his love on the thing he preferred. But God's love is the cause of every good found in a creature; consequently, the good in virtue of which one is preferred to another through election follows upon God's willing it—which pertains to his love. Consequently, it is not

---

3   *Super Rom*, no. 762: "Et ideo oportet dicere quod Deus ab aeterno Iacob" (Larcher trans., 252).

4   *Super Rom*, no. 764: "Sicut autem dilectio de qua hic loquitur, pertinet ad aeternam Dei praedestinationem, ita etiam odium, de quo hic loquitur, pertinet ad reprobationem qua Deus reprobat peccatores" (Larcher trans., 253).

in virtue of some good which he selects in a man that God loves him; rather, it is because he loved him that he prefers him to someone by election.[5]

Shortly thereafter, Thomas considers a respect in which reprobation critically differs from predestination:

> It is different in that predestination implies preparation of the merits by which glory is reached, but rejection implies preparation of the sins by which punishment is reached. Consequently, a foreknowledge of merits cannot be the reason for predestination, because the foreknown merits fall under predestination; but the foreknowledge of sins can be a reason for rejection on the part of the punishment prepared for the rejected, inasmuch as God proposes to punish the wicked for the sins they have from themselves, not from God; the just he proposes to reward on account of the merits they do not have from themselves: *destruction is your own, O Israel; your help is only in me* (Hos 13:9).[6]

The words of Thomas from *ST* I, q. 19, a. 9, ad 3, are pertinent here, "God therefore neither wills evil to be done, nor wills it not to

---

[5]   *Super Rom*, no. 763: "Electio autem et dilectio aliter ordinantur in Deo et in homine. In homine enim electio praecedit dilectionem, voluntas enim hominis movetur ad amandum ex bono quod in re amata considerat, ratione cuius ipsam praeelegit alteri et praeelectae suum amorem impendit. Sed voluntas Dei est causa omnis boni quod est in creatura et ideo bonum per quod una creatura praefertur alteri per modum electionis, consequitur voluntatem Dei, quae est de bono illius, quae pertinet ad rationem dilectionis. Unde non propter aliquod bonum quod in homine eligat Deus eum diligit, sed potius eo quod ipsum diligit, praefert eum aliis eligendo" (Larcher trans., 253).

[6]   *Super Rom*, no. 764: "Differt autem quantum ad hoc quod praedestinatio importat praeparationem meritorum quibus pervenitur ad gloriam, sed reprobatio importat praeparationem peccatorum quibus pervenitur ad poenam. Et ideo praescientia meritorum non potest esse aliqua ratio praedestinationis, quia merita praescita cadunt sub praedestinatione; sed praescientia peccatorum potest esse aliqua ratio reprobationis ex parte poenae, quae praeparatur reprobatis, inquantum scilicet Deus proponit se puniturum malos propter peccata quae a seipsis habent, non a Deo; iustos autem proponit se praemiaturum propter merita quae a seipsis non habent. Os. XIII, 9: *perditio tua ex te, Israel, tantum in me auxilium tuum*" (Larcher trans., 253).

be done, but wills to permit evil to be done; and this is a good."[7]

Commenting on Romans 9:15—"I will have mercy on whom I will have mercy"—Thomas observes that one might be thought worthy of merit by reason of preexisting works, but that this would be tantamount to the Pelagian heresy.[8] He then considers whether God might not bestow grace because he foresees the good use that the creature will make of it, and observes that this, too, is inadequate. As he writes:

> But it seems that not even this is a suitable explanation. For it is clear that nothing which is an effect of predestination can be taken as a reason for a predestination, even if it be taken as existing in God's foreknowledge, because the reason for a predestination is presupposed to the predestination, whereas the effect is included in it. But every benefit God bestows on a man for his salvation is an effect of predestination. Furthermore, God's benefits extend not only to the infusion of grace, by which a man is made righteous, but also to its use, just as in natural things God not only causes their forms but also all the movements and activities of those forms, inasmuch as God is the source of all movement in such a way that when he ceases to act, no movement or activity proceeds from those forms. But sanctifying grace and the accompanying virtues in the soul are related to their use as a natural form is related to its activity. Hence, it is said: *O Lord, you have wrought for us all our works* (Isa 26:12).[9]

---

[7] *ST* I, q. 19, a. 9, ad 3: "Deus igitur neque vult mala fieri, neque vult mala non fieri, sed vult permittere mala fieri. Et hoc est bonum."

[8] *Super Rom*, no. 771: "Sed misereri cui dignum est, potest intelligi dupliciter. Uno modo ut intelligatur aliquis dignus misericordia propter opera praeexistentia in hac vita, licet non in alia, ut posuit Origenes, quod pertinet ad haeresim Pelagianorum, qui posuerunt gratiam Dei hominibus secundum merita dari"; "But having mercy on one who is worthy can be understood in two ways: in one way so that one is counted worthy of mercy on account of preexisting works in this life, though not in another life, as Origen supposed. This belongs to the Pelagian heresy which taught that God's grace is given to men according to their merits" (Larcher trans., 255–56).

[9] *Super Rom*, no. 772: "Sed videtur quod nec hoc convenienter dici possit. Manifestum est enim quod nihil potest poni ut ratio praedestinationis, quod est praedestinationis effectus, etiam si accipiatur prout est in Dei praescientia, quia ratio praedestinationis praeintelligitur praedestinationi, effectus autem in ipsa inclu-

It is worth noting here that, for Thomas, everything that is said of God is said by way of identity with the divine simple substance, for no creature can determine the divine essence.[10] As God is Pure Act subject to no limiting principle of potency, it is impossible that God be subjected to real determined reciprocal relations with creatures.[11] Thus, although creation has a real relation to God, and truly depends on God in order to be, God does not have a real and determined relation to the creature, but only a conceptual relation. For example, it is true to call God "Lord" because the creature can exist only as ordered to him in this way. This is what Thomas refers to in *ST* I, q. 13, a. 7, resp. and ad 4, as a "temporal predicate" that pertains only conceptually to God, owing to something that is true of the creature. Further, Thomas affirms that God is the first and principal cause of the application of every power to act[12]—or, as he says above, "God not only causes their forms but also all the movements and activities of those forms, inasmuch as God is the source of all movement in such a way that *when he ceases to act, no movement or activity proceeds*

---

ditur. Manifestum est autem quod omne Dei beneficium quod homini confert ad salutem, est divinae praedestinationis effectus. Divinum autem beneficium non solum extendit se ad infusionem gratiae, qua homo iustificatur, sed etiam ad gratiae usum: sicut etiam in rebus naturalibus non solum Deus causat ipsas formas in rebus, sed etiam ipsos motus et operationes formarum, eo quod Deus est principium omnis motus, cuius operatione cessante a movendo, ex formis nullus motus vel operatio sequitur. Sicut autem se habet habitus gratiae vel virtutis in anima ad usum ipsius, sic se habet forma naturalis ad suam operationem. Et ideo dicitur Is. XXVI, 12: *omnia opera nostra operatus es in nobis, Domine*" (Larcher trans., 256).

[10] *ST* I, q. 28, a. 2, ad 1: "Nihil autem quod est in Deo, potest habere habitudinem ad id in quo est, vel de quo dicitur, nisi habitudinem identitatis, propter summam Dei simplicitatem"; "But nothing that exists in God can have any relation to that wherein it exists or of whom it is spoken, except the relation of identity; and this by reason of [propter] God's supreme simplicity."

[11] *ST* I, q. 13, a. 7, resp.: "Cum igitur Deus sit extra totum ordinem creaturae, et omnes creaturae ordinentur ad ipsum, et non e converso, manifestum est quod creaturae realiter referuntur ad ipsum Deum; sed in Deo non est aliqua realis relatio eius ad creaturas, sed secundum rationem tantum, inquantum creaturae referuntur ad ipsum"; "Since therefore God is outside the whole order of creation, and all creatures are ordered to Him, and not conversely, it is manifest that creatures are really related to God Himself; whereas in God there is no real relation to creatures, but a relation only in idea, inasmuch as creatures are referred to Him."

[12] Cf. *Summa contra gentiles* [*SCG*] III, ch. 67: "Sed omnis applicatio virtutis ad operationem est principaliter et primo a Deo"; "But every application of power to its operation is principally and first from God."

from those forms."[13] But, owing to the divine simplicity,[14] the only distinction between God acting and God not acting is the *being* of the effect. A purely and completely indeterminate effect being indistinguishable from no effect whatsoever, to speak of "divine grace" or "divine agency" always implies a determinate effect.[15]

Citing Aristotle's analysis, that human deliberation is an effect of God, Thomas argues in his commentary that, "consequently, it is impossible that the merits which follow grace are the reason for showing mercy or for predestination; the only reason is God's will, according to which he mercifully delivers certain ones,"[16] and that, "in this way, then, the very use of grace is from God."[17] He writes:

---

[13] *Super Rom*, no. 772: "Divinum autem beneficium non solum extendit se ad infusionem gratiae, qua homo iustificatur, sed etiam ad gratiae usum: sicut etiam in rebus naturalibus non solum Deus causat ipsas formas in rebus, sed etiam ipsos motus et operationes formarum, eo quod Deus est principium omnis motus, cuius operatione cessante a movendo, ex formis nullus motus vel operatio sequitur" (Larcher trans., 256).

[14] Of course, the teaching of the divine simplicity, and that God has no real reciprocal determined relation with creation, is to be found throughout Thomas's works. Thus for example in *ST* I, q. 13, a. 7: "Since therefore God is outside the whole order of creation, and all creatures are ordered to Him, and not conversely, it is manifest that creatures are really related to God Himself; whereas in God there is no real relation to creatures, but a relation only in idea, inasmuch as creatures are referred to Him. Thus there is nothing to prevent these names which import relation to the creature from being predicated of God temporally, not by reason of any change in Him, but by reason of the change of the creature; as a column is on the right of an animal, without change in itself, but by change in the animal." Likewise, in *ST* I, q. 28, a. 2, ad 1, we find Thomas teaching that "nothing that exists in God can have any relation to that wherein it exists or of whom it is spoken, except the relation of identity; and this by reason of [*propter*] God's supreme simplicity."

[15] As Thomas points out in *ST* I-II, q. 109, a. 1, resp.: "Now not only is every motion from God as from the First Mover, but all formal perfection is from Him as from the First Act. And thus the act of the intellect or of any created being whatsoever depends upon God in two ways: first, inasmuch as it is from Him that it has the form whereby it acts; secondly, inasmuch as it is moved by Him to act." And thus, "no matter how perfect a corporeal or spiritual nature is supposed to be, it cannot proceed to its act unless it be moved by God." Indeed, as Thomas notes in ad 3 of the same article, "we need God's help for every thought, insofar as is it God who moves the understanding to act."

[16] *Super Rom*, no. 773: "Sic igitur non potest esse quod merita consequentia gratiam sint ratio miserendi aut praedestinandi, sed sola Dei voluntas, secundum quam misericorditer aliquos liberat" (Larcher trans., 257).

[17] *Super Rom*, no. 773: "Sic igitur ipse usus gratiae est a Deo" (Larcher trans., 256).

"God moves all things, but in diverse ways, inasmuch as each is moved in a manner befitting its nature. And so man is moved by God to will and to perform outwardly in a manner consistent with free will. Therefore, willing and performing depends on man as freely acting; but on God and not on man, as initial mover."[18]

Freedom here does not imply absolute liberty of indifference to divine causality: every act of rational choice is of its nature free, because the intellect is ordered to universal good, whereas the proportionate objects of choice are all limited goods that can in some way be viewed as not-good, even precisely when they are good for us.[19] Thus, every choice is free, yet the least motion of the creature from potency to act presupposes ontologically prior divine motion.[20] Thus Thomas

---

[18] *Super Rom*, no. 778: "Deus omnia movet, sed diversimode, inquantum scilicet unumquodque movetur ab eo secundum modum naturae suae. Et sic homo movetur a Deo ad volendum et currendum per modum liberae voluntatis. Sic ergo velle et currere est hominis, ut libere agentis: non autem est hominis ut principaliter moventis, sed Dei" (Larcher trans., 258).

[19] Cf. *ST* I-II, q. 10, a. 2, corp.: "Unde si proponatur aliquod obiectum voluntati quod sit universaliter bonum et secundum omnem considerationem, ex necessitate voluntas in illud tendet, si aliquid velit, non enim poterit velle oppositum. Si autem proponatur sibi aliquod obiectum quod non secundum quamlibet considerationem sit bonum, non ex necessitate voluntas feretur in illud. Et quia defectus cuiuscumque boni habet rationem non boni, ideo illud solum bonum quod est perfectum et cui nihil deficit, est tale bonum quod voluntas non potest non velle, quod est beatitudo. Alia autem quaelibet particularia bona, inquantum deficiunt ab aliquo bono, possunt accipi ut non bona, et secundum hanc considerationem, possunt repudiari vel approbari a voluntate, quae potest in idem ferri secundum diversas considerationes"; "Wherefore if the will be offered an object which is good universally and from every point of view, the will tends to it of necessity, if it wills anything at all; since it cannot will the opposite. If, on the other hand, the will is offered an object that is not good from every point of view, it will not tend to it of necessity. And since lack of any good whatever, is a non-good, consequently, that good alone which is perfect and lacking in nothing, is such a good that the will cannot not-will it: and this is happiness. Whereas any other particular goods, insofar as they are lacking in some good, can be regarded as non-goods: and from this point of view, they can be set aside or approved by the will, which can tend to one and the same thing from various points of view."

[20] Cf. *De malo*, q. 3, a. 2, ad 4: "Similiter cum aliquid movet se ipsum, non excluditur quin ab alio moveatur a quo habet hoc ipsum quo se ipsum movet. Et sic non repugnat libertati quod Deus est causa actus liberi arbitrii"; "When anything moves itself, this does not exclude its being moved by another, from which it has **even this** that it moves itself. Thus it is not repugnant to liberty that God is the cause of the free act of the will." See also *ST* I, q. 83, a. 1, ad 3: "Dicendum quod liberum arbitrium est causa sui motus; quia homo per liberum arbitrium

observes in *ST* I-II, q. 10, a. 4, ad 3, that if God moves the creature to something, it is incompossible (*incompossibile est*)—not possible given such motion—that the creature not be moved,[21] and indeed, in *Summa contra gentiles* III, ch. 92, he writes that "a man does not always choose what his guardian angel intends, or that toward which a celestial body gives inclination. But a man does in all cases choose the object in accord with God's operation within his will."[22] In other words, human voluntary agency lies within the perfective causality of God.[23]

The will is free because its proportionate objects cannot compel it; but while the will moves itself, it is not the first cause of its self-motion, and must be moved from potency to act in regard to it,

---

seipsum movet ad agendum. Non tamen hoc est de necessitate libertatis, quod sit prima causa sui id quod liberum est; sicut nec ad hoc quod aliquid sit causa alterius, requiritur quod sit prima causa eius. Deus igitur est prima causa movens et naturales causas et voluntarias. Et sicut naturalibus causis, movendo eas, non aufert quin actus earum sint naturales; ita movendo causas voluntarias, non aufert quin actiones earum sint voluntariae, sed potius hoc in eis facit; operatur enim in unoquoque secundum eius proprietatem"; "Free-will is the cause of its own movement, because by his free-will man moves himself to act. But it does not of necessity belong to liberty that what is free should be the first cause of itself, as neither for one thing to be cause of another need it be the first cause. God, therefore, is the first cause, Who moves causes both natural and voluntary. And just as by moving natural causes He does not prevent their acts being natural, so by moving voluntary causes He does not deprive their actions of being voluntary: but rather is He the cause of this very thing in them; for He operates in each thing according to its own nature."

[21] *ST* I-II, q. 10, a. 4, ad 3: "Ad tertium dicendum quod, si Deus movet voluntatem ad aliquid, incompossibile est huic positioni quod voluntas ad illud non moveatur. Non tamen est impossibile simpliciter. Unde non sequitur quod voluntas a Deo ex necessitate moveatur."

[22] *SCG* III, ch. 92: "non semper homo eligit illud quod angelus custodiens intendit, neque illud ad quod corpus caeleste inclinat. Semper tamen hoc homo eligit secundum quod Deus operatur in eius voluntate."

[23] *De veritate*, q. 6, a. 3, ad 3: " . . . et ideo, quamvis nihil divinae voluntati resistat, tamen voluntas, et quaelibet alia res, exequitur divinam voluntatem secundum modum suum, quia et ipsum modum divina voluntas rebus dedit, ut sic eius voluntas impleretur; et ideo quaedam explent divinam voluntatem necessario, quaedam vero contingenter, quamvis illud quod Deus vult, semper fiat"; "Even though nothing can resist the divine will, our will, like everything else, carries out the divine will according to its own proper mode. Indeed, the divine will has given things their mode of being in order that His will be fulfilled. Therefore, some things fulfill the divine will necessarily, other things, contingently; but that which God wills always takes place."

something Thomas expressly teaches in many places.[24] While grace taken as an object of choice—as a good to be assented to—always is resistible, efficacious grace is grace that, perfecting human liberty without despoiling it, *is* not resisted, because absolutely speaking both grace and the perfection of human willing are *effects* of one merciful divine causality. Thus, when one says that, absolutely speaking, the divine will is not resistible, this does *not* mean that man has *no power* to resist, but that man's powers *are perfected by grace*. This is well expressed in the fourth of the canons on justification from the Council of Trent, which teaches:

> If anyone shall say that man's free will moved and aroused by God does not co-operate[25] by assenting [or: in no way co-operates by an assent] to God who rouses and calls, whereby it disposes and prepares itself to obtain the grace of justification, and that it cannot dissent, if it wishes, but that like someone inanimate it does nothing at all and is merely in a passive state: let him be anathema.[26]

---

[24] *De malo*, q. 3, a. 2, ad 4: "Similiter cum aliquid mouet se ipsum, non excluditur quin ab alio moueatur a quo habet hoc ipsum quo se ipsum mouet. Et sic non repugnat libertati quod Deus est causa actus liberi arbitrii"; "When anything moves itself, this does not exclude its being moved by another, from which it has even this that it moves itself. Thus it is not repugnant to liberty that God is the cause of the free act of the will."

[25] The phrase is *nihil cooperari*, which could be taken to mean, "does not cooperate by assenting," or "simply does not cooperate by assenting," or "in no way whatever cooperates by an assent"; in any case, the divine motion is said to be followed by animate cooperative assent. The phrase "nihil cooperari assentiendo Deo excitanti atque vocanti" can literally mean "in no way cooperate by assenting," which clearly makes *assent* to be implied. A clearer text defining efficacious grace—clearly quite different from the Calvinist irresistible grace, as likewise from any spurious absolute liberty of indifference of the will to divine causality—could not be sought. Sadly, North Americans in particular often are acquainted with this question only from the vantage points of apologetics, Molinist preoccupations, or analytic logical considerations, with these largely separated both from any normative metaphysical principles and frequently from the doctrinal tradition of the Church. But more is required to do justice to the theological riches of the Church than logic and apologetic concern.

[26] Council of Trent, *Decree Concerning Justification* (session 6), can. 4, as found in Heinrich Denzinger, *Enchiridion Symbolorum: The Sources of Catholic Dogma*, trans. Roy J. Deferrari (Fitzwilliam, NH: Loreto, 1955), which is translated from the 30th edition of Denzinger and will be abbreviated hereafter "Dz." The passage is translated differently in the 43rd edition, edited by Peter Hünermann, for

Man's free will *moved* and *aroused* by God cooperates by assenting.
The agent *can* dissent *if it wishes* and is not *inanimate*. But the agent
moved and aroused by grace *does not wish* to dissent and freely assents. Indeed, if anyone shall say that the will "moved" and "aroused"
by God "*does not* cooperate by assenting to God . . . let him be anathema" (emphasis added). The proposition not to be denied, whose denial brings anathematization, is not merely that those moved and
roused *may cooperate by assenting*, but that those moved and roused by
God do *actually cooperate by animate cooperation and assent*. In what
respect is there a grace if there is no positive effect? And if the positive effect is limited, more grace will be required for a further effect.
This is precisely what is affirmed by Thomas: that our free and animate cooperation is itself brought forth *through the perfecting motion
of grace.*

Thomas argues in his commentary on Romans that God can be
said to stir the human agent to good and to evil only in very different
ways, inclining the will directly to the good, but stirring to evil only
by placing before a person, interiorly or exteriorly, something good of
itself that owing to his own malice the agent uses for evil.[27]

> God is not said to harden anyone directly, as though he caus-
> es their malice, but indirectly, inasmuch as man makes an

---

the original bilingual edition, English trans. ed. Robert Fastiggi and Anne En-
glund Nash (San Francisco: Ignatius Press, 2012), commonly abbreviated "DH."
DH uses the phrase "in no way cooperates by an assent," which is just as strong,
for it indicates that the will moved and aroused or excited by God will cooperate
by some assent (which is the logical contrary); see DH no. 1554 (can. 4): "Si quis
dixerit, liberum hominis arbitrium a Deo motum et excitatum nihil cooperari
assentiendo Deo excitanti atque vocanti, quo ad obtinendam iustificationis gratiam se disponat ac praeparet, neque posse dissentire, si velit, sed velut inanime
quoddam nihil omnino agere mereque passive se habere: anathema sit" (Ignatius
ed., 385); cf. can. 4 in Dz no. 814 (Defarrari trans., 258; reproduced above in
main text).

27 *Super Rom*, no. 781: "However, he stirs them to good and to evil in different ways:
for he inclines men's wills to good directly as the author of these good deeds; but
he is said to incline or stir up men to evil as an *occasional* cause, namely, inasmuch
as God puts before a person, either in him or outside of him something which of
itself is conducive to good but which through his own malice he uses for evil: ***do
you not know that God's kindness is meant to lead you to repentance? But by your
hard and impenitent heart you are storing up wrath for yourself on the day of wrath***
(Rom 2:4–5) and *God gave his place for penance: and he abused it unto pride* (Job
24:23)" (Larcher trans., 258).

occasion of sin out of things God does within or outside the man; and this God himself permits. Hence, he is not said to harden as though by inserting malice, but by not affording grace.[28]

Commenting on the question at Romans 9:19—"You will say therefore to me: why does he still find fault? For who resists his will?"—Thomas observes that election and rejection suggests two questions, the first general (why does God will to show mercy, or to harden, *some*?) and the second particular (why does God show mercy to, or harden, a particular one?). He compares the ordering of predestination and reprobation to a builder's ordering of stones in an edifice. He affirms that a reason other than the divine will may be given as to why *some* are placed higher and others lower, owing to the nature of the intention of the whole. But as to why any *individual* stone is so placed, he argues that the reason seems to be "merely that the builder so willed," so that the answer about any given individual can be only "God's absolute will."[29] Yet for Thomas the divine will is always conformed to the divine goodness: whatever is either positively or permissively willed must final-

---

[28] *Super Rom*, no. 784: "Ad quod dicendum quod Deus non dicitur indurare aliquos directe, quasi in eis causet malitiam, sed indirecte, inquantum scilicet ex his quae facit in homine intus vel extra, homo sumit occasionem peccati, et hoc ipse Deus permittit. Unde non dicitur indurare quasi immittendo malitiam, sed non apponendo gratiam" (Larcher trans., 260).

[29] *Super Rom*, no. 788: "Et potest quidem ratio huius quaestionis assignari; secundae autem quaestionis non potest assignari ratio, nisi simplex Dei voluntas, cuius exemplum patet in rebus humanis. Si enim aliquis aedificare volens, haberet multos lapides similes et aequales congregatos, posset ratio assignari quare quosdam ponat in summo et quosdam in imo ex parte finis, quia ad perfectionem domus quam facere intendit, requiritur et fundamentum quod habet lapides in imo, et cacumen parietis quod habet lapides in summo. Sed quare ponat hos lapides in summo et hos in imo, non habet aliquam rationem, nisi quia artifex voluit"; "Although a reason other than God's will can be assigned in the first question, the only reason that can be assigned in the second question is God's absolute will. An example is found among humans. For if a builder has at hand many similar and equal stones, the reason why he puts certain ones at the top and others at the bottom can be gathered from his purpose, because the perfection of the house he intends to build requires both a foundation with stones at the bottom and walls of a certain height with stones at the top. But the reason why he put these stones on the top and those others at the bottom seems to be merely that the builder so willed" (Larcher trans., 263).

ly repose upon the divine goodness and what is due to it.[30]

Thomas comments on Romans 9:20—"Shall the thing formed say to him who formed it: why have you made me thus?"—that the goodness of a beautiful vessel made from base matter by an artisan is all ascribed to the goodness of the artisan, but that a vessel made from "base matter" and adapted to "meaner uses" would, if it could think, have no complaint.[31]

But human nature has baseness about it from its matter, because as Genesis says:

> *God formed man of dust from the ground* (Gen 2:7), and more baseness after being spoiled by sin, which entered this world through one man. That is why man is compared to dirt, in Job: *I am compared to dirt and I am likened to dust and ashes* (Job 30:19). Hence, any good that man possesses is due to God's goodness as its basic source: *O Lord, you are our Father, we are the clay, and you are the potter, we are all the work of your hands* (Isa 64:8). Furthermore, if God does not advance man to better things but leaves him in his weakness and reserves him for the lowliest use, he does him no injury such that he could justly complain about God.[32]

---

[30] *ST* I, q. 19, a. 1, ad 3: "Sed obiectum divinae voluntatis est bonitas sua, quae est eius essentia"; "The object of the divine will is his goodness, which is his essence."

[31] *Super Rom*, no. 790: "Here it should be noted that if an artisan uses base matter to make a beautiful vessel for noble uses, it is all ascribed to the goodness of the artisan; for example, if from clay he fashions pitchers and serving-dishes suited to a banquet table. If, on the other hand, from such base matter, say clay, he produced a vessel adapted to meaner uses, for example, for cooking or such, the vessel, if it could think, would have no complaint. But it could complain, if from precious metals, such as gold and precious stones, the artisan were to make a vessel reserved for base uses" (Larcher trans., 263–64).

[32] *Super Rom*, no. 790: "Humana autem natura vilitatem habet ex sua materia, quia, ut dicitur Gen. II, 7: *fecit Deus hominem de limo terrae*, sed maiorem vilitatem habet ex corruptione peccati, quae per unum hominem in hunc mundum intravit. Et ideo homo luto merito comparatur Iob XXX, 19: *comparatus sum luto, et assimilatus sum favillae et cineri.* Unde quicquid boni habet homo debet bonitati divinae quasi principali agenti adscribere. Is. LXIV, v. 8: *nunc, Domine, Pater es tu, nos vero lutum, et fictor noster tu, et opus manuum tuarum omnes nos.* Si vero Deus hominem ad meliora non promoveat, sed in sua infirmitate eum dimittens, deputat eum ad infimum usum, nullam ei facit iniuriam: ut possit iuste de Deo conqueri" (Larcher trans., 264).

He goes on to state that: "In the same way God has free power to make from the same spoiled matter of the human race, as from clay, and without any injustice, some men prepared for glory and some abandoned in wretchedness: *behold, like the clay in the potter's hand, so are you in my hand, O house of Israel* (Isa 18:6)."

Human nature has baseness about it from its matter. One notes that Thomas observes here not merely the defectibility of the human person *consequent upon sin*, but the prior defectibility that pertains to created human nature as such. This natural defectibility is *not* moral *defect*, but it is *ontological defect in the sense of limitation*. It is a capacity to fail owing to the composite nature of man, who learns discursively, with much admixture of error, and whose practical rational judgment is susceptible of being clouded by physical dispositions, whether of weariness, anger, desire, despondency, and so on. And it is not unjust that God permit the defectible creature to undergo some defect. God could have created man in the perfection of the beatific vision, but this is unfitting.[33] Permitting defectible creatures to undergo some measure of defect, he cannot fail to know what this implies, and

---

[33] *ST* I-II, q. 5, a. 7, resp. Thomas first acknowledges that the right order of the will to the end is necessary for happiness, and then states: "Sed ex hoc non ostenditur quod aliqua operatio hominis debeat praecedere eius beatitudinem, posset enim Deus simul facere voluntatem recte tendentem in finem, et finem consequentem; sicut quandoque simul materiam disponit, et inducit formam. Sed ordo divinae sapientiae exigit ne hoc fiat, ut enim dicitur in II *De caelo*, eorum quae nata sunt habere bonum perfectum, aliquid habet ipsum sine motu, aliquid uno motu, aliquid pluribus. Habere autem perfectum bonum sine motu, convenit ei quod naturaliter habet illud. Habere autem beatitudinem naturaliter est solius Dei. Unde solius Dei proprium est quod ad beatitudinem non moveatur per aliquam operationem praecedentem. Cum autem beatitudo excedat omnem naturam creatam, nulla pura creatura convenienter beatitudinem consequitur absque motu operationis, per quam tendit in ipsam"; "But this does not show that any work of man needs to precede his happiness, for God could simultaneously make the will to tend rightly toward the end and to attain the end: Thus at times God disposes the matter and simultaneously induces the form. But the order of divine wisdom necessitates that this not be, for as is said in II *De caelo*, of those things that have perfect good, some have it without motion, some by one motion, and others by many motions. But to have perfect good without motion belongs to that which naturally possesses it. But to have happiness naturally belongs solely to God. Wherefore it is proper to God alone that he not be moved to happiness by any preceding operation. For happiness exceeds every created nature, and no pure creature can fittingly achieve happiness without the motion of operation whereby it tends toward it."

is said to "reprobate" insofar as he has not bestowed unmerited aid upholding the creature from moral defect in that case where defect includes final impenitence.

The View That Scripture Speaks of the External, and Not the Internal, Economy

Fr. William Most is known for his remarkable work *Grace, Predestination, and the Salvific Will of God*. He offers a scriptural and systematic argument that Aquinas misread the Romans passage of which we have been speaking, and unequivocally views Thomas's view that the Jacob and Esau passage regards predestination to glory or reprobation as false. His scriptural argument hinges in part on his view that "St. Paul, in Romans 8–9, was not speaking about the infallible predestination of individuals to eternal glory, but about the plans of God for the call of peoples to be members of the Church, in the Old or New Testament, in the full sense, and about the divine plans for those who already are members of the Church in the full sense."[34] On his view, the predestination in question in the Romans passage is not predestination to glory or the beatific vision (the internal economy of providence), but merely predestination to membership in the Church (the external economy of providence). But he realizes that he can hold this only following on his judgment that, "since the principles of the two economies are not only different, but incompatible, it is illegitimate to infer that the principles of divine action in one economy are the same as in the other economy."[35] The principles governing these orders he thinks to be not only different, but literally "incompatible." So he argues:

> Now if God were to reject a man from eternal salvation as He rejected Esau, that is, before considering anything that the man would or would not do, and were to do it in such a way that, as the older Thomists say the rejected man could not "distinguish himself" in regard to being reprobated or

---

[34] Fr. William Most, *Grace, Predestination, and the Salvific Will of God: New Answers to Old Questions* (Front Royal, VA: Christendom, 1997), no. 4 (p. 4).

[35] Most, *Grace, Predestination, and the Salvific Will of God*, no. 16 (p. 31).

not: then he could not simultaneously say sincerely that He willed all men—including those reprobated—to be saved. Actually, as we shall see in chapters 4 and 5, God's desire for the salvation of all is so vehement that He bound Himself by a New and eternal Covenant in the blood of His Son to give graces to all that are in proportion to infinite objective titles or claims established at such great cost (the Cross) for each individual man.

So in one economy, God does not have mercy on all; but in the other, His mercy is universal. In one economy, even before a man has sinned, He may say: "Esau I hated," but in the other: you have "loathing for none of the things which thou hast made," for God "desires all men to be saved." Therefore, since the principles of the two economies are not only different, but incompatible, it is illegitimate to infer that the principles of divine action in one economy are the same as in the other economy, in which God has freely decreed to act differently, and has revealed that fact in Sacred Scripture.[36]

Sed contra. First, with regard to the narrow scriptural observation, *nothing whatsoever suggests that the principles articulated in Romans cannot proportionately apply both to membership in the Church and to final beatitude, and indeed there is a built-in reason to think this is so, insofar as the nobler elevation is precisely of its nature more perfectly merciful than is the preparatory elevation to communion with the Church.* The text of Romans 9:18 asserts that God has mercy "on whom he wills" and "hardens whom he wills," which clearly bears a relation to what is said in 9:23, "That he might show the riches of his glory on the vessels of mercy which he has prepared unto glory." *But God stirring to good, or "hardening" with respect to sin, quite clearly does not pertain solely to predestination to membership in the Church, but has its most significant application with respect to final contrition or impenitence.* Romans 9:23 also speaks not only of the grace of communion with the Church, but of the preparation for glory: "That he might show the riches of his glory on the vessels of mercy which he has prepared unto glory." "The riches of his glory" shown on those prepared *unto glory* is something rather more than membership in the Church, unless one wishes to argue that some possible reprobate soul dies

---

[36] Most, *Grace, Predestination, and the Salvific Will of God*, no. 16 (p. 31).

prepared unto glory.

The principles pertinent to the external economy cannot reasonably be opposed to the principles of the internal economy, because no divine effect whatsoever can be caused by God as purely indeterminate, for the simple reason that the indeterminate as such is not distinct from no effect whatsoever.

Two Objections

Two further objections to this teaching from within the Thomistic fold have developed which are close to one another: that of Jacques Maritain and that of Francisco Marín-Sola. Fr. Most concurs with both. Responding to the historico-doctrinal claims of Marín-Sola would, by itself, require a book-length manuscript. But the speculative center of each is comparatively simple.

Maritain famously held that the view of reprobation as a divine non-upholding in grace was unnecessary in order to sustain the principal concern of St. Thomas in affirming the transcendence of divine grace. He argued that, if only the agent does not negate an initial "shatterable" or "resistible" or "negatable" grace, then ordinarily God would bestow a grace unshatterable of itself. "Not to negate" was viewed as not any positive effect whatsoever, but merely the omission of resistance. Hence, Maritain viewed this account as preserving the dependence of the entirety of the effect of grace upon God. He held God *could* bestow an unshatterable grace to individuals without preceding this grace by a rejectable, negatable, shatterable grace, but that this was comparatively rare and exceptional.[37] This is a beautiful idea, well attuned to the language of the Gospel of St. John that, "without Me, you can do nothing" (15:5). Yet, it seems on reflection that it is impossible. The reason is that the negation of negation is, *in a real actually existing subject*, necessarily something positive. It is unintelligible to say of a real subject that, if only he does not *not*

---

[37] See Jacques Maritain, *Existence and the Existent*, trans. Lewis Galantiere and Gerald B. Phelan (New York: Pantheon, 1948), esp. 85–122 (ch. 4, "The Free Existent and the Free Eternal Purposes"), and more particularly 94 and 100n10. See also Maritain, *St. Thomas and the Problem of Evil* (Milwaukee, WI: Marquette University Press, 1942), 26–30, 33, 34, 36–38.

have a nose, then God will bestow a nose: because, in a real subject, the negation of a negation is ineluctably something positive, and every positive reality has God for its First Author. Thus, it would appear that this returns us to the starting line: either God mercifully upholds a creature from its own defectibility—defectibility in the natural order and in relation to revelation—by granting an aid that absolutely speaking is not due to any creature whatsoever, or else God permits the creature to suffer defect.

Marín-Sola, who speaks of the creature's resistance to grace in similar ways, added to this the idea that, in slight matters, the agent may take a grace ordained to one effect in the supernatural order and—without further divine aid—prolong or further extend it.[38] Indeed, he held that, with a merely sufficient and antecedent grace, the creature may further continue in some actual supernatural motion when dealing with easy things. He cites the Carmelite Salmanticenses in their *Cursus theologicus* as holding this view.[39] Yet,

---

[38] Michael D. Torre, *Do Not Resist the Spirit's Call: Francisco Marín-Sola on Sufficient Grace* (Washington, DC: Catholic University of America Press, 2013), 25–26; see also 29: "Well then: to *persevere* in the good or *not to place an impediment* to grace does not demand a new or special grace when one is dealing with easy things and for a *short time*. To affirm the contrary would be to suppose our [fallen] nature was not only weak, but rotten." But perseverance is itself *a grace*. Further, without the extension to some further effect, it is unclear why it would be described as a *continuation* in some prior grace, since one is not speaking simply of the state of grace, but of some particular graced motion which is extended. Speaking of sufficient grace, he says that it is efficacious for something, but calls this either actuation of the free will, *or* "incoaction of the imperfect act"—that it is "fallibly efficacious" or "proximately sufficient" for something including either "*continuation* or perseverance of the imperfect act" *or* "for not placing an impediment to the course of grace in easy things and for some time." Curiously, Marín-Sola says this despite expressly holding that created liberty cannot have more good than that to which God moves it, but it can have less (*Do Not Resist*, 128). Yet, the view that sufficient grace (which he views as an imperfect motion toward an end) can be extended by the creature without further aid is the idea that the scope of grace is decided by the creature.

[39] Marín-Sola, *Do Not Resist*, 155. But arguably the reason the Salmanticenses thought one in grace did not need a further grace in some light matter, or in facing even a minor temptation, was that this did not properly impinge on or impede the supernatural order: natural virtue is enough for the one in grace to do some slight good on which nothing noteworthy in the supernatural order hinges, or to avoid some slight temptation whose matter is natural and venial (e.g., overeating might be resisted by the one in grace through acquired natural temperance). The Salmanticenses were not minimalists about natural order, but they were also ar-

the Salmanticenses arguably affirm only that a *natural effect* achieved by someone in sanctifying grace requires only a divinely caused natural motion, unless either a further supernatural perfection or some significant temptation is involved.[40] Thus, eating a ham sandwich does not require further supernatural grace for the one in the state of sanctifying grace unless this poses some grave temptation or is connected by special circumstance to a supernatural good, because the natural powers of the agent suffice for eating the sandwich, while yet this does require *divine premotion in the natural order.* But even the slightest further effect in the supernatural order seems to require further grace. Here the observation of my old mentor, Fr. Jan Walgrave, seems to be vindicated, who commented that Marín-Sola "systematizes history," which "is not a bad thing, but it is a most dangerous enterprise."[41] However we construe the Salmanticenses, we have already seen Thomas's observation from his commentary on Romans that "God is the source of all movement in such a way that when he ceases to act, no movement or activity proceeds from those forms."[42] For God "to act" implies positing the being of an effect. Any further extension of agency designates a further divine aid either natural or supernatural.

Marín-Sola also thought of "antecedent" and "consequent" grace

---

dent premotivists, for whom every action whatsoever requires prior divine motion either in the natural or the supernatural order.

[40] I say "arguably" because the passage indicates that any light temptation does not exceed the power of free will to resist, which power is natural to the human person and, taken in itself simply as natural power, suggests that it is premotion in the natural order and not supernatural grace that would be at stake; see Salmanticenses, *Cursus theologicus, de gratia*, disp. 2, dub. 2, no. 49: "Ratio quad primam partem est: quia supposito, quod tentatio sit levis (undecunque proveniat) non excedit ejus resistentia facultatem liberi arbitrii" (Paris: V. Palme, 1870–1883). This seems to concern a light matter besetting someone already in the state of grace, not the continuance of some particular motion *in* the order of grace without further divine aid. In other words, the continued *upholding* in sanctifying grace is supposed, but the act in question of pursing some light good or brushing away some light temptation is natural, proportionate to the natural power. See also the last paragraph of no. 48 in *Cursus theologicus, de gratia*, disp. 2, dub. 2.

[41] Fr. Jan Walgrave, *Unfolding Revelation* (Philadelphia: Westminster, 1972), 168: "He does not look at the data of history in a strict historical perspective, and he too often accommodates them to fit into his own system. He systematizes history. In itself this is not a bad thing, but it is a most dangerous enterprise."

[42] See note 13 above.

as authentically *in* God,[43] and like Fr. Most, he thought of the antecedent will *in* God as needing to be "sincere." But as Thomas observes in the *Summa theologiae*,[44] there is neither antecedent nor consequent *in God*, and antecedent grace is named "antecedent" because it brings about *a thing* that is proximate or antecedent to a yet *further thing* which thus may—or may not—be attained, as remorse is an antecedent grace vis à vis possible confession.[45] (Indeed, the antecedent

---

[43] Marín-Sola, *Do Not Resist*, 254n109, referring critically to Báñez as denying that the antecedent will in God is a "true" will.

[44] See *ST* I, q. 19, a. 6, ad. 1: "Tertio, secundum Damascenum, intelligitur de voluntate antecedente, non de voluntate consequente. Quae quidem distinctio non accipitur ex parte ipsius voluntatis divinae, in qua nihil est prius vel posterius; sed ex parte volitorum"; "Third, according to Damascene (*De Fide Orth*. ii, 29), they are understood of the antecedent will of God; not of the consequent will. This distinction must not be taken as applying to the divine will itself, in which there is nothing antecedent nor consequent, but to the things willed."

[45] My emphases in the quote below (again, in bold) make clear that there is no dubiety about Thomas's text, which is clear beyond all peradventure of doubt. Thomas's words are quite precise in *ST* I, q. 19, a. 6, ad 1: "The words of the Apostle, 'God will have all men to be saved,' etc. can be understood in three ways. First, by a restricted application, in which case they would mean, as Augustine says (*De praed. sanct*. i, 8: *Enchiridion* 103), 'God wills all men to be saved that are saved, not because there is no man whom He does not wish saved, but because there is no man saved whose salvation He does not will.' Secondly, they can be understood as applying to every class of individuals, not to every individual of each class; in which case they mean that God wills some men of every class and condition to be saved, males and females, Jews and Gentiles, great and small, but not all of every condition. Thirdly, according to Damascene (*De Fide Orth*. ii, 29), they are understood of the antecedent will of God; not of the consequent will. **This distinction must not be taken as applying to the divine will itself, in which there is nothing antecedent nor consequent, but to the things willed.**

"To understand this we must consider that everything, in so far as it is good, is willed by God. A thing taken in its primary sense, and absolutely considered, may be good or evil, and yet when some additional circumstances are taken into account, by a consequent consideration may be changed into the contrary. Thus that a man should live is good; and that a man should be killed is evil, absolutely considered. But if in a particular case we add that a man is a murderer or dangerous to society, to kill him is a good; that he live is an evil. Hence it may be said of a just judge, that antecedently he wills all men to live; but consequently wills the murderer to be hanged. In the same way God antecedently wills all men to be saved, but consequently wills some to be damned, as His justice exacts. **Nor do we will simply, what we will antecedently, but rather we will it in a qualified manner; for the will is directed to things as they are in themselves, and in themselves they exist under particular qualifications. Hence we will a thing simply inasmuch as we will it when all particular circumstances are consid-**

will is more of a willingness than an absolute will.[46]) Marín-Sola, both in his own thought and in his interpretation of prior commentators, seems to designate antecedent grace as a motion "to" the same end as is given in efficacious grace. But there is a difference here that we would express in English as the difference between moving *toward* and moving *to*. I move *toward* queening my pawn when I move my pawn one square forward toward the other side of the board; but I

---

ered; and this is what is meant by willing consequently. Thus it may be said that a just judge wills simply the hanging of a murderer, but in a qualified manner he would will him to live, to wit, inasmuch as he is a man. **Such a qualified will may be called a willingness rather than an absolute will. Thus it is clear that whatever God simply wills takes place; although what He wills antecedently may not take place**"; "Ad primum ergo dicendum quod illud verbum apostoli, quod Deus vult omnes homines salvos fieri etc., potest tripliciter intelligi. Uno modo, ut sit accommoda distributio, secundum hunc sensum, Deus vult salvos fieri omnes homines qui salvantur, non quia nullus homo sit quem salvum fieri non velit, sed quia nullus salvus fit, quem non velit salvum fieri, ut dicit Augustinus secundo potest intelligi, ut fiat distributio pro generibus singulorum, et non pro singulis generum, secundum hunc sensum, Deus vult de quolibet statu hominum salvos fieri, mares et feminas, Iudaeos et gentiles, parvos et magnos; non tamen omnes de singulis statibus. Tertio, secundum Damascenum, intelligitur de voluntate antecedente, non de voluntate consequente. Quae quidem distinctio non accipitur ex parte ipsius voluntatis divinae, in qua nihil est prius vel posterius; sed ex parte volitorum.

Ad cuius intellectum, considerandum est quod unumquodque, secundum quod bonum est, sic est volitum a Deo. Aliquid autem potest esse in prima sui consideratione, secundum quod absolute consideratur, bonum vel malum, quod tamen, prout cum aliquo adiuncto consideratur, quae est consequens consideratio eius, e contrario se habet. Sicut hominem vivere est bonum, et hominem occidi est malum, secundum absolutam considerationem, sed si addatur circa aliquem hominem, quod sit homicida, vel vivens in periculum multitudinis, sic bonum est eum occidi, et malum est eum vivere. Unde potest dici quod iudex iustus antecedenter vult omnem hominem vivere; sed consequenter vult homicidam suspendi. Similiter Deus antecedenter vult omnem hominem salvari; sed consequenter vult quosdam damnari, secundum exigentiam suae iustitiae. **Neque tamen id quod antecedenter volumus, simpliciter volumus, sed secundum quid. Quia voluntas comparatur ad res, secundum quod in seipsis sunt, in seipsis autem sunt in particulari, unde simpliciter volumus aliquid, secundum quod volumus illud consideratis omnibus circumstantiis particularibus, quod est consequenter velle.** Unde potest dici quod iudex iustus simpliciter vult homicidam suspendi, sed secundum quid vellet eum vivere, scilicet inquantum est homo. **Unde magis potest dici velleitas, quam absoluta voluntas. Et sic patet quod quidquid Deus simpliciter vult, fit; licet illud quod antecedenter vult, non fiat.**"

[46] Note particularly the next to last sentence of the Latin in note 45: "Unde magis potest dici velleitas, quam absoluta voluntas."

move my pawn *to* queen it only when I move it into any of the squares on the last opposed row on the board. The first suggests growing *proximity*, whereas the other designates *actual attainment*. It is typical of the rejection of what I believe to be Thomas's own account that this rejection requires failing to see the distinction between potency and act.

CONCLUSION

Because *glory* is not necessarily attained by all those who are members of the Church, Thomas takes up the implications of the Romans passages with a view toward the maximal formal radiance and import of its principles, which is found in the crucial consideration of individual predestination and reprobation. Thomas's treatment does not "wall off" the proximate material consideration from his analysis, but this material consideration is necessarily an application of the nature and teleology of grace as such. Hence, Thomas principally considers what is most formally important and prepossessing about these passages in Romans: namely, certain principles that are necessary to the understanding of revelation and grace itself, and that proportionately apply both to communion in the Church and to the divine providence over the fulfilling fruition of grace as such, rendering the former to be a *type* of the latter. In discerning that these passages articulate principles of greater profundity than their proximate material application, St. Thomas arguably harvests their most profound and persistently crucial teaching.

"Obedient unto Death": The Function of Philippians 2 in St. Thomas's Theology of the Cross

Roger Nutt
Ave Maria University

Preliminary Considerations on Aquinas as a Biblical Theologian

In 1939, the publication of Marie-Dominique Chenu's study of the *ordo* of the *Summa theologiae* [*ST*], reprinted later as a chapter in his influential *Toward Understanding Saint Thomas*,[1] stimulated interest in Aquinas as a theologian and student of the Scriptures that has continued to attract the attention of scholars and students. Thomas's love for Aristotle, Boethius, and Dionysius, *inter alii*, is well known. One of the difficulties of the present state of scholarship is that familiarity with Thomas's commentaries on the works of Aristotle, Boethius, and Dionysius, not to mention his commentary on the *Book of Causes*, the *De ente et essentia*, and his other philosophical works, make it overly convenient for theological readers of Aquinas to chide scholars who seem to forget that his status in the academy for most of his career was that of a lecturer on the Bible—a criticism

---

[1] M.-D. Chenu, *Toward Understanding Saint Thomas*, trans. Albert M. Landry and Dominic Hughes (Chicago: Regnery, 1964).

that has become stale. Moreover, even noting the quantity of biblical references in Aquinas's work over against references of a philosophical province does little to establish him as a biblical theologian of any merit, let alone distinguish him from any other Christian thinker from the first through the sixteenth centuries. The question remains: what makes Aquinas a biblical theologian?

Without attempting to claim it as a definitive answer to the above, allow me to say that one thing that is unique and underappreciated about Thomas's theology is the intrinsic fashion in which the Bible stands at the epicenter of the structure of his thought, especially as he sets it forth in the *Summa theologiae*. As John Boyle gently points out to post-Chenu readers of Aquinas, especially in light of Thomas's creative ordering of the *tertia pars* of the *Summa theologiae*, "a distinction between the scientific and the scriptural," in the structure of Thomas's thought, "is problematic [and] needs to be evaluated critically in light of Thomas's conception of *sacra doctrina*."[2] Indeed, to turn to two examples from the first two questions of his *Summa theologiae*, Thomas was not perplexed about whether the Bible's use of multiple senses and metaphors was appropriate (I, q. 1, aa. 9–10), and the question "Does God Exist" (I, q. 2, a. 3) was certainly not a matter about which he entertained doubt. The *sed contra* to the latter question—"it is said in the person of God: 'I am Who am' (Exodus 3:14)"—indicates that Thomas often asked questions for the sake of scientifically explaining biblical revelation. His use of questions, as Colman O'Neill explains, is "an artificial method, typical of the literary genre of a *Summa*, for presenting the teaching of the Scriptures."[3]

In the last generation, one noteworthy contribution to this growing field of scholarship on the influence of the Bible in Thomas's theology is Wilhelmus Valkenberg's *Words of the Living God: Place and Function of Holy Scripture in the Theology of St. Thomas Aquinas*.[4]

---

[2]   John F. Boyle, "The Twofold Division of St. Thomas's Christ in the *Tertia Pars*," *The Thomist* 60 (1996): 439. See also Boyle's *Master Thomas Aquinas and the Fullness of Life*, Dallas Aquinas Lecture Series 1 (South Bend, IN: St. Augustine's Press, 2014).

[3]   See editorial note *a* in Thomas Aquinas, *Summa theologiae* [*ST*], vol. 50, ed. Colman E. O'Neill (London: Blackfriars, 1965), 137.

[4]   Wilhelmus G. B. M. Valkenberg, *Words of the Living God: Place and Function of Holy Scripture in the Theology of St. Thomas Aquinas* (Leuven, BE: Peeters, 2000), 2.

As the title of his book indicates, Valkenberg identifies a distinction between Aquinas's quantitative use of Scripture—the sheer number of citations to the Bible—and his qualitative use. To use his terminology, there is a distinction between the "place" and the "function" of Scripture in Aquinas's theology: "The term 'place' refers to a quantitative analysis in which the contribution of all sorts of quotations from Scripture to the theological text can be measured. The term 'function' refers to the qualitative analysis of the role Scripture plays in the text, not only as a contributing factor in its surface structure, but also as the main source in its deep structure."[5] Valkenberg's work offers scholars who are interested in further exploring the biblical contours of Aquinas's thought perhaps the most promising path to continued progress and development in this fertile field of speculation, and to understanding him as a biblical theologian.[6]

In the present essay, the qualitative "function" of Philippians 2 in Aquinas's soteriology is considered both as a paradigmatic example of his scientific biblical theology and as an enduring resource for engaging perennial challenges to the faith in relation to how Christ's suffering and death bring about salvation.

The Role of Philippians 2 as a Foundational Point of Reference for Aquinas's Treatment of the Scandal of the Cross

While the Cross has indeed been a scandal since the Apostolic Age, it is also true that the axis of the scandal has shifted. The reasons that made the crucifixion a stumbling block for the Jews and folly to the Gentiles of Paul's day (1 Cor 1:23) are not the same reasons for which it is often "a stumbling block" for the contemporary theologian or philosopher of religion.[7] Rik Van Nieuwenhove observes

---

[5]   Valkenberg, *Words of the Living God*, 2.
[6]   Perhaps the best example of the fruitfulness of pursuing the function of Scripture in Aquinas's theology, with a developed treatment of Philippians 2, is Matthew Levering's *Paul in the Summa Theologiae* (Washington, DC: Catholic University of America Press, 2014).
[7]   For an example of an unsuccessful (in my opinion) contemporary engagement with this question from a theological perspective, see Henri Blocher, *Evil and the Cross: An Analytical Look at the Problem of Pain* (Grand Rapids, MI: Kregel, 1994).

one of the reasons that Christ's Cross is a stumbling block today: "Modern soteriology puts less emphasis on salvation from sin than is the case in more traditional soteriologies. For Jürgen Moltman, for instance, the perspective has shifted from sin to suffering."[8] In fact, by forgetting the need for redemption from sin, the value of the suffering of Christ, and all suffering for that matter, becomes unintelligible—perhaps intolerable.[9] An example of this disquiet over Christ's sufferings can be discerned in Gerald O'Collins's assessment of Thomas's soteriology in his book *Christology: A Biblical, Historical, and Systematic Study of Jesus*. Citing Thomas's teaching that Christ's sacrifice to God on the Cross was aimed at meeting the demands of God's justice (III, q. 49, a. 4), O'Collins argues that "this helped to open the way, sadly, to the idea of Christ propitiating an angry God by paying a redemptive ransom."[10] In particular, although he acknowledges that Aquinas improved upon Anselm's doctrine of satisfaction, O'Collins accuses him of paving the way for the arresting substitution theories of the Lutheran tradition: "The way Aquinas adjusted Anselm's theory helped open the door to a monstrous version of redemption: Christ as the penal substitute propitiating divine anger."[11]

---

[8] See Rik Van Nieuwenhove, "Bearing the Marks of Christ's Passion: Aquinas' Soteriology," in *The Theology of Thomas Aquinas*, ed. Rik Van Nieuwenhove and Joseph Wawrykow (Notre Dame, IN: University of Notre Dame Press, 2005), 277.

[9] For a fruitful engagement with the tension between the Christian virtue of hospitality and the violence of the Cross, which treats both ancient and modern soteriologies, see Hans Boersma, *Violence, Hospitality, and the Cross: Reappropriating the Atonement Tradition* (Grand Rapids, MI: Baker Academic, 2004). Boersma does not engage Aquinas's theology of the Cross in a developed manner, adverting only briefly to Thomas's distinction between the antecedent and consequent will in God, and he is not in substantive dialogue with the recent scholarly interest in Aquinas as a biblical theologian, but the book is helpful for outlining how different approaches to atonement have addressed the question of the violence of the Cross.

[10] Gerald O'Collins, S.J., *Christology: A Biblical, Historical, and Systematic Study of Jesus* (Oxford: Oxford University Press, 1995), 206.

[11] O'Collins, *Christology*, 207. Another, more recent attempt to address this problem is Fr. Nicholas Lombardo's *The Father's Will: Christ's Crucifixion and the Goodness of God* (Oxford: Oxford University Press, 2013). Lombardo follows closely the analytic doctrine of intention so as to situate Christ's death on the Cross as an example of a complex action to which "double effect" reasoning is applicable. Lombardo's argument is as follows: "Being all good, God never wants moral evil,

In light of this acute and perennial question about the will of the Father in the death of the Son, the position of Van Nieuwenhove seems well stated: "In my view, Aquinas' soteriology still proves useful because it can accommodate these modern concerns while remaining more faithful than some of the recent soteriologies to the way the New Testament views the central role of cross."[12]

Van Nieuwenhove's understanding that Thomas's soteriology accommodates modern concerns while remaining faithful to the biblical narrative is especially true in light of the function of Philippians 2 within Thomas's teaching. The "hymn" of Philippians 2:5–11 looms as large as any biblical text in the tradition of the Church, especially after Nicaea, in the adjudication of the Nestorian and Monophysite controversies. Paul's affirmation of Christ's twofold "form"—"though he was in the form of God, he did not deem equality with God a thing to be grasped, but emptied himself, taking the form of a servant, being born in the likeness of men"—was a standard point of reference for the "two natures, one person" orthodoxy affirmed at Ephesus and Chalcedon.[13] The doctrine of the kenosis or humiliation of the Word in taking on the form of a servant is likewise dependent upon this passage.

The remainder of this essay focuses on the function of verses 7–9a of Philippians 2 in Aquinas's theology of the Cross.[14] In these verses, Paul declares of Christ: "He emptied himself, taking the form of a servant, being born in the likeness of men, and being found in

---

and even *cannot* want moral evil. Sound Christian theology, therefore, must keep a clear distance between God's will and the moral evil of Christ's crucifixion" (80). While Lombardo grants that the Cross "happens according to both God's (θέλημα) and God's plan (βουλή)," he adds: "The New Testament always stops short of claiming that God wants, intends, or wills the actual crucifying of his Son. It places the full weight of moral responsibility on the shoulders of those who crucify Christ, and it does not sanitize the violence of the crucifixion or diminish its injustice" (142). As a result, the reasoning of double effect, in Lombardo's analysis, avoids implicating God in the moral evil of Christ's suffering and death. More is said about Lombardo's work vis-à-vis Christ's obedience "unto to death" below at the start of my third section.

12 Van Nieuwenhove, "Bearing the Marks," 278.

13 On the function of Philippians 2 in Aquinas's theology of the hypostatic union, see Roger Nutt, "Introduction," in Thomas Aquinas, *De unione verbi incarnati*, trans. Roger W. Nutt with introduction (Leuven, BE: Peeters, 2015), 22–23.

14 For a treatment of every instance of Aquinas's engagement with Philippians 2 in the *Summa theologiae*, see Levering, *Paul in the Summa Theologiae*.

human form he humbled himself and became obedient unto death, even death on a cross. Therefore God highly exalted him and bestowed on him the name above every name."

In his commentary on Philippians, Thomas uncovers four interrelated points that, not surprisingly, reappear in his systematic works.[15] As a result, it is worth noting some of the things Thomas underscores in his commentary, because in doing so, the reciprocity between his reading of the Bible and the contours of his systematic theology becomes immediately evident.

Firstly, Thomas reads the revelation of Christ in Philippians 2 against the backdrop of the pride that led to the fall of Satan and Adam. With implicit reliance on the teaching of Romans 5 on Christ as the new Adam, Thomas sees the references to the divine Word emptying himself by becoming a "servant" and to his obedience unto death as revelations of Christ as an antidote to the pride of Adam, who sought to be like God.[16] In particular, Thomas especially reads the emptying as a revelation of Christ's humility: "How beautiful to say that he *emptied himself,* for the empty," Thomas reasons, "is opposed to the full."[17] It is important to recognize that Thomas does not consider the Cross and justification abstractly and ahistorically. Rather, Christ's obedience unto death is a work of providence in human history to redeem humanity from the concrete condition resulting from the fall of Adam.

Secondly, when Paul says that Christ "humbled himself," Thomas comments that Paul *"commends* Christ's humility as indicated in

---

[15] For a summary treatment of Thomas's commentaries on Paul's letters, see Pasquale Porro, *Thomas Aquinas: A Historical and Philosophical Profile*, trans. Joseph G. Trabbic and Roger W. Nutt (Washington, DC: Catholic University of America, 2016), 188–90.

[16] On this point, Romanus Cessario explains: "There [in Phil 2] Thomas makes another comparison between the roles played by the devil in seducing man away from God and the role played by Christ in leading man back to God. . . . Thomas remarks that one can contrast the humility of the Logos who sought to lower himself with the audacity of man, who being filled with pride, sought to 'grasp' ('rapina') at divinity" (*The Godly Image: Christ and Salvation in Catholic Thought from Anselm to Aquinas* (Petersham, MA: St. Bede's Publications, 1990), 36.

[17] *Super Eph* 2, lec. 2 (Marietti no. 57.2), in *Super Epistolas S. Pauli Lectura*, vol. 2, ed. P. Raphaelis Cai (Rome: Marietti, 1953); paragraph numbers in citations of Thomas's Scripture commentaries will be Marietti numbers. I have loosely followed the translations that can be found at dhspriory.org/thomas/SSPhilippians.htm, with frequent modifications of my own to the translations.

the mystery of His Passion."[18] That is to say, Thomas recognizes from Paul's words that, in Christ, we encounter an especially noteworthy mode of humility: "For He was man, yet an exceedingly great one, because the same one is God and man; and yet He *humbled himself* . . . 'Learn from me, for I am gentle and lowly in heart' (Matt 11:29)."[19] This point is especially important in clarifying the moral content of Christ's action in his passion and death. Christ's agency is superlative in an area (humility) that the state of sin normally compromises.

Thirdly, Thomas joins Christ's humility with his obedience in contrast to the sin of pride: "The way of humility and the sign of humility is obedience, whereas the characteristic of the proud is to follow their own will. Since the proud person seeks the highest places . . . as a result, obedience is the opposite of pride."[20] In addition to being humble, Christ's actions are doubly opposed to the vice of pride, because his humility is complimented by a free and willing obedience to the will of another.

Fourthly, Thomas sees in Christ's humility and obedience the source of the efficacy of the Cross: "If [Christ] had not suffered out of obedience, His passion would not be so praiseworthy, for obedience gives merit to our sufferings."[21] It is Christ, in the form of a servant, suffering out of obedience that conforms his actions to the will of God: "not as I will, but as you will" (Matt 26:39). On this point, Thomas explicitly connects Christ's obedience and humility with the pride and disobedience of the fall: "It is fitting that He bring obedience into His passion, because the first sin was accomplished by disobedience: 'For as by one man's disobedience many were made sinners, so by one man's obedience many will be made righteous' (Rom 5:19)."[22] Thomas does not see Christ's obedience and humility as mere external exemplars of the Christian moral life. Even more than being a good moral example, Christ's humility and obedience unto death explain the saving power of the Cross. His action not only shows his followers how to act rightly; his action merits salvation and gives the actions of those joined to him the character of merit.

This recognition of Christ's humility as manifest in his obedi-

---

[18] *Super Eph* 2, lec. 2 (no. 63).
[19] *Super Eph* 2, lec. 2 (no. 64).
[20] *Super Eph* 2, lec. 2 (no. 65).
[21] *Super Eph* 2, lec. 2 (no. 65).
[22] *Super Eph* 2, lec. 2 (no. 65).

ence, which, in turn, makes his suffering and death meritorious, exercises a formative function on all of Thomas's thinking about salvation in Christ.

Philippians 2 and Thomas's Teaching in the *Summa theologiae*

As was noted above, many contemporary scholars have blanched at theories of atonement and satisfaction that implicate the will of God in the suffering and death of Christ. Nicholas Lombardo, for example, argues:

> If we determine that a particular human action is inherently evil, we can rule out the possibility that God would or could ever will it. On the basis of these considerations, we can rule out any theological narrative in which God wills the actual crucifying of Christ, or Christ intends his own death. Yet as long as he does not intend his death, theological narratives in which Christ knowingly causes his death, or even provokes it, can nonetheless be philosophically viable.[23]

Commenting directly on Paul's affirmation that Christ was "obedient unto death," Lombardo equivocates: "Paul does not specify what exactly this obedience entails, however. Consequently, considering the passage on its own, it is not clear whether becoming 'obedient unto death' means that Christ was so tenaciously obedient to God's will that he ended up crucified, or that Christ was obedient to a command that necessarily involved his crucifixion."[24] What Lombardo leaves out of his consideration is the possibility that the will of God (and the human will of Christ) could intend the suffering and death of Christ without willing the evil of his unjust condemnation or the malice of his accusers. Pinpointing the object of the Father's will, the object of Christ's obedience, and the charity that animated Christ's suffering enables Aquinas to articulate how the human will of Christ and the will of the Father meet in the passion without

---

[23] Lombardo, *The Father's Will*, 92.
[24] Lombardo, *The Father's Will*, 134.

succumbing to the conclusion that either must be implicated in evil agency.[25]

Philippians 2 influences Aquinas's teaching on Christ's death in several places in the *Summa theologiae* in a manner that enables him to unravel the tension between the violence of his sufferings and the will of the Father. There are no less than twenty-seven explicit citations of these verses in the *Summa theologiae*, and twenty-two of these references, not surprisingly, appear in the treatise on Christ in the *tertia pars*.[26]

Leading up to his use of Philippians 2 in the treatise on Christ, Aquinas introduces some key components of the function of the text in his teaching on Christ's death in his exposition of martyrdom in the *secunda secundae*. It might be said that Thomas makes a Christological deposit in his treatment of martyrdom in conjunction with the virtue of fortitude with an eye to cashing it in the *tertia pars*.

In his treatment of martyrdom, Aquinas calls it "an act of the greatest perfection." Before doing so, however, Thomas concedes that undergoing death "is not praiseworthy in itself, but only in so far as it is directed to some good . . . such as faith or the love of God."[27] Martyrdom belongs to the perfection of the life of virtue, not simply because of the passivity of undergoing suffering and death, but

---

[25] Already in his early *Literal Exposition on Job*, Aquinas develops an underappreciated response to the problem of evil in relation to the scene in Job 1 in which God permits Satan to inflict suffering upon Job. Aquinas allows that God wills Job's suffering without implicating God in Satan's malevolence. "From what has been said already it is clear that the cause of the adversity of blessed Job was that his virtue should be made clear to all. So Scripture says of Tobias, 'Thus the Lord permitted him to be tempted so that an example might be given to posterity of his patience, like blessed Job' (Tob. 2:12). Be careful not to believe that the Lord had been persuaded by the words of Satan to permit Job to be afflicted, but he ordered this from his eternal disposition to make clear Job's virtue against the false accusations of the impious. Therefore, false accusations are placed first and the divine permission follows" (*Literal Exposition on Job*, commentary on Job 1:10–12a [dhspriory.org/thomas/SSJob.htm#012]). For further development of this point, see Roger W. Nutt, "Providence, Wisdom, and the Justice of Job's Afflictions: Considerations from Aquinas' *Literal Exposition on Job*," *Heythrop Journal* 56, no. 1 (2015): 44–66.

[26] Levering, *Paul in the Summa Theologiae*, 268.

[27] *ST*, II-II, q. 124, a. 3. English translations of the *Summa theologiae* are from Thomas Aquinas, *Summa theologiae*, trans. Laurence Shapcote, O.P., ed. John Mortensen and Enrique Alarcón (Lander, WY: Aquinas Institute for the Study of Sacred Doctrine, 2012).

rather, Thomas teaches, because it "is the greatest proof of the perfection of charity."[28] What makes martyrdom an act of perfection is that the martyr's love for God exceeds the natural inclination to maintain biological life. To vindicate this point, Thomas argues that martyrdom is the highest form of religious obedience by appealing to the Philippians hymn. "The highest possible degree of obedience," Thomas teaches, is "obedience unto death; thus we read of Christ (Philippians 2:8) that he became 'obedient unto death.'"[29] Paul's understanding of Christ's obedience animates Aquinas's understanding of martyrdom.

Philippians 2 and the connection between love and obedience in Thomas's assessment of martyrdom reappears in the *tertia pars*, this time directly in relation to the Cross. This occurs for the first time in his treatment of the union of body and soul in Christ. In his question on the subject, the objections all deny a union of body and soul in Christ for reasons raised by the major Christological heresies (he could not have enjoyed a body–soul union without being a second hypostasis; he did not need a soul because the Word was the animating principle of the union; and so on). Thomas's response to these questions is the affirmation by Paul in Philippians 2:7 that Christ was "born in the likeness of men." This indicates, Thomas explains, that Scripture reveals Christ to be a man "univocally" with the rest of the species precisely by having a body and a soul.[30] Thomas's reasoning, however, is more subtle than merely affirming with the Tradition that Christ is true God and true man. If Christ did not have a human soul, he could not have offered to the Father his exemplary martyrdom; without a human soul, he could not have died in loving obedience.[31] Thomas makes this line of reasoning explicit when treating the various parts of human nature assumed by Christ.

---

[28] *ST*, II-II, q. 124, a. 3.

[29] In *The Glory of God's Grace: Deification According to St. Thomas Aquinas* (Ave Maria, FL: Sapientia Press of Ave Maria University, 2015), Daria Spezzano explains Aquinas's teaching on the moral significance of obedience in Christ's life: "A graced life of sacrificial filial obedience, shaped by charity and wisdom to be like that of Christ crucified, makes one participate more fully in the interior reality of Christ's priesthood, so that one's whole life can be said to be directed toward the worship of God" (311).

[30] *ST*, III, q. 2, a. 5.

[31] For a global treatment of Aquinas's doctrine of Christ's soul and passions, see Paul Gondreau, *The Passions of Christ's Soul in the Theology of St. Thomas Aquinas* (Scranton, PA: University of Scranton Press, 2009).

In the first article of question 2, an objection to the truth of Christ's human nature cites Philippians 2:7 to argue that Jesus was born not with a true human nature, but merely "in the likeness of men." Aquinas responds to this docetic use of the word "likeness" by citing the next verse, verse 8, which affirms that Christ "became obedient unto death, even death on a cross." His argument is that Paul's use of the term "likeness" is not docetic but rather intended to indicate the truth of Christ's human nature. "All that truly exists in human nature," Thomas reasons, "[is] said to be like in species—and not a mere imaginary likeness." For Thomas, this is not merely a question of semantics. The "likeness" that Christ has with humanity is essential to his unity with the fallen human race in death. Christ's death, Thomas reasons, "would have been impossible" had his human nature not been integral—in other words, he could not have been "obedient unto death," as Paul affirms.[32] Paul's witness to Christ's death in Philippians 2 confirms the doctrine of his integral human nature.

Paul's witness to the truth of Christ's humanity—body and soul—in relation to the truth of his obedient death is also foundational for Thomas's understanding of how Christ's death merits his own exaltation and the salvation of others. Thomas approaches the question of the merit of Christ's death via the objection that, if Christ knew God fully, his death could not merit the treasure of heaven, which he already possessed in the beatific form of knowledge. Such a robust doctrine of Christ's human knowledge as Thomas famously held would seem to diminish the saving merits of Christ's death. The unseen nature of faith (as opposed to beatific knowledge) would likewise seem to lie at the heart of the virtuous perfection of martyrdom. "The merit of faith," he argues, "consists in this—that man through obedience assents to what things he does not see"—which would seem to exclude Christ from the order of merit as a comprehensor. This objection, however, allows Thomas to clarify Christ's uniqueness while also more clearly affirming the truth of his human nature. Christ, Thomas reasons, was obedient to the truth as he knew it through the *lumen gloriae*, while the believer is obedient to the light of faith. Thomas also affirms that Christ necessarily "has most perfect obedience to God, according to Philippians 2:8: '[he became] obedient unto death.'" Like the believer who follows God in faith, therefore, Christ, "taught nothing pertaining to merit

---

[32] *ST*, III, q. 5, a. 1, obj. 1 and ad 1.

which he did not fulfil more perfectly himself."[33] Though the mode of knowledge is different, adherence to the will of God by loving obedience is common to both orders.

Philippians 2 also enters into Thomas's defense of Christ's operational unity against the historical errors of the monoenergists and monothelites. Further pressing the integrity of Christ's human nature, Thomas asks whether, by his earthly life and death, Christ did anything that was meritoriously beneficial for himself.[34] For, if Christ truly is the Son of God and he truly enjoyed union with God, what could he have done during his earthly journey that would have merited anything that he did not already enjoy? Merit, Thomas teaches, regards the bestowal of "what is not yet possessed."[35] This would seem to exclude Christ from any possible merit on his own behalf. Thomas, however, affirms that Christ did merit for himself "the glory of his body and whatever else pertained to His outward excellence."[36] In support of his argument, he appeals to Philippians 2:9, which asserts that, because Christ was obedient unto death, "God has highly exalted him and bestowed upon him the name which is above every name." Thomas concludes that, by obeying, Christ "merited His exaltation and . . . merited something for Himself."[37]

These uses of Philippians 2 in the structure of Thomas's Christology underscore how Christ's possession of a human nature capable of suffering and death out of obedience influences how he ponders Christ's passion in itself, its causality, and salvific effects. In the sequence of questions on Christ's passion (*ST* III, qq. 46–49), Thomas cites Philippians 2 five times.[38] Four of these five citations are put forward authoritatively in *sed contras*. In this sequence, Thomas brings his reading of Philippians 2 directly into his account of the meaning of Christ's suffering and death.

---

[33] *ST*, III, q. 7, a. 3, ad 2.

[34] For a treatment of the soteriological significance of the doctrine of Christ's wills, see Corey Barnes, *Christ's Two Wills in Scholastic Thought: The Christology of Aquinas and Its Historical Contexts*, Studies and Texts 178 (Toronto: Pontifical Institute of Medieval Studies, 2012).

[35] *ST*, III, q. 19, a. 3.

[36] *ST*, III, q. 19, a. 3.

[37] *ST*, III, q. 19, a. 3, sc.

[38] For a helpful summary of these questions and Aquinas's soteriology, see Battista Mondin, *La Cristologia di San Tommaso d'Aquino: origine, dottrine principali, attualità* (Rome: Urbaniana University Press, 1997), 193–203.

Thomas uses a two-step argument to examine how the will of the Father and Christ's will come together in the passion. In question 47 of the *tertia pars*, he devotes one article (a. 2) to whether Christ died out of obedience and then follows it with an article (a. 3) that asks whether the Father delivered Christ up to the passion. Here Thomas confronts the dilemma of the Cross: how do Christ's suffering (and death) and the will of the Father come together coherently without implicating the Father in an act of injustice? In an objection, Thomas lays out the apparent problem with as much force as any contemporary theologian or philosopher of religion: "For it is a wicked and cruel act to hand over an innocent man to torment and death. But, as it is written (Deuteronomy 32:4): 'God is faithful, and without any iniquity.' Therefore [God the Father] did not hand over the innocent Christ to His Passion and death."[39]

Treating Christ's obedience in his passion, Thomas contemplates the Cross under the light of Philippians 2:9, which he cites authoritatively to affirm that Christ indeed died out of obedience to the Father. This account of how Christ's death was an act of obedience to the will of the Father enables him to reconcile the ugly and unjust nature of Christ's suffering—unjust at least on the part of his persecutors—with the Father's will and plan for redemption by affirming that Christ's death on the Cross was an act of obedience to the will of the Father as expressed in the moral, ceremonial, and judicial precepts of the Old Law.

Christ's obedience is not to an unjust and cruel plan of an angry God in need of appeasement, but to the will of God as expressed in the ordering of the Old Law to fulfillment in the New.[40] Jesus obeys God's will in his passion by fulfilling the moral precepts through his charity, the ceremonial precepts through his sacrificial self-offering, and the judicial precepts by accepting the penalty of death on behalf of those justly subject to it.[41] Jesus, Thomas explains, was not

---

[39] *ST*, III, q. 47, a. 3, obj. 1.

[40] The clearest treatment of Thomas's teaching on Christ's salvific fulfillment of the Old Law can be found in Matthew Levering's *Christ's Fulfillment of Torah and Temple: Salvation According to Thomas Aquinas* (Notre Dame, IN: University of Notre Dame Press, 2002).

[41] See *ST*, III, q. 47, a. 2, ad 1: "Christ received a command from the Father to suffer. For it is written (John 10:18): 'I have power to lay down My life, and I have power to take it up again: (and) this commandment have I received of My Father'—namely, of laying down His life and of resuming it again. 'From which,'

obedient to the Father as though the Father desired his death for its own sake, but was obedient under the *ratio* of the Father's desire for the consummation of the law in his Son and the redemption of man thereby through the establishment of justice (justification).

What of the will of the Father, which is the second step in his consideration? Thomas begins his treatment of the role of the Father's will in Christ's passion by invoking the previous article on Christ's obedience: "As observed above (article 2), Christ suffered voluntarily out of obedience to the Father."[42] Acknowledging again the cruelty of sending an innocent person to death against their will, Aquinas argues: "God the Father did not so deliver up Christ, but inspired Him with the will to suffer for us."[43] In other words, the Father did not impose the passion on Christ as an undeserved, yet required, punishment for the sins of others. Rather, Christ, as the protomartyr, accepted suffering and death as the just penalty of sin and obeyed God's will that it not be remitted without satisfaction because he intended to obey the full measure of the order of charity.

Question 48 (where Thomas treats the efficiency of Christ's pas-

---

as Chrysostom says (Hom. lix in Joan.), it is not to be understood 'that at first He awaited the command, and that He had need to be told, but He showed the proceeding to be a voluntary one, and destroyed suspicion of opposition' to the Father. Yet because the Old Law was ended by Christ's death, according to His dying words, 'It is consummated' (John 19:30), it may be understood that by His suffering He fulfilled all the precepts of the Old Law. He fulfilled those of the moral order which are founded on the precepts of charity, inasmuch as He suffered both out of love of the Father, according to John 14:31: 'That the world may know that I love the Father, and as the Father hath given Me commandment, so do I: arise, let us go hence'—namely, to the place of His Passion: and out of love of His neighbor, according to Galatians 2:20: 'He loved me, and delivered Himself up for me.' Christ likewise by His Passion fulfilled the ceremonial precepts of the Law, which are chiefly ordained for sacrifices and oblations, in so far as all the ancient sacrifices were figures of that true sacrifice which the dying Christ offered for us. Hence it is written (Colossians 2:16–17): 'Let no man judge you in meat or drink, or in respect of a festival day, or of the new moon, or of the sabbaths [*sic*], which are a shadow of things to come, but the body is Christ's,' for the reason that Christ is compared to them as a body is to a shadow. Christ also by His Passion fulfilled the judicial precepts of the Law, which are chiefly ordained for making compensation to them who have suffered wrong, since, as is written (Psalm 68:5): He 'paid that which' He 'took not away,' suffering Himself to be fastened to a tree on account of the apple which man had plucked from the tree against God's command."

42 *ST*, III, q. 47, a. 3.
43 *ST*, III, q. 47, a. 3, ad 1.

sion) applies this consideration to how Christ's passion actually saves from sin. This question can be perplexing to readers because Thomas asks the same question—"does Christ's passion bring about our salvation by way of?"—from four different perspectives and, seeming to equivocate, answers each question in the affirmative: Christ's passion brings about salvation by merit, atonement, sacrifice, and redemption. Thomas is not inconsistent by affirming that Christ's passion saves according to each aspect. Rather, the first article on Christ's merit lays a foundation for his affirmation of the other modes of efficiency.[44] Here Thomas hearkens back once more to his teaching on martyrdom: what happened to Christ, the suffering forced upon him by others, is not of itself a source of merit, yet that suffering can be beneficial, "inasmuch as one bears it willingly, [since] it has an inward principle."[45] As a result: "Whoever suffers for justice's sake, provided that he be in a state of grace, merits his salvation thereby, according to Matthew 5:10: 'Blessed are they that suffer persecution for justice's sake.' Consequently Christ by his Passion merits salvation, not only for himself, but likewise for all his members."[46] Governing Thomas's whole line of reasoning on this point is the affirmation in Philippians 2:9 that, because Christ obediently suffered death on a Cross, "God highly exalted him," which he quotes authoritatively in the *sed contra*.[47]

As Thomas shows in the subsequent articles of question 48, which draw their structure from all that has been harvested from Philippians 2, the meritorious nature of Christ's obedient suffering is the key to the other modes of efficiency as well: his passion is efficient in the order of atonement because, "by suffering out of love and

---

[44] For a dated but still valuable presentation of Thomas's teaching on Christ's merit, see William D. Lynn, "Christ's Redemptive Merit: The Nature of Its Causality According to St. Thomas" (STD diss., The Pontifical Gregorian University, 1962).

[45] *ST*, III, q. 48, a. 1, ad 1.

[46] *ST*, III, q. 48, a. 1, corp.

[47] Thomas also adopts this argument in relation to Christ's merit of his own exaltation: "Moreover (Philippians 2:8) it is written: 'He humbled Himself, becoming obedient unto death, even to the death of the cross: for which cause also God hath exalted Him, and hath given Him a name which is above all names'—that is to say, so that He shall be hailed as God by all; and all shall pay Him homage as God. And this is expressed in what follows: 'That in the name of Jesus every knee should bow, of those that are in heaven, on earth, and under the earth'" (*ST*, III, q. 49, a. 6).

obedience, Christ gave more to God than was required to compensate for the offense of the whole human race."[48] His passion worked efficiently as a sacrifice because he voluntarily offered himself to God out of love, thus making his suffering a true sacrifice.[49] His passion was efficient in the order of redemption because, by freely suffering death, Christ pays the penalty for sin, thereby redeeming the human race from the penalty of its guilt. In each case, Paul's teaching on the merit of Christ's obedience unto death is the efficient cause of salvation because, in satisfying for sin, redeeming from guilt, and uniting God and man in sacrifice, his obedience fulfills the will of God as revealed in the precepts of the law. This fulfillment establishes a saving order of justice or righteousness between God and humanity.

Conclusion

In a helpful treatment of the use and meaning of the word "satisfaction" in the *Rule of St. Benedict*, Guy Mansini uncovers some remarkable material that contextualizes not only the genesis of the soteriology of Anselm (or Aquinas and other adherents of satisfaction theory), but also the aims of monastic life in relation to Christ as the protomartyr. Mansini notes a distinction in the *Rule* between penances imposed upon monks by their abbot or superior for sins or wrongdoing and "satisfaction" done by monks (imposed penances and satisfactions are not the same thing in the *Rule*). The monk, Mansini explains, "does not 'incur' or is not 'subjected to' *satisfactio*; rather it seems that satisfaction is something he performs, does, executes as an active subject."[50] In a parallel manner, this sheds a great deal of light on the function of Philippians 2 in Thomas's teaching on salvation in Christ. Christ's death was not a penance imposed upon him by the wrath of the Father for a fault that he was not guilty of. Christ's willingness to die was a freely embraced act of loving obedience to the will of God, which St. Thomas makes

---

[48] *ST*, III, q. 48, a. 2, corp.

[49] *ST*, III, q. 48, a. 3.

[50] Guy Mansini, "St. Anselm, Satisfactio and the Rule of St. Benedict," in *The Word has Dwelt Among us: Explorations in Theology* (Ave Maria, FL: Sapientia Press of Ave Maria University, 2008), 77.

intelligible by the light of Paul's teaching. In fact, in answer to the question of whether or not Christ's suffering was necessary to save the human race, Thomas joins the mercy of God to his justice in an arresting claim:

> That man should be delivered by Christ's Passion was in keeping with both [God's] mercy and His justice. With His justice, because by His Passion Christ made satisfaction for the sin of the human race; and so man was set free by Christ's justice: and with His mercy, for since man of himself could not satisfy for the sin of all human nature, . . . God gave him His Son to satisfy for him. . . . *And this came of more copious mercy than if He had forgiven sins without satisfaction.*[51]

Mansini's argument about satisfaction in the *Rule* teases out a foundational Christological truth—a truth that Thomas finds in Philippians 2. It is precisely as a freely embraced, non-imposed act of satisfaction for sin (of others) that Christ's suffering and death are pleasing to the Father and meritorious for others.

Guided by the great hymn of Philippians 2, St. Thomas forges a theology of salvation in Christ that affirms a saving value of his suffering in the order of sacrifice, atonement, redemption, and merit without viewing the Cross as a means of placating divine anger. In this way, Christ's humble and obedient death saves humanity from the condition inherited by the pride and disorder introduced by the fall. As Matthew Levering observes, Philippians 2 teaches Aquinas that: "[Christ] renounces self-will in favor of following the will of God. He descends into death and hell so as to lead us out of death and hell and to enable us to share in the divine life. His exaltation reveals his glory as the incarnate Son, a glory of perfect love, and he becomes for us the path to eternal life."[52] This, Thomas teaches, is much more (and much better) than mere liberation from sin without suffering, because in Christ's obedience unto death, humanity is not merely forgiven but also fully reconciled to God in perfect justice. Indeed, with Paul's teaching that Christ's death was an act of humble and free obedience, the Cross did not reveal an angry God to St. Thomas, but a more copious mercy.

---

[51] *ST*, III, q. 46, a. 1, ad 3. Emphasis added.
[52] Levering, *Paul in the Summa Theologiae*, 280.